Jumping into C++

Alex Allain

Cprogramming.com

San Francisco

Jumping into C++. Copyright © 2012 by F. Alexander Allain

Printed in the United States of America

First Printing, 2013

ISBN 978-0-9889278-0-3

Cprogramming.com
355 1st St Unit S501
San Francisco, CA 94105
www.cprogramming.com

For inquiries, contact Cprogramming.com:
webmaster@cprogramming.com; (415) 857-4823

Contents

Part 1: Jumping into C++

Let's get ready to program! Programming, like other art forms, allows you to create—but in programming, your power is multiplied by the speed and capabilities of the computer. You can create engaging games like World of Warcraft, Bioshock, Gears of War and Mass Effect. You can create detailed and immersive simulations like The Sims. You can write programs that connect people together: web browsers like Chrome, email editors or chat clients, or websites like Facebook or Amazon.com. You can build apps that delight your users, taking advantage of new devices like iPhones or Android phones.

Those things, of course, take time to become skilled enough to create. But even in the beginning you can write interesting software—programs that solve your math homework for you, simple games like Tetris that you can show your friends, tools to automate tedious chores or complex calculations that would otherwise take days or weeks by hand. Once you understand the basics of programming a computer—which this book will teach you—you'll have the ability to pick up the graphics or networking libraries you need to in order to write the kinds of programs that interest you, whether they're games, scientific simulations or something in between.

C++ is a powerful programming language that will give you a strong grounding in modern programming techniques. In fact, C++ shares concepts with many other languages, so much of what you learn will transfer to other languages that you pick up later (almost no programmer works with a single language exclusively).

C++ programmers have a flexible skill set, with the ability to work on many different projects. Most of the applications and programs you use every day were written in C++. Incredibly, every one of these applications I listed earlier was either written entirely in C++ or has significant components written in C++.[1]

In fact, interest in C++ continues to grow even as new programming languages such as Java and C# gain popularity. I've seen a marked increase in traffic to my site, Cprogramming.com, over the last few years. C++ continues to be the language of choice for high performance applications, creating programs that run extremely fast, often faster than Java or similar languages. C++ continues to grow as a language, with a new language specification, C++11, adding new features that make it easier and faster to use as a developer while maintaining its high-performance roots.[2] A strong knowledge of C++ is also valuable on the job market, and jobs that require C++ skill are often both challenging and high-paying.

Are you ready to get started? Part 1 is all about getting you set up to start writing programs and getting you using the basic building blocks of C++. Once you're done with this section, you'll be able to write real programs that you can show your friends (your close and nice friends, anyway) and you'll understand how to think like a programmer. You won't be a C++ master, but you'll be well-prepared to learn the remaining language features that you'll need to make really useful and powerful programs.

I'll also give you just enough background and terminology to stay afloat, putting off the more complicated explanations for certain things until you've got the basics.

The other parts of this book will introduce you to increasingly advanced concepts. You'll learn how to write programs that work with large amounts of data, including taking input from files and learning how to process that data easily and efficiently (and learn numerous shortcuts along the way). You'll learn how to write larger, more complex programs without getting lost under a wave

---

[1] You can find these applications, and many more uses of C++, at http://www.stroustrup.com/applications.html

[2] This specification was ratified as this book neared completion, so I have not included any material from the new standard. You can find a series of articles introducing C++11 at http://www.cprogramming.com/c++11/what-is-c++0x.html

of complexity. You'll also learn about the tools that are used by professional programmers.

By the end of this book, you should be able to read and write real computer programs that do useful, interesting things. If you're interested in game programming, you'll be ready to take up the challenges specific to game programming. If you're taking, or preparing to take, a class on C++, you should have the information you need to survive and thrive. If you're a self-learner, you should have enough information to write just about any program you're interested in writing, having nearly all of the tools provided by C++ at the ready.

Errata and updates

While I've tried hard to make sure this book is accurate and up-to-date, some of the tools used in the book may be replaced by new versions, making the current instructions out of date, or there may be mistakes in the code or text. Updates and corrections will be posted at http://www.cprogramming.com/errata.html

Acknowledgements

I'd like to thank Alexandra Hoffer for her careful, patient editing and detailed suggestions throughout the production of this book. Without her efforts, this book would not exist. I'd also like to thank Andrei Cheremskoy, Minyang Jiang and Johannes Peter for invaluable feedback, suggestions and corrections.

Chapter 1
Introduction and Developer Environment Setup

What is a programming language?

When you want to control your computer, you need a way to speak to it. Unlike your dog or your cat, which have their own inscrutable languages, computers have programming languages created by people. A computer program is a piece of text—like a book, or an essay—but with its own particular structure. The language, while comprehensible to humans, is more strictly structured than a normal language, and the vocabulary is much smaller. C++ is one of these languages, and a popular one at that.

Once you have written a computer program, you need a way for the computer to run it—to interpret what you've written. This is usually called executing your program. The way you do this will depend on your programming language and environment—we'll talk more about how to execute your program soon.

There are many programming languages, each with their own different structure and vocabulary, but they are in many ways very similar. Once you have learned one, learning the next will be easier.

What's the difference between C and C++?

C is a programming language originally developed for developing the Unix operating system. It is a low-level and powerful language, but it lacks many modern and useful constructs. C++ is a newer language, based on C, which adds many more modern programming language features that make it easier to program than C.

C++ maintains all the power of the C language, while providing new features to programmers that make it easier to write useful and sophisticated programs.

For example, C++ makes it easier to manage memory and adds several features to allow "object-oriented" programming and "generic" programming. We'll talk about what that really means later. For now, just know that C++ makes it easier for programmers to stop thinking about the nitty-gritty details of how the machine works and think about the problems they are trying to solve.

If you're trying to decide between learning C and C++, I strongly suggest starting with C++.

Do I need to know C to learn C++?

No. C++ is a superset of C; anything you can do in C, you can do in C++. If you already know C, you will easily adapt to the object-oriented features of C++. If you don't know C, that's ok—there's no real advantage to learning C before C++, and you will be able to immediately take advantage of powerful C++-only features (the first among many being easier input and output).

Do I need to know math to be a programmer?

If I had a nickel for every time someone asked me this, I'd need a calculator to count my small fortune. Fortunately, the answer is, emphatically, No! Most of programming is about design and logical reasoning, not about being able to quickly perform arithmetic, or deeply understanding algebra or calculus. The overlaps between math and programming are primarily around logical reasoning and precise thinking. Only if you want to program advanced 3D graphics engines, write programs to perform statistical analysis or do other specialized numerical programming will you need mathematical skill.

Terminology

Throughout the book, I'll be defining new terms, but let's get started with some very basic concepts that you'll need to get started.

Programming
Programming is the act of writing instructions in a way that allows a computer to understand and execute those instructions. The instructions themselves are called **source code**. That's what you'll be writing. We'll see some source code for the very first time in a few pages.

Executable
The end result of programming is that you have an **executable** file. An executable is a file that your computer can run—if you're on Windows, you'll know these files as EXEs. A computer program like Microsoft Word is an executable. Some programs have additional files (graphics files, music files, etc.) but every program requires an executable file. To make an executable, you need a **compiler**, which is a program that turns source code into an executable. Without a compiler, you won't be able to do anything except look at your source code. Since that gets boring quickly, the very next thing we will do is set you up with a compiler.

Editing and compiling source files
The rest of this chapter is devoted to getting you set up with a simple, easy-to-use development environment. I'll get you set up with two specific tools, a compiler and an **editor**. You've already learned why you need a compiler—to make the program do stuff. The editor is less obvious, but equally important: an editor makes it possible for you to create source code in the right format.

Source code must be written in a **plain text** format. Plain text files contain nothing but the text of the file; there is no additional information about how to format or display the content. In contrast, a file you produce using Microsoft Word (or similar products) is not a plain text file because it contains information about the fonts used, the size of the text, and how you've formatted the text. You don't see this information when you open the file in Word, but it's all there. Plain text files have just the raw text, and you can create them using the tools we're about to discuss.

The editor will also give you two other nice features, **syntax highlighting** and **auto-indentation**. Syntax highlighting just means it adds color coding so that you can easily tell apart different elements of a program.   Auto-indentation means that it will help you format your code in a readable way.

If you're using Windows or a Mac, I'll get you set you up with a sophisticated editor, known as an **integrated development environment** (IDE) that combines an editor with a compiler. If you're using Linux, we'll use an easy-to-use editor known as nano. I'll explain everything you need in order to get set up and working!

A note about sample source code

This book includes extensive sample source code, all of which is made available for you to use, without restriction but also without warranty, for your own programs. The sample code is available from: http://www.cprogramming.com/c++book/code/sample_code.zip. All sample source code files are stored in a separate folder named after the chapter in which that source file appears (e.g. files from this chapter appear in the folder ch1). Each source code listing in this book that has an associated file has the name (but not the chapter) of the file as a caption.

Windows

We'll set up a tool called **Code::Blocks**, a free development environment for C++.

Step 1: Download Code::Blocks

- Go to this website: http://www.codeblocks.org/downloads
- Follow the link to "Download the binary release"
- Go to the Windows 2000 / XP / Vista / 7 section
- Look for the file that includes mingw in the name. (The name as of this writing was codeblocks-12.11mingw-setup.exe; the number may be different).
- Save the file to your desktop. As of this writing, It is roughly 74 megabytes.

Step 2: Install Code::Blocks

- Double click the installer.
- Hit next several times. Other setup tutorials will assume you have installed in **C:\Program Files\CodeBlocks** (the default install location), but you may install elsewhere if you like
- Do a Full Installation (select "Full: All plugins, all tools, just everything" from the "Select the type of install" dropdown menu)
- Launch Code::Blocks

Step 3: Running Code::Blocks

You will be prompted with a Compilers auto-detection window:

When you get the compilers auto-detection window, just hit OK. Code::Blocks may ask whether you want to associate it as the default viewer for C/C++ files—I suggest you do. Click on the File menu, and under "New", select "Project..."

The following window will come up:

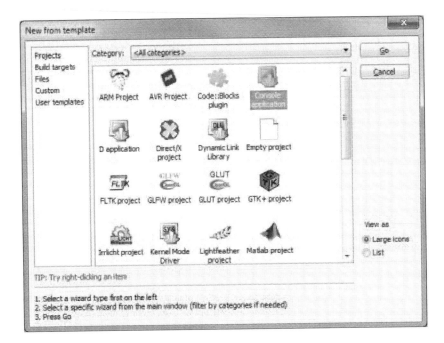

Click on "Console Application" and hit the "Go" button. All sample code from this book can be run as a console application.

Click next until you get to the language selection dialog:

You'll be asked to choose whether you want to use C or C++. Since we're learning C++, pick C++.

After clicking "Next", Code::Blocks will then prompt you with where you'd like to save the console application:

I'd recommend you put it in its own folder, as it may create several files (this is especially true if you create other types of projects). You will need to give your project a name; anything will be fine.

Clicking "Next" again will prompt you to set up your compiler:

You don't need to do anything here. Just accept the defaults by hitting "Finish".

You can now open the main.cpp file on the left:

(You may need to expand the contents of the "Sources" folder if you don't see main.cpp.)

At this point, you will have your main.cpp file, which you can modify if you like. Notice the file extension: .cpp is the standard extension for C++ source files—not .txt—even though cpp files are plain text. For now, it just says "Hello World!", so we can run it as is. Hit F9, which will first compile it and then run it. (You can also go to the Build|Build and Run menu option.)

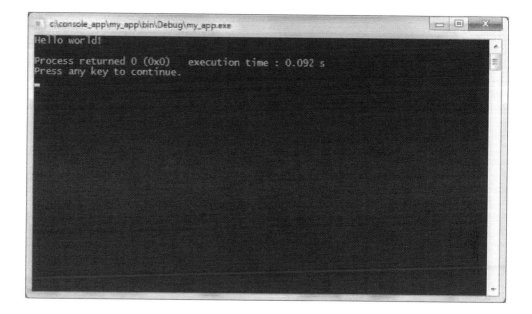

You now have a running program! You can simply edit main.cpp and then hit F9 to compile it and run it again.

Troubleshooting

If for some reason you don't get a running program, it probably means that there were compiler errors or that the environment wasn't set up correctly.

Environment Setup

The most common error people see if things don't work is a message like "'CB01 – Debug" uses an invalid compiler. Probably the toolchain path within the compiler options is not setup correctly?! Skipping..."

First, make sure that you downloaded the right version of Code::Blocks, the one that included MinGW. If that doesn't solve the problem, it is likely a problem with compiler auto-detection. To check your current "auto-detected" state, go to "Settings|Compiler and Debugger...". Then on the left, choose "Global Compiler Settings" (it has a gear icon) and on the right, select the "Toolchain executables" tab. This tab has an "Auto-detect" button that you can use. That might fix the problem—if it doesn't, you can manually fill out the form. Here's a screenshot demonstrating what things look like on my system. Change the path marked "Compiler's installation directory" if you installed to a different location, and make sure everything else is filled in as shown.

Once you've done that, try pressing F9 again to see if you get a running program.

Compiler Errors

Compiler errors could happen if you've modified the main.cpp file in a way that confuses the compiler. To figure out what is wrong, take a look at the "Build messages" or "Build log" windows. The "Build messages" window will show you just compiler errors, the "Build log" will show you other issues too. Here's what it will look like if you have an error:

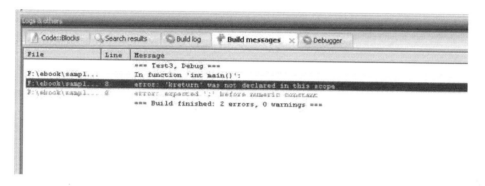

In this case, it shows you the name of the file, the line number, and then a brief string of text explaining the error. Here, I changed the line `return 0;` to be `kreturn 0;` and that is not valid C++, so I got an error.

Whenever you are programming, you will find it useful to check this window when your program doesn't compile in order to figure out what happened.

Throughout this book, you will see lots of sample code. For each one, you can either create a new console application or modify the source file of your original program. I'd recommend making a new console application for each program so that you can make changes to the sample code and save it for later review.

What exactly is Code::Blocks?

Earlier, I introduced the idea of an integrated development environment. Code::Blocks is an integrated development environment because it makes it easy to write source code and build your program from the same application. One thing you should be aware of is that Code::Blocks itself is not a compiler. When you downloaded Code::Blocks, the installation package you chose *also* included a compiler, in this case GCC from MinGW, which is a free compiler for Windows. Code::Blocks handles all the messy details of setting up and calling the compiler, which is doing the real work.

Macintosh

This section covers only setting up development on an OS X system.[3]

OS X already comes with a powerful Unix-based shell environment that you can use, so many of the tools that are covered in the Linux section of this book are available to you. However, you may also want to try out Apple's Xcode development environment. Regardless of whether you choose to use the Xcode environment itself, installing Xcode is a prerequisite to using the standard Linux tools as well.

While using the Xcode environment itself is not required for developing C++ programs on the Mac, if you want to venture into Mac UI programming, then you should learn to use Xcode.

Xcode

Xcode comes for free as part of Mac OS X, but by default, Xcode is not actually installed. You can either find Xcode on your Mac OS X DVD, or download the latest version. The download that includes documentation is very large, so you should try to find Xcode on your Mac OS X CD if you have a slow network connection. Note that even the basic compilers, such as gcc and g++, which you normally have installed by default on a Linux environment, are not installed by default on Mac OS X; to get them, you must download Xcode Developer Tools.

Below are instructions for installing and getting started with Xcode 3 and Xcode 4. If you are using Snow Leopard (10.6) or earlier, follow the instructions for Xcode 3. Otherwise, skip ahead to the section on installing Xcode 4.

Installing Xcode 3

To download Xcode:

- Register as an Apple developer at
  http://developer.apple.com/programs/register/
- Registering as an Apple developer is free. The Apple website may make it seem like you have to pay, but the link above should take you directly

---

[3] If you're using Mac OS 9 or earlier, and are unable to upgrade, you can try the Macintosh Programmer's Workshop, available directly from Apple: http://developer.apple.com/tools/mpw-tools/ Since OS 9 is so old, I cannot walk you through the setup.

to the free signup page. You will have to fill out some basic personal information as part of signing up.

- Go to https://developer.apple.com/downloads/index.action and search for Xcode 3.2.6. One result will show up; click on it and then click the download link, Xcode 3.2.6 and iOS SDK 4.3.

Xcode comes as a standard disk image file that you can open. Open this disk image, and run the file Xcode.mpkg.

The installation process will ask you to agree to a licensing agreement, and then present you with a list of components to install. The default components should be fine. Go ahead and accept all the defaults and run the rest of the installer.

Running Xcode

Once you've run the installer, you can find Xcode in Developer|Applications|Xcode. Go ahead and run the Xcode application. Xcode comes with extensive documentation, and you may wish to take some time and go through the "Getting Started with Xcode" tutorial. However, the rest of this section will not assume that you have read any other documentation.

Creating your first C++ program in Xcode

So let's get started—from the main Xcode window that comes up when you start Xcode, choose "Create a new Xcode project". (You can also go to "File|New Project..." or press Shift-⌘-N).

Choose "Application" from the left sidebar under "Mac OS X", and then choose "Command Line Tool". (You may also see "Application" under iOS—you don't want that right now.)

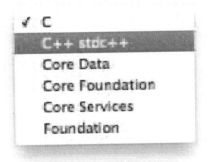

You will also need to change the "Type" of the project from C to C++ stdc++.

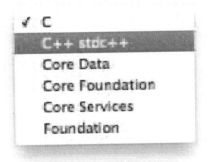

Once you've done that, press "Choose…" and select a name and a location for your new project. This will create a new directory under the location that you choose, with the same name as the name of your project. For this sample program, I will use the project name HelloWorld.

Then press Save.

After pressing save, a new window will come up that looks like this:

This view shows you quite a few things. The right sidebar gives you access to Source, Documentation and Products. The "Source" folder contains the actual C++ files associated with your project, the "Documentation" folder contains any documentation you have—usually the source for a "man page". You can ignore it for now. The "Products" folder stores the result of compiling your program. You can also see the contents of these folders displayed in the top middle window.

For now, let's work on the source file itself. Go ahead and select "main.cpp" either from the top middle window or from the Source folder on the left. (Notice the file extension: .cpp is the standard extension for C++ source files— not .txt—even though cpp files are plain text.) If you single-click you will bring up the source in the window that currently reads "No Editor". You can then start typing directly into the file.

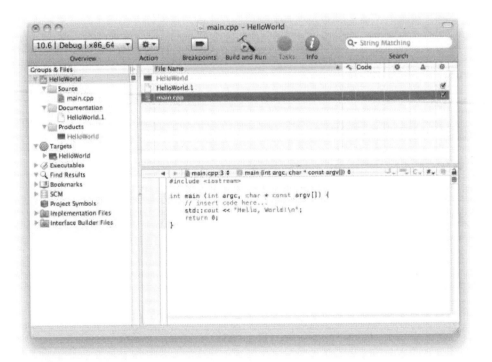

You can also double-click on the file in order to bring up a larger editor window, if you want more space.

By default Xcode provides a small sample program that you can start with. Let's compile and then run this sample program. First click on the "Build and Run" button on the toolbar.

When you press this button, the program will compile, meaning that the executable file will be created. In Xcode 3, you won't actually see anything run. In order to do that, you need to double-click on the "HelloWorld" executable. You'll notice that it used to be colored red, but after doing the build it should be colored black:

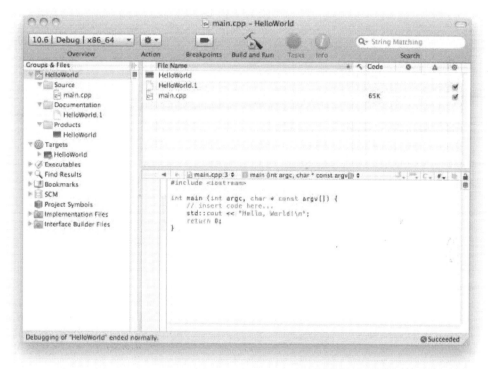

Go ahead and double click it to run your first program!

You should see some output that looks something like this (I've covered the username for the privacy of the person who lent me their Macintosh for this screenshot):

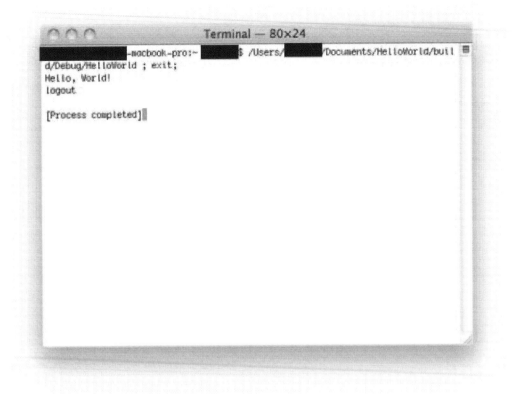

And there you go—you've run your first program!

From here on out, whenever you have a sample program you want to run, you can use the project we just created, or you can create a new project for it. In either case, when you want to add your own code, you can start by modifying the sample program that Xcode creates in main.cpp.

Installing Xcode 4

To download Xcode 4, you can simply search for it in the Mac App Store and install it. It is about 4.5 GB.

The download from the Mac App Store will put an "Install Xcode" icon into your Dock. Run this to start the install process.

The installation process will ask you to agree to a licensing agreement, and then present you with a list of components to install. The default components should be fine. Go ahead and accept all the defaults and run the rest of the installer.

Running Xcode

After running the installer, you'll find Xcode in Developer|Applications|Xcode. Go ahead and run the Xcode application. Xcode comes with extensive documentation, and you may wish to take some time and go through the "Xcode Quick Start Guide", which you can reach from the "Learn about using Xcode" link on the startup screen. However, the rest of this section will not assume that you have read any other documentation.

Creating your first C++ program in Xcode

So let's get started—from the main Xcode window that comes up when you start Xcode, choose "Create a new Xcode project". (You can also go to "File|New|New Project..." or press Shift-⌘-N). This will bring up a screen that looks like this.

Choose "Application" from the left sidebar under "Mac OS X", and then choose "Command Line Tool". (You may also see "Application" under iOS—you don't want that right now.) Then press "Next".

After pressing "Next", you will see this screen:

I've already filled it out with a product name, "HelloWorld", and I've chosen the Type to be C++ (it defaults to C). Do that, and then press "Next" again.

After pressing "Next", you'll be brought to this screen:

If "Create local git repository for this project" is checked, you can uncheck it. Git is a "source control" system that allows you to keep multiple versions of your project, but git is outside the scope of this book. You should also choose a location for your project—I put this one in Documents. Once you've made these choices, press "Create".

After pressing "Create", a new window will come up that looks like this:

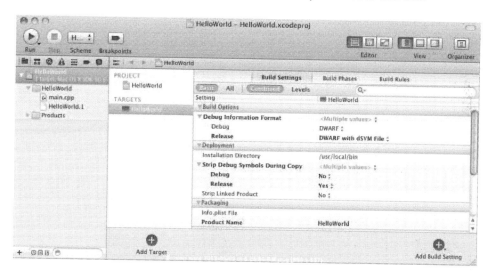

This view shows you quite a few things. The right sidebar gives you access source code and Products. The source code is under the directory named after your project, in this case "HelloWorld". Most of the rest of this screen is displaying compiler configuration, which we don't need to do anything with right now.

Let's work on the source file itself. Go ahead and select "main.cpp" in the folder on the left sidebar. (Notice the file extension: .cpp is the standard extension for C++ source files—not .txt—even though cpp files are plain text.) If you single-click you will bring up the source in the main window. You can then start typing directly into the file.

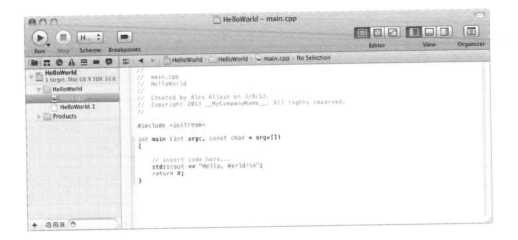

You can also double-click on the file in order to bring up an editor window that can be moved around.

By default Xcode provides a small sample program that you can start with. Let's compile and then run this sample program. All you need to do is click the "Run" button on the toolbar! The output will be displayed in the lower right:

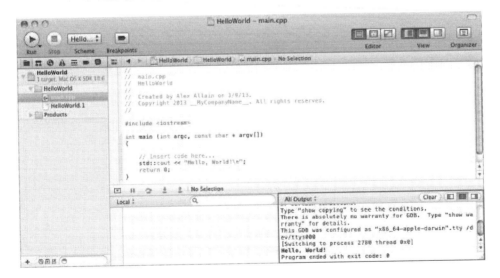

And there you go—you've run your first program!

From here on out, whenever you have a sample program you want to run, you can either use the project we just created, or you can create a new project for it. In either case, when you want to add your own code, you can start by modifying the sample program that Xcode creates in main.cpp.

Troubleshooting

[This section uses screenshots from Xcode 3. I have noted where Xcode 3 and Xcode 4 are different.]

It's possible that your program will fail to compile for some reason, usually because of a compiler error (for example, perhaps a typo in the sample program or a real error in your own program). If this happens, then the compiler will display one or more compiler error messages.

Xcode displays compiler error messages directly alongside the source code, at the line where the error occurred. In the below example, I modified the original program so that instead of `std::cout`, it has simply `c`.

In the rectangle, you can see the compiler error—that Xcode doesn't know what 'c' is. You can also see a message that the build failed, in the lower left corner, and again in the lower right corner, along with a count of the number of errors (1, in this case). (In Xcode 4, the icon is similar, but it appears in the upper-right corner.)

If you want to see a full list of errors, in Xcode 3 you can click on the hammer icon in the lower-right corner and bring up a dialog box that shows all errors the compiler discovered, as a list:

Again I've highlighted the place where you can see the actual error, and if you click on it, it will show a small editor window where you can see the error in the code itself.

In Xcode 4, the right-hand panel where the source files were located is replaced with compiler errors if the build fails.

Once you fix the error, you can simply press the "Build and Run" button again to try again.

Linux

If you are running on Linux, you almost certainly already have a C++ compiler installed. Typically, Linux users use the C++ compiler g++, which is part of the GNU Compiler Collection (GCC).

Step 1: Installing g++

To check if you have g++ installed, bring up a terminal window. Type in g++ and hit enter. If you have your compiler already installed, you should see:

```
g++: no input files
```

If you see a phrase like this one:

```
command not found
```

then you will probably need to install g++. Installing g++ will depend on your particular Linux distribution's package management software. If you are running Ubuntu, for example, you may need to simply type:

```
aptitude install g++
```

Other Linux distributions may have similarly easy package management or may require additional steps. Read the documentation from your Linux distro for more.

Step 2: Running g++

Running g++ is relatively easy. Let's create your very first program right now. Create a simple file with a .cpp extension that contains exactly this text:

```
#include <iostream>
```

```
int main ()
{
        std::cout << "Hello, world" << std::endl;
}
```
Sample Code 1: hello.cpp

Save this file as `hello.cpp`, and remember the directory where you put it. (Notice the file extension: .cpp is the standard extension for C++ source files—not .txt—even though cpp files are plain text.)

Go back to the terminal window, and change to the directory where you saved the file.

Type:

```
g++ hello.cpp -o hello
```

Then hit enter.

The `-o` option to g++ provides a name for the output file. If you don't use it, the name defaults to `a.out`.

Step 3: Running your program
In this case, we gave the file the name `hello`, so you can now run your new program by typing

```
./hello
```

And you should see the output

```
Hello, world
```

And there is your first program, saying hi to the brave new world.

Troubleshooting
It's possible that your program may fail to compile for some reason, usually because of a compiler error (for example, if you entered the sample program with a typo). If this happens, then the compiler will display one or more compile error messages.

For example, if you put an x before `cout` in the sample program, the compiler would come back with these errors:

```
gcc_ex2.cc: In function 'int main ()':
gcc_ex2.cc:5: error: 'xcout' is not a member of 'std'
```

Each error shows you the file name, a line number, and an error message. Here, the issue is that the compiler doesn't know anything about xcout since it should just be cout.

Step 4: Setting up a text editor

If you're using Linux, you will also want to find a good text editor to use. Linux has some very high end text editors available, such as Vim and Emacs (I use Vim when I'm working on Linux). But they are relatively difficult to learn, and require a real time investment. In the long run, it's worth it, but you may not want to take the time when you're also starting to learn to program. If you are already familiar with either of these tools, feel free to continue using them.

If you don't already have a favorite editor, you may want to try a text editor like nano. Nano is a comparatively simple text editor, but it does have certain valuable features like syntax highlighting and automatic indentation (so that you don't have to keep pressing tab all the time when you go to a new line in your program—sounds trivial, but you really do want it). Nano is based on an editor called pico, which is a very simple editor to learn to use but that lacks many features needed for programming. You may even have used pico if you've used the mail program Pine. If not, that's ok, no prior experience is necessary to start working with nano.

You may already have nano—to find out, type nano in a terminal window. It may launch automatically. If not, and you get a variant of

```
command not found
```

then you will need to install nano—you should follow the instructions for getting nano using your Linux distribution's package manager. I've written this section with version 2.2.4 of nano in mind, but later versions should be fine.

Configuring Nano

In order to take advantage of some features of nano, you will need to set up a nano configuration file. The configuration file for nano is called .nanorc and like most Linux configuration files, your user-specific configuration resides in your home directory (~/.nanorc).

If this file already exists, you can simply edit it—otherwise, you should create it. (If you have no experience at all using text editors on Linux, you can use nano to do this configuration—read below if you need help with the basics of nano!)

To configure nano properly, use the sample `.nanorc` file that comes with this book. It will provide you will nice syntax highlighting and auto-indentation, which will make editing source code much easier.

Using Nano

You can run nano without providing an argument if you wish to create a new file, or you can specify a filename at the command line to start editing that file:

```
nano hello.cpp
```

If the file doesn't exist, nano will start editing a new buffer associated with the file. It will not, however, create the file on disk until you actually save your changes.

Here's an example of what nano should look like when you run it.

In the rectangle at the top is the title of the current file being edited or "New Buffer" if you ran nano without providing a file.

In the rectangle at the bottom are a bunch of keyboard commands. Any time you see the ^ character in front of a letter, that means you need to press the Control key on your keyboard in combination which the letter—for example, exit is shown as ^X, so to exit you press Ctrl-X. The capitalization is not important.

If you're coming from a Windows world, you may not be familiar with some of the terminology used by nano, so let's look at some basic nano operations.

Editing text

When you launch nano, you can either bring up a new file or open an existing file. At this point, you can simply begin typing into the file—in this respect nano is very similar to Notepad on Windows. If you want to use copy and paste, though, the terms are different—Cut Text (Ctrl-K) and UnCut Text (Ctrl-U). These commands default to cutting a single line of text if you haven't selected any text.

You can also search for text in a file using "Where Is" by pressing Ctrl-W. This brings up a new set of options, but the simplest of them is to simply type in the string you're looking for and hit enter.

You can navigate a page at a time using Prev Page (Ctrl-Y) and Next Page (Ctrl-V). Notice that the keyboard shortcuts have little in common with Windows.

The only major feature that nano lacks, that most other text editors have, is that nano currently (in version 2.2) has only experimental support for undo/redo functionality. All undo/redo functionality is disabled by default.

You can use nano to do a file wide search/replace by pressing Alt-R—you'll first be prompted with text to find, and then the text to replace it with.

Saving files

Saving a file is called, in nano parlance, WriteOut (Ctrl-O).

```
File Name to Write:
^G  Get Help          ^T  To Files      M-M  Mac Format      M-P  Prepend
^C  Cancel            M-D DOS Format    M-A  Append          M-B  Backup File
```

When you invoke WriteOut, you will always be prompted for the name of the file to write to, even if you have a file already open. If you are already editing a file, the name of the file will be shown by default, so you can just hit Enter and it will save the file. If you want to save to a new location, can type in the name of the file to save, or you can use the To Files menu option (Ctrl-T) to select a file to write to. Cancel (Ctrl-C) speaks for itself—most commands will have the option of cancelling them—but unlike a Windows machine, the default cancel button is Ctrl-C rather than Escape. Don't worry about the other options that are available for now—you shouldn't need to use them most of the time.

Opening files

If you want to actually open a file for editing, you use Read File (Ctrl-R). Read File brings up a new set of menu options.

If you want to open the file, rather than insert the text directly into the file you're currently editing, choose New Buffer at this menu, before selecting a file. The shortcut for New Buffer is M-F. The M stands for meta key—in this case, you'd normally use the Alt key on your keyboard: Alt-F.[4] This tells nano that you are going to open the file. Once you've done that, you can either type in the name to a file, or you can use Ctrl-T to bring up a file list that will let you select the file you want to edit. As usual, you can use Ctrl-C to cancel the operation.

Looking at a source file

Now that you've learned a bit about editing in nano, you should be able to open a source file and start working on it. If you've got your .nanorc file configured properly, when you open a source file that has some text in it, it should look something like this if you open the file hello.cpp we ran earlier:

---

[4]Some folks may have trouble using the Alt key for the meta key; if you find that using the Alt key doesn't work, you can always press and release Esc before pressing the letter—for example Esc F is the same as pressing Alt-F.

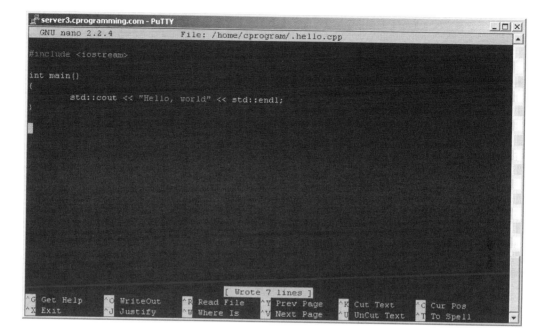

You should see that the text is displayed in different colors depending on what its function is; for example, if you put the above "Hello world" program into your editor, you should see that the text is pink. This syntax highlighting is file extension based, so until you save the file as a source file (.cpp), it won't have highlighting.

From here on out, whenever you have a sample program you want to run, you can simply create a new text file for that program using nano and compile it using the steps above.

Learning more
You should now be able to edit basic files in nano, but if you want to learn more, the built-in help is simply a Ctrl-G away. I also found this website to be particularly useful for explaining more advanced nano features:
http://freethegnu.wordpress.com/2007/06/23/nano-shortcuts-syntax-highlight-and-nanorc-config-file-pt1/

Chapter 2
The Basics of C++

Intro to the C++ language

If you have set up your development environment as laid out in the previous chapter, you've already had a chance to run your first program. Congratulations! That's a big step.

In this chapter, I will walk you through the basic building blocks of C++, allowing you to start making your own simple programs. I'll introduce several concepts that you will see again and again: how a program is structured, the `main` function, the idea of standard functions provided by your compiler, how to add comments to your program, and a short introduction to how to think like a programmer.

The simplest C++ program

Let's start off by simply looking at the simplest possible program—one that doesn't do anything—and walk through it step by step:

```cpp
int main ()
{
}
```
Sample Code 2: empty.cpp

See, not too scary!

The first line

```
int main ()
```

tells the compiler that there is a function named **main**, and that the function returns an integer, abbreviated in C++ to `int`. A **function** is a piece of code that someone wrote, usually using other functions or possibly simply basic language features. In this case, our function doesn't do anything, but we'll soon see a function that does.

The `main` function is a special function; it's the only function that must be included in all C++ programs, and it's the point where your program will start when you run it. The main function is preceded by the type of its return value, `int`. When a function returns a value, the code that calls that function will be able to access the value returned from the function. In the case of main, the value returned goes to the operating system. Normally we would need to explicitly return a value here, but C++ allows the main function to omit the return statement and it will default to returning 0 (a code that tells the operating system everything went ok).

The **curly braces**, { and }, signal the beginning and end of functions (and, as we'll see soon, other code blocks). You can think of them as meaning *begin* and *end*. In this case, we know that the function doesn't do anything because there is nothing between the two curly braces.

When you run this program, you won't see any output, so let's move on to a program that is a little bit more interesting (but only a little bit).

```
#include <iostream>

using namespace std;

int main ()
{
     cout << "HEY, you, I'm alive! Oh, and Hello
World!\n";
}
```
Sample Code 3: hello.cpp

First of all, notice that there is something between the curly braces—this means that the program will *do* something! Let's walk through the program step-by-step.

The first line

```
#include <iostream>
```

is an **include statement** that tells the compiler to put code from the header file called `iostream` into our program before creating the executable. The `iostream` header file comes with your compiler and allows you to perform input and output. Using `#include` effectively takes everything in the header file and pastes it into your program. By including header files, you gain access to the many functions provided by your compiler.

Whenever we need access to basic functions, we'll need to include the header file that gives access to that function—for now, most of the functions we need are in the `iostream` header file, and you'll see it at the start of almost every program, but nearly every program you write will start off with one or more include statements.

Following the include statement is this line:

```
using namespace std;
```

This is boilerplate code that almost all C++ programs will include. For now, just use it at the top of all your programs, right under the include statements. The statement itself makes it easier to use shorter versions of some of the routines provided by the `iostream` header file. We'll talk later about exactly how this works—for now, just don't forget to include it.

Notice that this line ends with a semicolon. The semicolon is part of the syntax of C++. It tells the compiler that you're at the end of a statement. The semicolon is used to end most statements in C++. Not putting in semicolons is one of the most common problems for new programmers, so if your program doesn't work for some reason, make sure that you didn't leave out a semicolon. Whenever I introduce new concepts, I'll tell you whether you need to use a semicolon or not when you use them.

Next we have the `main` function, where the program will start:

```
int main ()
```

The next line of the program may seem strange, with the funny << symbol.

```
    cout << "HEY, you, I'm alive! Oh, and Hello
World!\n";
```

What's going on is that C++ uses the `cout` object (pronounced "C out") to display text. Getting access to `cout` is the reason that we included the `iostream` header file.

It uses the << symbols, known as "insertion operators", to indicate what to output. In short, `cout` << results in a function call with the text as an argument to the function. A function call runs the code associated with the function. Functions usually take **arguments** used by their code. In this case, the text string we provided is the argument. You can think of function arguments like the parameters to an equation. If you want to know the area of a square, you might have a formula that squares the length of the side; here, the side length is the argument to your formula. Functions, like formulas, take variables as arguments. In this case, the function will put the argument provided onto the screen.

The quotes tell the compiler that you want to output the literal string as-is, except for certain special sequences. The \n sequence is one of those special sequences—it is actually treated as a single character that stands for a newline, basically, like hitting the enter key (we'll talk about this later in more detail). It moves the cursor on your screen to the next line. You will also sometimes see the special value `endl` used instead of a newline: `cout << "Hello" << endl` and `cout << "Hello\n"` are essentially equivalent. The word `endl` stands for "**end** line", and the last letter is L, not 1. Writing end1 with a 1 instead of an L is an easy mistake to make, so be careful.

Finally, notice the semicolon again; we need to put it here since we're calling a function.

The final curly brace closes off the function. You should try compiling this program and running it. Go ahead and type it into your compiler, or open up the sample source file that came with this book. You could copy and paste it, but I recommend actually typing the program yourself—it's not very long, and it will help you notice the small details that matter to the compiler, like remembering to use semicolons.

Once you've got your first program running, why don't you try playing around with the `cout` function to get used to writing C++? Output different text, output multiple lines—see what you can make the computer do.

What happens if you don't see your program?

Depending on the operating system and compiler that you are using, when you run the programs that come with this book, you may not see the result of the program—it might flash by very quickly and then close. If you are using one of the environments recommended by this book, you shouldn't run into this problem, but if you are using another environment, it might. If this happens, you can fix the problem by adding the line:

```
cin.get();
```

at the end of your program. This will cause the program to wait for you to press a key before exiting, so that you can see the result before the window closes.

The basic structure of a C++ program

Whew, there was a surprising amount going for such a short program! Let's cut out all the details and look at the outline of a basic C++ program:

```
[include statements]
using namespace std;

int main()
{
    [your code here];
}
```

Now what happens if you leave out any of these pieces?

If you leave out the `include` statement or the `using namespace std`, your program will fail to compile. If the program doesn't compile, that means there is something that the compiler did not understand—perhaps you had bad syntax (like a missing semicolon) or perhaps you were missing a header file. Failures to compile can be quite challenging to track down when you are first starting to program. Any compiler failure will generate one or more **compiler errors**, which will explain the reason for the failure. Here's a very basic example of a compiler error message:

```
error: 'cout' was not declared in this scope
```

If you see a message like this, make sure that you both have your include statement for `iostream` and `using namespace std;` at the top of your program!

Compiler error messages are not always so easy to interpret. If you leave out the semicolon, you're likely to get all kinds of compiler errors—usually, the errors will be right *after* the line where you forgot the semicolon. If you see a lot of incomprehensible errors, try looking at the previous line and make sure it has a semicolon. Don't worry, over time you'll become very good at interpreting compiler errors, and you'll start to see fewer of them. Don't feel bad if you have a lot of them when you start out, learning to work out these errors is almost a rite of passage!

Commenting your programs

As you are learning to program, you should also start to learn how to document your programs (for yourself, if no one else). You do this by adding **comments** to code; moreover, I'll also use comments very frequently to help explain code examples.

When you tell the compiler a section of text is a comment, it will ignore it when running the code, allowing you to use any text you want to describe the real code. To create a comment use either //, which tells the compiler that the rest of the line is a comment, or /* and then */ to block off everything between as a comment.

```
// this is a one line comment
This code is not part of the comment

/* this is a multi-line comment
This line is part of the comment
*/
```

Certain compiler environments will change the color of a commented area to make it easier to tell it isn't executable code. This is an example of syntax highlighting at work.

Sometimes it is useful to be able to **comment out** sections of code in order to see how the output is affected. Commenting out code just means putting comment markers around lines of code that you don't want to be compiled. For example, if you wanted to see the effect of not having your cout statement, you could just comment it out:

```
#include <iostream>

using namespace std;

int main ()
{
//    cout << "HEY, you, I'm alive! Oh, and Hello
// World!\n";
}
```
Sample Code 4: hello_comment.cpp

Just be certain not to accidentally comment out code you need!

If you do comment out some code that is required, for example if you commented out the header file, the program may not properly compile. If you're having a lot of trouble compiling a piece of code, you can try commenting out parts of the program that you think might not be valid; if the program compiles without that code, you know the problem is coming from the code that you commented out.

Thinking like a programmer and creating reusable code

Let's take a moment away from the syntax of programming to talk about the experience of programming. There used to be a State Farm commercial where a car wash company returned cars to customers with the soap suds still on the car. The car wash washed the car, but they didn't rinse the car.[5] In the commercial, the point was that some insurance companies will write policies that make it hard to collect claims because they're written to exclude lots of things that seem like they ought to be covered.

This commercial is also a perfect metaphor for how you need to think in order to program. Computers, like the car wash company from the commercial, are very literal. They do exactly, and only, what you tell them to do; they do not understand implicit intentions. If you say wash the car, they wash the car. If you want the car rinsed, you'd better say that too. The level of detail required can

---

[5] You can watch it here, it's only 57 seconds:
http://www.youtube.com/watch?v=QaTx1J7ZeLY

be daunting at first because it requires thinking through every single step of the process, making sure that no steps are missing.

Fortunately, when you program, once you tell the computer how to do something, you can name it and refer to it, rather than repeating the steps again and again. So it is not as tedious as it sounds—you don't have to repeat yourself again and again, you can just write down very precise instructions once and reuse them. You'll see this shortly, when we get to functions.

A few words on the joys and pain of practice

You're just getting started with the book, but even this chapter has several practice problems at the end. In my experience, there is very little better for learning to program than working on practice problems. First of all, programming requires attention to detail, and I know from experience that it's easy to read a piece of text and think, "hey, that all makes sense" only to find out that I didn't get the details. You can't really get good at dealing with the syntax of C++ and the nuances of the language without writing your own code. Since it's not always easy to come up with good ideas for simple programs when you're just learning to program, most of the chapters in this book include practice problems for you do to. There aren't an overwhelming number, so I would strongly recommend that after each chapter, you attempt all of the practice problems before moving on to the next chapter.

Congratulations! You've just finished learning about your first program and even a little bit about how to start thinking like a programmer—there's a lot of material here, and there's already some room for you to play with the sample code to see what you can do. In the next chapter, we'll learn more about how to interact with the user, including how to take user input into our programs.

Quiz yourself

1. What is the correct value to return to the operating system upon the successful completion of a program?

A. -1

B. 1

C. 0

D. Programs do not return a value.

2. What is the only function all C++ programs must contain?

A. `start()`

B. `system()`
C. `main()`
D. `program()`

3. What punctuation is used to signal the beginning and end of code blocks?
A. `{ }`
B. `->` and `<-`
C. `BEGIN` and `END`
D. `(` and `)`

4. What punctuation ends most lines of C++ code?
A. `.`
B. `;`
C. `:`
D. `'`

5. Which of the following is a correct comment?
A. `*/ Comments */`
B. `** Comment **`
C. `/* Comment */`
D. `{ Comment }`

6. What header file do you need to use to get access to cout?
A. `stream`
B. nothing, it is available by default
C. `iostream`
D. `using namespace std;`

(View solution on page 480)

Practice problems

1. Write a program that prints out your name.

2. Write a program that displays multiple lines of text onto the screen, each one displaying the name of one of your friends.

3. Try commenting out each line of code in the first program we created together and see whether the program can compile without it. Look at the

errors you get—do they make any sense? Can you see why they happened because of the line of code you changed?

Chapter 3
User Interaction and Working with Variables

So far you've learned how to write a simple program to display information typed in by you, the programmer, and how to describe your program with comments. That's great, but what if you want to interact with your user?

Introduction to Variables

To interact with your user, you need to accept **input**, information that comes from outside the program. To do that, you must have a place to store that input. In programming, input, as well as other data, is stored in **variables**. There are several different types of variables that store different kinds of information (e.g. numbers versus letters); when you tell the compiler you are declaring a variable, you must include the **data type**, or just **type**, along with the name of the variable.

The most common basic types available to you are `char`, `int`, and `double`. A variable of type **char** stores a single character, variables of type **int** store integers (numbers without decimal places), and variables of type **double** store numbers with decimal places (weird name, eh?). Each of these variable types is the keyword that you use when you declare a variable.

Declaring variables in C++

Before you can use a variable, you need to tell the compiler about it by declaring it (the compiler is very picky about being told about things in advance). To declare a variable you use the syntax "type <name>;" (notice that semicolon again!)

Here are some examples of declaring variables:

```
int whole_number;
char letter;
double number_with_decimals;
```

You can declare multiple variables of the same type on the same line; each variable name should be separated by a comma.

```
int a, b, c, d;
```

I recommend declaring each variable on its own line, though, to make it easier to read.

Using variables

Ok, so you now know how to tell the compiler about variables, but what about using them?

You use cin (pronounced "C in") to accept input, and it is followed by an insertion operator going in the other direction, >>, followed by the variable into which you want to "insert" the value typed by the user.

Here is a sample program demonstrating using a variable:

```
#include <iostream>

using namespace std;

int main ()
{
      int thisisanumber;

      cout << "Please enter a number: ";
      cin >> thisisanumber;
      cout << "You entered: " << thisisanumber << "\n";
}
```
Sample Code 5: readnum.cpp

Let's break apart this program and examine it line by line. You've already seen the first part, so I'll focus on the body of the main function.

```
int thisisanumber;
```

This line declares that `thisisanumber` is of type integer. The next new line is

```
cin >> thisisanumber;
```

The function `cin >>` stores the value the user typed into `thisisanumber`. The user must press enter before the number is read by the program.

What if your program exits immediately?

If you previously had to use `cin.get()` to keep your program from exiting immediately, you may have seen that the above program immediately quit when you ran it, even if you included the `cin.get()` call. You can fix it by adding this line before the call to `cin.get()`:

```
cin.ignore();
```

This is a function that reads and discards a character, in this case, the enter key that the user pressed. Yes, when the user types input into your program, it takes the enter key too. We don't need this, so we throw it away. This line is generally only needed if you need to add a `cin.get()` to keep your program open and wait for a key press. Without it, the `cin.get()` will read in the newline character and your program will still exit immediately.

Keep in mind that the variable was declared to be integer; if the user attempts to type in a decimal number, it will be **truncated** (the decimal component of the number will be ignored; for example, 3.1415 would become 3). Try typing in a sequence of characters or a decimal number when you run the example program; the response will vary from input to input, but in no case is it particularly pretty. For now, we'll ignore the error handling that you would need to do to deal with this situation.

```
cout << "You entered: " << thisisanumber << "\n";
```

Is the line that prints back the user's input. Notice that when printing out a variable quotation marks are not used. If we'd used quotation marks around `thisisanumber`, the output would be, "You Entered: thisisanumber." The lack of quotation marks tells the compiler that there is a variable, and therefore that the program should check the value of the variable in order to replace the variable name with the variable when displaying the result.

By the way, do not be confused by the inclusion of two separate insertion operators on one line. Including multiple insertion operators on one line is perfectly acceptable and all of the output will go to the same place. In fact, you must separate string literals (strings enclosed in quotation marks) and variables by giving each its own insertion operators (<<). Trying to display a variable together with a string literal with only one << will also give you an error message:

BAD CODE
```
cout << "You entered: " thisisanumber;
```

Finally, the line ends with a semicolon, just like all other function calls. If you forget the semicolon, the compiler will give you an error message when you attempt to compile the program.

Changing, using and comparing variables
Reading in and printing back variables gets dull pretty quickly. Let's add the ability to modify variables and change your program's behavior based on the values of those variables. We'll be able to respond to different user inputs in different ways.

You can assign a value to a variable using the **assignment operator**, =.

```
int x;

x = 5;
```

Sets x equal to 5. You might have thought that the equals sign would *compare* the value of the left and right values, but it does not. In C++ a separate operator, with two equals signs, ==, is used for checking equality. You will often use == in such constructions as if statements or loops. We'll use comparisons a lot in the next couple of chapters when we learn about how to choose different paths through the program depending on the user's input.

```
a == 5      // Does NOT assign five to a. Rather, it checks
            // to see if a equals 5.
```

You can also perform arithmetic operations on variables

*	Multiplies two values
−	Subtracts two values
+	Adds two values
/	Divides one value by another

Here are a few examples:

```
a = 4 * 6; // (Note use of comments and of semicolon) a is
           //24
a = a + 5; // a equals the original value of a with five
           // added to it
```

Shorthand for adding and subtracting one
In C++, it is very common to add one to a variable:

```
int x = 0;
x = x + 1;
```

You'll see this pattern all the time later in the book, as we start to work with concepts like loops. The pattern is so common that there's an operator whose sole purpose is to add one to a variable—the ++ operator.

The code above could be written

```
int x = 0;
x++;
```

And x would have the value 1 at the end. This operator is commonly called the **increment** operator and adding one to a variable is commonly called **incrementing** the variable.

The −− operator works the same way, but subtracts one from the variable. The −− operator is commonly called the **decrement** operator, and subtracting one from a variable is called **decrementing** the variable.

Knowing this, you may be able to guess where the name C++ came from. C++ is based on a programming language called C; C++ literally means "C plus one".

C++ is C with some additions rather than an entirely new language. I think if the creators of C++ knew just how much more powerful it would be than C, they might have wanted to call it C-squared instead.

There are similar shortcut operators for adding any value to a variable:

```
x += 5; // adds 5 to x
```

As well as dividing, subtracting, and multiplying:

```
x -= 5; // subtract five from x
x *= 5; // multiply x by 5
x /= 5; // divide x 5 by five
```

Finally, not only can you use ++ or -- after a variable, you can also use it in front of the variable:

```
--x;
++y;
```

The difference between the two is the value that is returned from the expression. If you write:

```
int x = 0;
cout << x++;
```

The output is 0. The reason is that even though x is modified, the expression x++ returns the original value of x. Since the ++ appears after the variable, you can think of it being executed after getting the value of the variable.

If you put the operation before the variable, you get the new value:

```
int x = 0;
cout << ++x;
```

Will print 1 because it first adds 1 to x, and then gets the value of x. With these operations, you can make a small calculator in C++:

```
#include <iostream>

using namespace std;
```

```cpp
int main()
{
    int first_argument;
    int second_argument;
    cout << "Enter first argument: ";
    cin >> first_argument;
    cout << "Enter second argument: ";
    cin >> second_argument;
    cout << first_argument << " * " << second_argument
         << " = " << first_argument * second_argument
         << endl;
    cout << first_argument << " + " << second_argument
         << " = " << first_argument + second_argument
         << endl;
    cout << first_argument << " / " << second_argument
         << " = " << first_argument / second_argument
         << endl;
    cout << first_argument << " - " << second_argument
         << " = " << first_argument - second_argument
         << endl;
}
```

Sample Code 6: calculator.cpp

The use and misuse of variables

Common errors when declaring variables in C++

Declaring variables gives your program a lot of new things it can do, but getting a variable declaration wrong can cause some initial problems. For example, if you attempt to use a variable that you have not declared, the compile will fail and you will get a compiler error complaining about an **undeclared variable**. The compiler will usually emit an error like this:

```
error: 'x' was not declared in this scope
```

if you use a variable (x, in this case) that was not declared. The exact text will depend on your compiler; this example was taken from MinGW and Code::Blocks.

While you can have multiple variables of the same type, you cannot have multiple variables with the same name. For example, you cannot have both a double and an `int` called `my_val`. The error message from declaring two variables with the same name may look something like this:

```
error: conflicting declaration 'double my_val'
```

```
error: 'my_val' has a previous declaration as `int my_val'
error: declaration of `double my_val'
error: conflicts with previous declaration `int my_val'
```

A third compile-time issue is forgetting to put a semi-colon at the end of the line:

BAD CODE
```
int x
```

Such an error can result in wildly different error messages from the compiler, depending on what follows the variable declaration. Typically, the compiler error will mention the line right after the variable declaration.

Finally, some kinds of errors come at runtime, rather than during compilation. When you first declare a variable, the variable is **uninitialized**. You must **initialize** the variable before you use it. To initialize the variable you must assign a value to the variable before using it; if you do not, your program will behave unexpectedly. A common problem is to do something like this:

```
int x;
int y;
y = 5;
x = x + y;
```

Here, the value of y is set to 5 before y is used, but the initial value of x is unknown. It will be chosen essentially at random when the program runs, so the resulting value of x in the above code could be anything at all! Don't assume that variables are initialized to a convenient value, like 0.

One technique you can use is to always initialize your variables upon declaration:

```
int x = 0;
```

Would be enough to ensure that the variable has a known value when it is created. Getting into this habit now will definitely save you from some nasty bugs later on, and what's a few extra keystrokes among friends?

Case sensitivity

Now is a good time to talk about another important concept that can easily throw you off—**case sensitivity**. In C++, whether you use uppercase or lowercase letters matters. The names `Cat` and `cat` mean different things to the compiler. In C++, all language keywords, all functions and all variables are case sensitive.

A difference in case (`X` vs. `x`) between your variable declaration and the places where you use the variable is one reason you might get an undeclared variable error even if you think you did declare it.

Naming variables

Choosing meaningful, descriptive names for your variables is also very important. Here's an example of some bad variable naming:

```
val1 = val2 * val3;
```

What's that mean? Nobody can tell; the names of in the equation are next to useless. Whenever you program, you'll think that the code you're writing is pretty obvious—the day you write it. You'll think it's incomprehensible the next day. Coming up with descriptive variable names makes you feel just a little less confused the next time you go read the code. For example:

```
area = width * height;
```

Is much clearer than the first equation, and all without changing anything but the names.

Storing strings

You might have noticed that all of the data types so far only allow you to hold really simple values—for example, a single integer or a character. You can actually get quite a bit done with those basics, but C++ also provides other data types.[6]

One of the most useful data types is the **string**. A string can hold multiple characters. You've already seen them used when displaying text on the screen:

---

[6] C++ actually provides the ability to make your own data types, but we'll get to that later when we talk about structures

```
cout << "HEY, you, I'm alive! Oh, and Hello World!\n";
```

But the C++ string class allows you to save, modify and otherwise work with strings.

Declaring a string is easy:

```
#include <string>

using namespace std;

int main ()
{
        string my_string;
}
```
Sample Code 7: string.cpp

Notice however, that unlike when you use other built-in types, to use the string, you must use the <string> header file. The reason is that the string type is not built directly into the compiler in the way that integers are. Strings are provided to you by the C++ standard library, a large library of re-usable code.

Just like other basic types provided by C++, you can read in a string from the user using cin.

```
#include <iostream>
#include <string>

using namespace std;

int main ()
{
      string user_name;

      cout << "Please enter your name: ";
      cin >> user_name;
      cout << "Hi " << user_name << "\n";
}
```
Sample Code 8: string_name.cpp

This program creates a string variable, prompts the user to enter his or her name, and then prints back out the name.

Just like other variables, strings can be initialized with a value:

```
string user_name = "<unknown>";
```

If you want to put two strings together, known as **appending** one string onto another, you can use the + sign:

```cpp
#include <iostream>
#include <string>

using namespace std;

int main ()
{
    string user_first_name;
    string user_last_name;

    cout << "Please enter your first name: ";
    cin >> user_first_name;
    cout << "Please enter your last name: ";
    cin >> user_last_name;
    string user_full_name =
        user_first_name + " " + user_last_name;

    cout << "Your name is: " << user_full_name << "\n";
}
```
Sample Code 9: string_append.cpp

This program takes the values of three separate strings, the user's first name, a single space, and the user's last name, and appends them all together into a single value.[7]

When you read in strings, sometimes you want to read a whole line at a time. There is a special function, getline, which can be used to read in the whole line. It will even automatically discard the newline character at the end.

To use getline, you pass in a source of input, in this case cin, the string to read into, and a character on which to terminate input. For example, the following code reads the user's first name:

```cpp
getline( cin, user_first_name, '\n' );
```

---

[7] Terminology note: you will sometimes see the word **concatenate** used to mean appending two strings together. Concatenate comes from the Latin for "to chain together", catena meaning chain in Latin.

`getline` could also be useful if you wanted to read user input only up to another character, such as a comma (the user still has to hit enter before the program will actually accept the data, though):

```
getline( cin, my_string, ',' );
```

Now if the user types:

```
Hello, World
```

The value "`Hello`" will go into `my_string`. The rest of the text, in this case, "`World`", will remain in the input buffer until your program reads it with another input statement.

Okay, I get strings—but why all those other types?
Note: This section is advanced material that you don't need to use quite yet. If you find it confusing, it's fine to move on and come back to it later.

At this point, you might be wondering why we have so many different types of basic variables.

Let's take a moment to introduce two basic building blocks for all computer programs: the **bit** and the **byte**. The bit is the fundamental unit of storage on a computer—a bit is an on/off switch, holding either a one or a zero, depending on which way the switch is set. A byte is made up of eight bits. Because there are eight bits in a byte, there are 256 possible configurations of 1 and 0. This is because there are eight positions, each of which can have two values. Let's break that down. One bit can store 0 or 1—two values. A second bit gives us twice as many: 00, 01, 10, and 11. A third bit doubles it again by pairing a zero or a one with any of the two-bit combinations. So each bit doubles the number of representable values. In order words, for n bits, we can represent 2^n values. A byte is eight bits, so it can represent 2^8 possible configurations. If you have two bytes, you have 16 bits, so you can represent 2^{16} (65536) values.

If you didn't follow all of that, it's ok, the main takeaway is that the more bytes you have, larger the range of data you can store.

For example, a char can store only a limited range of data—256 different values. It's a single byte. An integer typically uses four bytes, meaning it can represent about four billion different numbers.

A good example of two variables that differ only in the amount of space they require are the double, and its lesser twin, the **float**. The float was actually the original variable type that could store decimal numbers, and the name float came from the fact that it has a decimal that can "float" into different positions in the number. In other words, you can have two digits before the decimal and four after (12.2345), or you can have four digits before the decimal and two after (3421.12). You aren't limited to a specific number of digits before and a specific number of digits after the decimal.

If you didn't quite get that, it's ok—the name is mostly historical. Just know that floating-point numbers mean "numbers with decimal places". But floats have only four bytes of space, so they cannot store as many different values as doubles, which have eight bytes of space. Back when computers had less memory than they do today, this was a bigger deal, and programmers would often go to great lengths to save a few bytes. Nowadays, you will almost always be better off using a double, but in cases where space is critical (perhaps on low-memory systems like cell phones), you still have the option of using a float.

The smallest data type is the char—a single byte. You might be thinking, if space doesn't matter, why do we still have chars? The answer is that chars also have special meaning—input and output is done in terms of characters rather than numbers. When you read a value into a char variable, the user can type a character, and when you print a character `cout` displays the character represented by the number stored in the variable rather than printing the actual number in the variable. "What," you ask, "does that mean? Why are numbers characters? Huh?" The answer is that when a computer stores what we think of as a character (the letter 'a', for example), it actually stores a number that represents that character. There is a table of pairings between numbers and characters, called the **ASCII table**, which tells you what numbers correspond to which characters. When your program prints out a character, rather than displaying the number, it goes and finds the character to display in the ASCII table.[8]

---

[8] I would be remiss in not saying that the ASCII table is quite small—it has only 256 values. This means that ASCII is not suitable for use with languages like Japanese or

The dirty little secret of floating-point numbers

I want to let you in on something about floating-point numbers like float or double—they sure sound good in practice, since they can represent a huge range of values. The maximum value a double can represent is about 1.8×10^{308}. That's a number with 308 zeros at the end of it. But a double is only 8 bytes—doesn't that mean it holds only 2^{32} (18,446,744,073,709,551,616) possible values? (That's a LOT of zeros, but it's not 308 zeros.)

Yes, that's right! In fact, a double can only represent about 18 quintillion numbers. That's very large—so large I had to look up what was the name for a number with 18 zeros. But it's still not 308 zeros. Floating-point numbers allow you to exactly represent only a small number of the values that are in their actual overall range by using a format similar to scientific notation.

In scientific notation, you write out numbers in the form $x \times 10^y$. The x usually stores the first few digits of the number, and the y value, the **exponent**, stores the power to raise the number to. For example, you could write the distance between the sun and the earth as 9.2956×10^7 miles (approximately 93 million miles).

This allows the computer to store really big numbers by putting a very large number in the exponent. But the non-exponent part can't store 300 digits, it can only store about 15 digits. So you can only get 15 digits of **precision** when you work with floating-point numbers. If you're dealing with relatively small values, then the difference between the number the computer stores, and the actual number, will be very small. If you're working with huge values, well, you're going to have large absolute error, even if the relative error is small. For example, if I had only two digits of precision, I could write that the earth is 9.3×10^7 miles from the sun. That's very close, in relative terms, to the right value (less than .1% off). But in absolute terms, it's 44 thousand miles! That's nearly twice the circumference of the earth. But of course, that's using only 2 digits of precision. With 15, you can get a lot closer for numbers as small as a million.

Chinese, which have many more characters than 256. Dealing with these complications involves introducing the idea of Unicode, which is outside the scope of this book. You can read more about it here:

http://www.cprogramming.com/tutorial/unicode.html

In most cases, the inexactness of floating-point numbers won't affect you unless you're doing some serious number crunching or scientific computing, but when it matters, it matters.

The dirty little secret of integers

Integers, too, have their own dirty laundry. The fact is, integers and floating-point numbers don't get along. Integers, unlike floating-point numbers, always store exactly the integer value you put into them; but they truly hate the decimal point. When you do math with an integer, and the result is not another integer, the result is truncated. The non-decimal component is exact, but the rest is thrown out.

For example, you would probably fail any math test where you said that 5/2 = 2. But this is actually exactly what the computer will do! If you want to get the answer with decimal places, you need to use a non-integer type.

When you actually write numbers into your program, they are assumed to be integers—that's why 5/2 evaluates to 2. But if you put a decimal point in the number, for example, 5.0/2.0, then the compiler will interpret the operation as a floating-point equation, and give you back the answer you expect—2.5.

Quiz yourself

1. What variable type should you use if you want to store a number like 3.1415?
A. `int`
B. `char`
C. `double`
D. `string`

2. Which of the following is the correct operator to compare two variables?
A. `:=`
B. `=`
C. `equal`
D. `==`

3. How do you get access to the string data type?
A. It is built into the language, so you don't need to do anything
B. Since strings are used for I/O, you include the `iostream` header file
C. You include the `string` header file
D. C++ doesn't support strings

4. Which of the following is not a correct variable type?

A. `double`

B. `real`

C. `int`

D. `char`

5. How can you read in an entire line from the user?

A. use `cin>>`

B. Use `readline`

C. use `getline`

D. You cannot do this easily

6. What would be displayed on the screen for this expression in C++: `cout <<` `1234/2000`?

A. 0

B. .617

C. Roughly .617, but the result cannot be precisely stored in a floating-point number

D. It depends on the types of the two sides of the equation

7. Why does C++ need a char type if there are already integers?

A. Because characters and integers are completely different kinds of data, one is a number, one is a letter

B. For backward compatibility with C

C. To make it easy to read in, and print out, actual characters rather than numbers, even though chars are stored as numbers

D. For internationalization support, to handle languages like Chinese and Japanese, that have many characters

(View solutions on page 483)

Practice problems

1. Write a program that outputs your name.

2. Write a program that reads in two numbers and adds them together.

3. Write a program that performs division of two numbers read from the user and prints out an exact result. Make sure to test your program with both integer inputs and decimal inputs.

Chapter 4
If Statements

So far you've seen how to make a program that marches directly from one statement to the next, with no way of varying what happens other than displaying different values calculated from input by the user. **If statements** allow you to control whether a program enters a section of code or not based on whether a given condition is true or false. In other words, the if statement allows the program to select different actions based upon the user's input. For example, by using an if statement to check whether a user entered a correct password, your program can decide whether a user is allowed access to the program.

Basic syntax for if
The structure of an if statement is simple:

```
if ( <expression is true> )
     Execute this statement
```

Or

```
if ( <expression is true> )
{
     Execute everything in this block
}
```

The code that follows the if statement (and that is conditionally executed) is called the **body** of the if statement (just like the code in the main function was called the body of the main function).

Here is a simple and silly example that shows the syntax:

```
if ( 5 < 10 )
   cout << "Five is now less than ten, that's a big
surprise";
```

Here, we're just evaluating the statement, "is five less than ten", to see if it is true or not; with any luck, it's not! If you want, you can write your own full program including `iostream` and put this in the main function and run it to test that out.

Here's an example showing the use of curly braces with multiple statements:

```
if ( 5 < 10 )
{
      cout << "Five is now less than ten, that's a big
surprise\n";
      cout << "I hope this computer is working
correctly.\n";
}
```

If you have more than one line after an if statement, you need to use the curly braces to make sure the whole block is executed only if the if statement evaluates to true. I recommend always putting the curly braces around the body of the if statement. If you do this, you never have to remember to put them in when you want more than one statement to be executed, and you make the body of the if statement more visually clear. A common mistake is to add a second statement to the body of an if statement without adding the curly braces, which causes that second statement to always execute.

```
if ( 5 < 10 )
      cout << "Five is now less than ten, that's a big
surprise\n";
      cout << "I hope this computer is working
correctly.\n";
```

Because of the indentation, it can be difficult to spot these errors. It's safer to always go with the braces.

These if statements that we've looked at so far are pretty dull; let's look at a real if statement that works with user input.

```
#include <iostream>

using namespace std;

int main ()
{
     int x;
     cout << "Enter a number: ";
     cin >> x;
     if ( x < 10 )
     {
          cout << "You entered a value less than 10"
               << '\n';
     }
}
```

Sample Code 10: variable.cpp

This program differs from our previous example by reading a value from the user rather than hard coding a value in the comparison. This should be exciting, since it's the first time we've had a program whose behavior was substantially different depending on what the user did. But now let's look at the flexibility of if statements.

Expressions

If statements test a single expression. An **expression** is a statement, or a series of statements linked together, that evaluates to a single value. Most places that take variables or constant values (like numbers) can also take expressions. In fact, both variables and constant values are just simple expressions. Operations like addition or multiplication are also just slightly more complex forms of expressions. When used in the context of a comparison (such as in an if statement), the result of the expression is turned into either true or false.

What is truth?

To poets, truth is beauty and beauty is truth, and that's all you need to know.[9] But compilers aren't poets. To the compiler, an expression is **true** if it evaluates to a nonzero number. A **false** statement evaluates to zero. So, yes, a statement such as

```
if ( 1 )
```

will always cause the body of the if statement code to execute whereas

---

[9] http://www.bartleby.com/101/625.html

```
if ( 0 )
```

will cause the body of the if statement to **never** be executed.

C++ has specific keywords, `true` and `false`, that you can also write directly into your code. If you were to display the integer value associated with `true`, it is 1; the integer value associated with `false` is, of course, 0.

When you perform a comparison using one of the **relational operators**, the operator will return true or false. For example, the check `0 == 2` evaluates to false. (Notice that checking for equality uses two equals signs, `==`. Using a single equals sign is the equivalent of doing an assignment of a value to a variable.) The check `2 == 2` evaluates to true. There is no need to check the result of a relational operation directly against true or false when using it in an if statement:

```
if ( x == 2 )
```

is the same as

```
if ( ( x == 2 ) ==   true )
```

and the first version is much easier to read!

When programming, you'll often need to check if one value stored by a variable is larger than, smaller than, or equal to another value.

Here is a table of the relational operators that allow you to compare two values.

>	greater than	5 > 4 is true
<	less than	4 < 5 is true
>=	greater than or equal	4 >= 4 is true
<=	less than or equal	3 <= 4 is true
==	equal to	5 == 5 is true
!=	not equal to	5 != 4 is true

The bool type

C++ allows you to store the results of comparisons by using a special type called a **bool**.[10] The bool type is not that different from an integer, but it has one advantage: it makes it very clear that you are only ever going to use two possible values, `true` and `false`. These keywords, and the bool type, make your intentions more clear. The result of all comparison operators is a Boolean.

```
int x;
cin >> x;
bool is_x_two = x == 2; // note double-equals for
comparison

if ( is_x_two )
{
      // take some action because x is two!
}
```

Else statements

In many cases, you will want your program to perform a single test, and then take either one action if the test is true (e.g. a password read in from the user is correct) or another action if the test is false (the password was wrong).

The **else** statement allows you to do these if/else comparisons. The code after an else (whether a single line or code between brackets) is executed when the condition checked by the if statement is false. Here's an example that tests whether the user provided a negative number or not:

```
#include <iostream>

using namespace std;

int main()
{
      int num;
      cout << "Enter a number: ";
      cin >> num;
      if ( num < 0 )
      {
            cout << "You entered a negative number\n";
      }
```

---

[10]The bool type is named for George Boole, a mathematician who designed Boolean logic, a kind of logic that uses only the values true and false, and was fundamental in the design of digital computers.

```
        else
        {
              cout << "You entered a non-negative number\n";
        }
}
```
Sample Code 11: non_negative.cpp

Else-if

Another use of else is when there are multiple conditional statements that may all evaluate to true, yet you want only one if statement's body to execute. For example, you might want to modify the above code to detect three separate cases: negative numbers, zero, and positive numbers. You can use an **else-if** statement following an if statement and its body; that way, if the first statement is true, the else-if will be ignored, but if the if statement is false, it will then check the condition for the else-if statement. If the if statement was true the else statement will not be checked. It is possible to use a series of else-if statements to ensure that only one block of code is executed.

Here's how we could change the above code to use an else-if to check for zero:

```
#include <iostream>

using namespace std;

int main()
{
        int num;
        cout << "Enter a number: ";
        cin >> num;
        if ( num < 0 )
        {
              cout << "You entered a negative number\n";
        }
        else if ( num == 0 )
        {
              cout << "You entered zero\n";
        }
        else
        {
              cout << "You entered a positive number\n";
        }
}
```
Sample Code 12: else_if.cpp

String comparisons

C++ string objects allow you to use all of the comparisons that you learned about earlier in this chapter. By comparing string objects, we can write our password checker!

```cpp
#include <iostream>
#include <string>

using namespace std;

int main ()
{
    string password;

    cout << "Enter your password: " << "\n";
    getline( cin, password, '\n' );
    if ( password == "xyzzy" )
    {
        cout << "Access allowed" << "\n";
    }
    else
    {
        cout << "Bad password. Denied access!" << "\n";
        // returning is a convenient way to stop the
        // program
        return 0;
    }
    // continue onward!
}
```
Sample Code 13: password.cpp

This program reads in a line from the user and compares it with a password, "xyzzy". If the line entered is not the same as the password, then the program immediately returns from main.[11]

You can also use the other comparison operators on string, such as comparing two strings to see which comes first in alphabetical order, or using != to check if one string is different from another.

More interesting conditions using Boolean operators

So far, you've only been able to check one condition at a time. If you want to check two things, such as checking both for the right password and the right

---

[11] Of course, no real password checker is quite this simple. You wouldn't want to put the password directly into the source code, for one thing!

username, you'd have to write some kind of weird if/else statement. Fortunately, C++ supports the ability to perform multiple checks at once using a feature called **Boolean operators** (the name is related to the bool type from earlier; Boolean operators work on Boolean values).

Boolean operators allow you to create more complex conditional statements. For example, if you wish to check if a variable called `age` is both greater than five and less than ten, you could use the Boolean AND to ensure both `age > 5` and `age < 10` are true.

The Boolean operators work like the comparison operators, returning either true or false, depending on the result of the expression.

Boolean not

The **Boolean not** operator accepts one input. If that input is true, it returns false, and if that input is false, it returns true. For example, not(true) evaluates to false, and not(false) evaluates to true. Not(any number but zero) evaluates to false.

The actual symbol for NOT in C++ is ! (yes, an exclamation mark)

For example:

```
if ( ! 0 )
{
      cout << "! 0 evaluates to true";
}
```

Boolean and

Boolean and returns true if both inputs are true (if 'this' AND 'that' are true). `true` AND `false` would evaluate to false because one of the inputs is false (both must be true for it to evaluate to true). `true` AND `true` evaluates to true. (any number but 0) AND false evaluates to false.

The AND operator is written `&&` in C++. Do not be confused by thinking it checks equality between numbers: it does not. It only makes checks if both arguments are true.

```
if ( 1 && 2 )
{
      cout << "Both 1 and 2 evaluate to true";
```

```
}
```

Short circuiting checks

If the first expression of a Boolean and is false, the second expression will not be evaluated. In other words, it **short circuits** its checking.

Short circuiting is useful because you can write expressions where the second condition should only be checked if the first condition is true—for example, to guard against division by zero. Take this if statement that checks whether 10 divided by x is less than 2:

```
if ( x != 0 && 10 / x < 2 )
{
    cout << "10 / x is less than 2";
}
```

When the if statement is evaluated, the program first determines if x is 0 or not. If it is zero, then it doesn't need to check the next condition, so it skips it. This means that you don't need to worry about the fact that division by zero would cause your program to crash. If there were no short-circuiting, you'd have to write:

```
if ( x != 0 )
{
    if ( 10 / x < 2 )
    {
        cout << "10 / x is less than 2";
    }
}
```

With short-circuiting, we can write clearer, more concise code.

Boolean or

Boolean or return true if either, or both, of the two values provided are true. For example, true OR false evaluates to true. false OR false evaluates to false. Boolean or is written as || in C++. Those are the pipe characters. On your keyboard, they may look a bar with a small space in the middle, although most fonts display them as a solid bar. On many keyboards the pipe shares its key with \ character and requires pressing shift.

Like Boolean and, Boolean or short-circuits; if the first condition is true, it does not check the second.

Combining expressions

With the basic Boolean operators, you can check two conditions at a time. What if you want even more power? Remember how expressions can be made up of variables, operators and values? Expressions can also be made up of other expressions.

For example, you can check that x is two and y is three by combining equality comparisons with a Boolean and:

```
x == 2 && y == 3
```

Let's look at an example of using Boolean and to create a password program that checks for both a username and a password.

```cpp
#include <iostream>
#include <string>

using namespace std;

int main ()
{
    string username;
    string password;
    cout << "Enter your username: " << "\n";
    getline( cin, username, '\n' );

    cout << "Enter your password: " << "\n";
    getline( cin, password, '\n' );
    if ( username == "root" && password == "xyzzy" )
    {
        cout << "Access allowed" << "\n";
    }
    else
    {
        cout << "Bad username or password. Denied
access!" << "\n";
        // returning is a convenient way to stop the
        // program
        return 0;
    }
    // continue onward!
}
```
Sample Code 14: username_password.cpp

When run, this program will allow access only to a user named root, who has the right password. You could easily extend the program to allow multiple different users, each with his or her own password, using else-if statements.

Order of evaluation

In C++, operators have a **precedence** that determines the order in which they are evaluated. In the arithmetic operators (+, −, / and *), the precedence is the same as normal mathematics: division and multiplication operations are evaluated before addition and subtraction.

With Boolean operators, the not operation is evaluated first, followed by comparisons. Boolean and is then evaluated before Boolean or.

In table form, the precedence order for Boolean operators and comparison operators is

!
==, <, >, <=, =>, !=
&&
||

You can always use parentheses to control the order of evaluation for both Boolean operators and arithmetic operators like addition and subtraction.

For example, take our previous example:

```
x == 2 && y == 3
```

If you wanted to say, "when this condition is NOT true", you could use parentheses:

```
! ( x == 2 && y == 3 )
```

Example Boolean expressions

Let's look at some more complex Boolean expressions that you can use to test your understanding of the Boolean operators.

What does this expression evaluate to?

```
! ( true && false )
```

It would be true. It is true is because `true && false` evaluates to `false` and `! false` evaluates to `true`.

Here are a few more problems, with answers included in the footnotes:

```
! ( true || false )¹²
! ( true || true && false )¹³
! ( ( true || false ) && false )¹⁴
```

Quiz yourself
1. Which of the following is true?
A. 1
B. 66
C. .1
D. -1
E. All of the above

2. Which of the following is the Boolean operator for Boolean and?
A. `&`
B. `&&`
C. `|`
D. `|&`

3. What does the expression `! ( true && ! ( false || true ) )` evaluate to?
A. `true`
B. `false`

4. Which of the following shows the correct syntax for an if statement?
A. `if expression`
B. `if { expression`
C. `if ( expression )`
D. `expression if`

(View solution on page 485)

---

[12] false
[13] false (AND is evaluated before OR)
[14] true

Practice problems

1. Ask the user for two users' ages, and indicate who is older; behave differently if both are over 100.

2. Implement a simple "password" system that takes a password in the form of a number. Make it so that either of two numbers is valid, but use only one if statement to do the check.

3. Write a small calculator that takes as input one of the four arithmetic operations, the two arguments to those operations, and then prints out the result.

4. Expand the password checking program from earlier in this chapter and make it take multiple usernames, each with their own password, and ensure that the right username is used for the right password. Provide the ability to prompt users again if the first login attempt failed. Think about how easy (or hard) it is to do this for a lot of usernames and passwords.

5. Think about what kind of language constructs or features would make it easier to add new users without recompiling the password program. (Note: don't feel like you need to solve these problems with the C++ you've learned so far, the goal is to think about how you might use tools we'll pick up in future chapters.

Chapter 5
Loops

So far, you've learned how to make your program behave differently based on the user's input, but it will still only run once through. You can't yet write a program that will keep prompting the user for new inputs again and again. If you worked on the password program practice problem at the end of the last chapter that asked you to re-prompt the user on a failed password entry, you probably had to hard-code in a series of if-statements to recheck the password; there was no way to allow a user to re-enter a password until he enters the correct password.

That's what loops are for. Loops repeatedly execute a block of code. Loops are extremely powerful and core parts of most programs. Many programs and websites that produce extremely complex output (such as a message board) are really only executing a single task many times. Now, think about what this means: a loop lets you write a very simple statement to produce a significantly greater result simply by repetition. You can prompt a user for a password as many times as the user is willing to try to enter a password; you can display a thousand posts on an Internet forum. It's pretty sweet.

C++ has three kinds of loops, each of which has a slightly different purpose: while, for, and do-while. We'll go through each in turn.

While loops
While loops are the simplest kind of loop. The basic structure is

```
while ( <condition> )
{
      [Code to execute while the condition is true]
}
```

In fact, a while loop is almost exactly like an if statement, except that the while loop causes its body to be repeated. Just like an if statement, the condition is a Boolean expression. For example, here's a while loop with two conditions:

```
while ( i == 2 || i == 3 )
```

Here's a really basic example of a while loop:

```
while ( true )
{
      cout << "I am looping\n";
}
```

Warning: if you run this loop, it will never stop! The condition will always evaluate to true. This is called an **infinite loop**. Because an infinite loop never stops, you have to kill your program to stop it (you can do this by either pressing Ctrl-C, Ctrl-Break or closing the console window). To avoid infinite loops, you should be sure your loop condition won't always be true.

A common mistake

Now is a good time to point that a common cause of infinite loops is using a single equals sign instead of two equals signs in a loop condition:

BAD CODE
```
int i = 1;
while ( i = 1 )
{
      cin >> i;
}
```

This loop attempts to read inputs from the user until the user enters something other than 1. Unfortunately, the loop condition is

```
i = 1
```

Rather than

```
i == 1
```

The expression `i = 1` will just assign the value of 1 to `i`. As it turns out, an assignment expression acts as if it also returns the value assigned—in this case, 1. Since 1 is not zero, it is true, so this loop will go on forever.

Let's look at a loop that actually works well! Here's a full program demonstrating while loops by displaying the numbers from 0 to 9:

```cpp
#include <iostream>

using namespace std;

int main ()
{
      int i = 0;  // Don't forget to declare variables

      while ( i < 10 ) // While i is less than 10
      {
            cout << i << '\n';
            i++;  // Update i so the condition can be met
                  // eventually
      }
}
```
Sample Code 15: while.cpp

If you're having trouble getting your mind around loops, try thinking about it this way: when the program reaches the brace at the end of the loop's body it jumps back up to the beginning of the loop, which checks the condition again and decides whether to repeat the block another time, or stop and move to the next statement after the block.

For loops
For loops are incredibly versatile and convenient. The syntax for a for loop is

```cpp
for ( variable initialization; condition; variable update )
{
      // Code to execute while the condition is true
}
```

That's a lot of stuff going on in the loop, so let's look at short example and talk through each element of the loop. In fact, this loop behaves exactly like the while loop we just saw:

```
for ( int i = 0; i < 10; i++ )
{
    cout << i << '\n';
}
```

Variable initialization

The variable initialization, in this case `int i = 0`, allows you to declare a variable and give it a value (or give a value to an already existing variable). Here, we declared the variable `i`. When the value of a single variable is checked in a loop, `i` in this case, that variable is sometimes called a **loop variable**. In programming, it is traditional to use the letters `i` and `j` as loop variables. A variable that is incremented by one each time through the loop is called a **loop counter** because the variable counts up from one value to another.

Loop condition

The loop condition tells the program that while the conditional expression is true the loop should repeat itself (just like a while loop). In this case, we are checking whether x is less than 10. Just like the while loop, the condition is checked before ever executing the body of the loop, and then after each run through the loop to determine if the loop should repeat again.

Variable update

The variable update section is where the loop variable can be updated. It is possible to do things like `i++`, `i = i + 10`, or make a function call; if you really wanted to, you could call functions that do nothing to the variable but still have a useful effect on the code.

Since a great many loops have a single variable, a single condition, and a single variable update, the for loop is a compact way of writing out a loop so that everything that matters to the loop can go on a single line.

Notice that this single line uses semicolons to separate the sections; you cannot leave out the semicolon. Any or all of the sections may be empty, but the semicolons still have to be there. If the condition is empty, it is evaluated as true and the loop will repeat until something else stops it—that's another way of writing an infinite loop.

To really understand when each part of a for loop happens, compare it with the while loop that we saw earlier that does the same thing:

```
int i = 0; // variable declaration and initialization
while ( i < 10 ) // condition
{
    cout << i << '\n';
    i++; // variable update
}
```

The for loop is just a more compact way of doing it.

Let's look at one more example of a for loop that does something a bit more interesting than just printing out a basic series of numbers. Here's a full program that prints out the square of all numbers from 0 to 9:

```
#include <iostream>

using namespace std;

int main ()
{
    // The loop goes while i < 10, and i increases by one
    // every loop

    for ( int i = 0; i < 10; i++ )
    {
        // Keep in mind that the loop condition checks
        // the conditional statement before it loops
        // again. Consequently, when i equals 10 the
        // loop breaks. i is updated before the
        // condition is checked.

        cout<< i << " squared is " << i * i << endl;
    }
}
```
Sample Code 16: for.cpp

This program is a very simple example of a for loop. To understand exactly when each part of a for loop executes, let's go through it:

1. The initialization step is run: i is set to zero
2. The condition is checked; since i is less than 10, the body is executed
3. The update step runs, adding 1 to i
4. The condition is checked and the loop ends unless the condition is true
5. If the condition is true, the body is executed and then everything is repeated, starting at step 3 until i is no longer less than 10.

Remember that the update step happens only after the loop runs. It doesn't take place the first time, before the loop body has run.

Do-while loops

Do-while loops are special-purpose and fairly rare. The main purpose of do-while loops is to make it easy to write a loop body that happens at least once. The structure is

```
do
{
      // body...
} while ( condition );
```

The condition is tested at the end of the loop body instead of the beginning; therefore, the body of the loop will be executed at least once before the condition is checked. If the condition is true, we jump back to the beginning of the block and execute it again. A do-while loop is basically a reversed while loop. A while loop says, "Loop while the condition is true, and execute this block of code", a do-while loop says, "Execute this block of code, and then loop back while the condition is true". Here's a simple example that lets a user enter the password until it is correct:

```
#include <string>
#include <iostream>

using namespace std;

int main ()
{
      string password;
      do
      {
            cout << "Please enter your password: ";
            cin >> password;
      } while ( password != "foobar" );
      cout << "Welcome, you got the password right";
}
```
Sample Code 17: dowhile.cpp

This loop will execute the body at least once, allowing the user to enter the password; if the password is incorrect, the loop will repeat, prompting the user for the password again until the user enters the correct password.

Notice the trailing semi-colon after the while in the above example! It's easy to forget to add the semicolon because the other loops do not require it; in fact, the other loops should **not** be terminated with a semicolon, adding to the confusion.

Controlling the flow of loops

While you normally decide to exit a loop by checking the loop condition, sometimes you want to exit out of the loop early. C++ has just the keyword for you: **break**. A break statement will immediately terminate whatever loop you are in the middle of.

Here's an example that uses break to end what would otherwise be an infinite loop, a basic rewrite of the password example code:

```
#include <string>
#include <iostream>

using namespace std;

int main ()
{
        string password;
        while ( 1 )
        {
            cout << "Please enter your password: ";
            cin >> password;
            if ( password == "foobar" )
            {
                break;
            }
        }
        cout << "Welcome, you got the password right";
}
```
Sample Code 18: break.cpp

A break statement immediately ends the loop, jumping to the closing brace. In this example, once the correct password is entered, the loop terminates. Because the break statement can appear anywhere in the loop, including at the very end, you can use infinite loops as an alternative way of writing a do-while loop, as we did here. The break statement effectively acts like the condition check at the end of the do-while loop.

Break statements are useful when you need an escape route from within a large loop, but too many break statements can make your code hard to read.

A second way of controlling loops is to skip a single iteration by using **continue**. When the continue statement is hit, the current loop iteration ends early, but the loop is not exited. For example, you could write a loop that skips printing out the number 10:

```
int i = 0;
while ( true )
{
     i++;
     if ( i == 10 )
     {
          continue;
     }
     cout << i << "\n";
}
```

Here, the infinite loop will never end, but when i reaches 10, the **continue** statement will cause it to jump back to the starting line of the loop, skipping the call to cout. The loop condition will still be tested, though. When using continue with a for loop, the update step occurs immediately after the continue.

The continue statement is most useful when you want to skip some code in the middle of the body of a loop. For example, you might do some checks on a user's input, and if they enter something wrong, you can skip processing that input with a loop structure that looks like this:

```
while ( true )
{
     cin >> input;
     if ( ! isValid( input ) )
     {
          continue;
     }
     // go on to process the input as normal
}
```

Nested loops

In C++, it is very common that you want to loop over not just one value, but two different, related values. For example, you might want to print out a list of posts in an internet forum (one loop) and for each post, you want to print out a bunch of different values like the subject line of the post, the author, and the body. You could do this inside of a second loop. But you need your second loop to execute inside of the other loop—once for each message. These kinds of loops are called **nested** loops, because one loop is nested inside the other.

Let's look at a simpler example that doesn't require as much complexity as a forum post: printing out a multiplication table works great with nested loops:

```cpp
#include <iostream>

using namespace std;

int main ()
{
    for ( int i = 0; i < 10; i++ )
    {
        // \t represents a tab character, which will
        // format our output nicely
        cout << '\t' << i;
    }

    cout << '\n';

    for ( int i = 0; i < 10; ++i )
    {
        cout << i;

        for ( int j = 0; j < 10; ++j )
        {
            cout << '\t' << i * j;
        }
        cout << '\n';
    }
}
```
Sample Code 19: nested_loops.cpp

When you use nested loops, you can talk about the **outer loop** and the **inner loop,** to distinguish the two loops. Here, the loop with variable `j` is the inner loop, and the loop containing it, with the loop variable `i`, is the outer loop.

Just be careful not to use the same loop variable for both your inner and your outer loop:

BAD CODE
```cpp
for ( int i = 0; i < 10; i++ )
```

```
{
        // oops, accidentally redeclared i here!
        for ( int i = 0; i < 10; i++ )
        {
        }
}
```

You can nest more than two loops—you can have as many nesting levels as you like—a loop, within a loop, within a loop, within a loop—loops all the way down!

Choosing the right kind of loop

So you've seen the three different kinds of loops in C++. You're probably wondering: so what? Why do you need three kinds of loops anyway?

And the truth is that you don't really need all three kinds of loops. I see do-while loops more often in textbooks than I do in real code. For loops and while loops are far more common.

Here are some quick guidelines for picking the right loop type. These are just rules of thumb—over time, you will get a better feel for what makes a loop the right choice in a particular piece of code, and you shouldn't let these guidelines win out over your experience.

For loop

Use a for loop if you know the exact number of times you want to loop—for example, when counting from 0 to 100, a for loop is perfect or when you're doing multiplication tables. For loops are also the standard way of iterating over arrays—which you'll see when we get to arrays (see   Arrays on page 133). On the other hand, you wouldn't use a for loop if the variable needs to be updated in a really complicated way—a for loop is good for showing everything about how the loop works in a single succinct statement. If the update step requires multiple lines of code, then you lose the advantage of the for loop.

While loops

On the other hand, if you have a complicated loop condition, or you have to do a lot of math to get the next value of the loop variable, consider a while loop. While loops make it very simple to see when a loop is going to terminate, but they make it harder to see what changes each time you loop. If the change is complicated, you're better off using a while loop since the reader will at least know that it wasn't a simple update.

For example, if you have two different loop variables:

```
int j = 5;
for ( int i = 0; i < 10 && j > 0; i++ )
{
        cout << i * j;
        j = i - j;
}
```

Notice that not everything that matters fits into the single line of the for loop. Some of it appears at the end of loop body. This is misleading to the reader; it would be better to make this a while loop.

```
int i = 0;
int j = 5;

while ( i < 10 && j > 0 )
{
        cout << i * j;
        j = i - j;
        i++;
}
```

It's still not pretty, but at least it's not misleading.

A while loop is also perfect if you want to continue looping nearly indefinitely—for example, if you have a program that plays chess and you want to allow each side to make a turn until the end of the game.

Do-while loops

As I said, these are the black swans of programming—they show up every one in a long while. The only real reason to use a do-while loop is if you want to do something at least once. A good example is the earlier sample code that prompts a user for a password, or, more generally, any kind of user interface that requires input and repeatedly presents a prompt to the user until the input is correct. In some cases, even if you do want the body of a loop to be repeated, it still might not be the best choice if the body needs to be slightly different the first time through—for example, if you want to have a different message if the user entered the wrong password.

For example, how would you write something like this with a do-while loop?

```
string password;

cout << "Enter your password: ";

cin >> password;
while ( password != "xyzzy" )
{
        cout << "Wrong password--try again: ";
        cin >> password;
}

string password;

do
{
        if ( password == "" )
        {
                cout << "Enter your password: ";
        }
        else
        {
                cout << "Wrong password--try again: ";
        }
        cin >> password;
} while ( password != "xyzzy" );
```

See how the do-while loop makes this more complicated, rather than less? The point is that the "body" is not the same—even though we're reading in the user's input, we need to display a different message to the user.

Quiz yourself
1. What is the final value of x when the code int x; for(x=0; x<10; x++) {} is run?

A. 10

B. 9

C. 0

D. 1

2. When does the code block following while(x<100) execute?

A. When x is less than one hundred

B. When x is greater than one hundred

C. When x is equal to one hundred

D. While it wishes

3. Which is not a loop structure?
A. for
B. do-while
C. while
D. repeat until

4. How many times is a do-while loop guaranteed to loop?
A. 0
B. Infinitely
C. 1
D. Variable

(View solution on page 486)

Practice problems

1. Write a program that prints out the entire lyrics to a full rendition of "99 Bottles of Beer".[15]

2. Write a menu program that lets the user select from a list of options, and if the input is not one of the options, reprint the list.

3. Write a program that computes a running sum of inputs from the user, terminating when the user gives an input value of 0.

4. Write a password prompt that gives a user only a certain number of password entry attempts—so that the user cannot easily write a password cracker.

5. Try writing each practice problem with each kind of loop—notice which loops work well for each kind of problem.

6. Write a program that displays the first 20 square numbers.

7. Write a program that provides the option of tallying up the results of a poll with 3 possible values. The first input to the program is the poll question; the

---

[15] In case you don't know this song, the words are here:
http://en.wikipedia.org/wiki/99_Bottles_of_Beer

next three inputs are the possible answers. The first answer is indicated by 1, the second by 2, the third by 3. The answers are tallied until a 0 is entered. The program should then show the results of the poll—try making a bar graph that shows the results properly scaled to fit on your screen no matter how many results were entered.

Chapter 6
Functions

Now that you've seen loops, you're able to write some fairly interesting programs. Unfortunately, your programs must be written entirely in the main function. If you try to do anything complicated within main, it will start to get really big and hard to understand. Perhaps you even noticed this when working on some of the more complicated exercises from earlier chapters. Moreover, you'll run into situations where you want to do the same thing in multiple places and have to copy and paste the code again and again.

That's where **functions** come in—by breaking your program up into functions, you will be able to reuse the code from those functions in many places without copying and pasting. In fact, you've already used several standard functions for doing input and output.

Most of what you've learned so far has been about being able to do new stuff; functions are about how to organize things, making it easy to reuse them, and making your code nicer to read.

Function syntax

You've already seen how to create a function; every single one of your programs has had a main function in it!

Let's take another function, to have something to talk about and really pull apart all the pieces of a function:

```
int add (int x, int y)
{
      return x + y;
}
```

Okay, so what's going on? First, notice that this looks a lot like the main function that you've written several times already. There are only two real differences:

1. This function takes two arguments, x and y. Main did not take any arguments.
2. This function explicitly returns a value (remember that main also returns a value, but you don't have to put in the return statement yourself).

The line

```
int add (int x, int y)
```

gives the return type first, before the function name. The two arguments are listed after the name. If you take no arguments, you'd simply write a pair of parentheses, like this:

```
int no_arg_function ()
```

If you want a function that does not return a value—for example, a function that just prints something to the screen—you can declare its return type as **void**. This will prevent you from using your function as an expression (such as in variable assignments or the condition of an if statement).

The return value is provided by using the return statement; this function consists of only a single line,

```
      return x + y;
```

But you can have more than one line, just like in main, and the function will stop only when the return statement runs, providing the value to the caller.

Once you've declared your function, you can then call your newly-minted function like this:

```
add( 1, 2 ); // ignore the return value
```

You can also use the function as an expression to assign it to a variable or output it:

```
#include <iostream>

using namespace std;

int add (int x, int y)
{
    return x + y;
}

int main ()
{
    int result = add( 1, 2 );   // call add and assign the
                                // result to a variable

    cout << "The result is: " << result << '\n';
    cout << "Adding 3 and 4 gives us: " << add( 3, 4 );
}
```
Sample Code 20: add_function.cpp

In this example, it might look like `cout` will output the `add` function. But as with variables, `cout` prints the result of the expression rather than the literal phrase "add(3, 4)". The result would be the same as if we had run this line of code:

```
cout << "Adding 3 and 4 gives us: " << 3 + 4;
```

In the example program, notice that we call the `add` function several times, rather than repeating the code again and again. For such a short function, that doesn't really help us much, but if we later decide to add some more code to the add function (maybe some debugging statements to print out the arguments and result) it means we'd have to change much less code—just the function, rather than every place that had the duplicated code.

Local variables and global variables
Now that you can have more than one function, you will probably have many more variables, some in each function. Let's talk for a minute about the names you give variables. When you declare a variable inside a function, you give it a name. Where can you use that name to refer to that variable?

Local variables

Let's take a simple function:

```
int addTen (int x)
{
      int result = x + 10;
      return result;
}
```

There are two variables here, x and `result`. Let's talk about `result` first—the variable `result` is available only within the curly braces in which it is defined—basically, the two lines within the add function. In other words, you could also write another function with the variable result:

```
int getValueTen ()
{
      int result = 10;
      return result;
}
```

You could even use `getValueTen` inside `addTen`

```
int addTen (int x)
{
      int result = x + getValueTen();
      return result;
}
```

There are two different variables called `result`, one that belongs to the `addTen` function and another that belongs to the `getValueTen` function. The variables do not conflict—while `getValueTen` executes, it has access only to its own copy of the `result` variable, and vice-versa.

The visibility of a variable is called its **scope**. The scope of a variable simply means the section of code where the variable's name can be used to access that variable. Variables declared within a function are available only in the scope of the function—when the function itself is executing. Variables declared in the scope of one function are not available to other functions that are called during execution of the first function. When one function calls another, the new function's variables are the only ones available.

Arguments to functions are also declared in the scope of the function. These variables are not available to the caller of the function—even though the caller is providing the value. The variable x, in the addTen function, is an argument to the function, and can only be used inside the addTen function. Morever, like any other variable declared within one function, the variable x cannot be used by the function that addTen calls. In the example above, the variable x, an argument to addTen, is not available to the getValueTen function.

Function arguments are like the stunt-doubles of the variables passed in to the function; changing a function argument has no effect on the original variable. To make this happen, when a variable is passed into a function, it is copied into the function argument:

```
#include <iostream>

using namespace std;
void changeArgument (int x)
{
     x = x + 5;
}

int main ()
{
     int y = 4;
     changeArgument ( y ); // y will be unharmed by the
                           // function call

     cout << y; // still prints 4
}
```
Sample Code 21: local_variable.cpp

The scope of a variable can be even narrower than an entire function. Every set of curly braces defines a new, more narrow scope. For example:

```
int divide (int numerator, int denominator)
{
     if ( 0 == denominator )
     {
          int result = 0;
          return result;
     }
     int result = numerator / denominator;
     return result;
}
```

The first declaration of result is in scope only within the if statement's curly braces. The second declaration of result is in scope only from the place where it was declared to the end of the function. In general, the compiler won't stop you from creating two variables with the same name, as long as they are used in different scopes. In cases such as in the `divide` function, multiple variables with the same name in similar scopes can be confusing to someone trying to understand the code.

Any variable declared in the scope of a function, or inside of a block, is called a **local variable**. You can also have variables that are available more widely, called global variables.

Global variables

Sometimes you want to have a single variable that is available to all of your functions. For example, if you have a board game, you might want to store the board as a global variable so that you can have multiple functions that use the board without having to pass it around all the time.

You can accomplish this by using a global variable. A **global variable** is a variable that is declared outside of any function. These variables are available everywhere in the program past the point of the variable's declaration.

Here's a basic example of a global variable showing how you declare it, and how you can use it.

```
#include <iostream>

using namespace std;
// just a small function to demonstrate scope
int doStuff ()
{
      return 2 + 3;
}

// global variables can be initialized just like other
// variables

int count_of_function_calls = 0;

void fun ()
{
      // and the global variable is available here
      count_of_function_calls++;
}
int main ()
{
```

```
        fun();
        fun();
        fun();
        // and the global variable is also available here!
        cout << "Function fun was called "
             << count_of_function_calls << " times";
}
```

Sample Code 22: global_variable.cpp

The variable `count_of_function_calls` begins its scope right before the function `fun`. The function `doStuff` does not have access to the variable because the variable was declared after `doStuff`, and both `fun` and `main` do have access because they were declared after the variable.

A warning about global variables

Global variables might seem like they make things easier, because everyone can use them. But using global variables makes your code more difficult to understand: to know how a global variable is really used, you have to look everywhere! Using a global variable is rarely the right thing to do. You should use them only when you truly need something to be very widely available. Prefer passing arguments to functions, rather than having functions access global variables. Even when you think that a particular thing is going to be globally used, it may turn out later that it isn't.

Take the game board example from earlier—you might decide to create a function to display the board and have that function access a global variable. But what happens if you want to display some board other than the current board—for example, to show an alternative move? Your function doesn't take the board as an argument; it shows only the single global board. Not very convenient!

Making functions available for use

The rules of scoping that apply to variables—such as a variable being usable only after it is declared—also apply to functions. (Isn't consistency great?)

For example, this program would not compile:

BAD CODE

```
#include <iostream>    // needed for cout

using namespace std;
```

```
int main ()
{
      int result = add( 1, 2 );
      cout << "The result is: " << result << '\n';
      cout << "Adding 3 and 4 gives us: " << add( 3, 4 );
}

int add (int x, int y)
{
      return x + y;
}
```
Sample Code 23: badcode.cpp

If you compile this program, you will see this error message (or something like it):

```
badcode.cpp:7: error: 'add' was not declared in this scope
```

The problem is that at the point where the add function is called, it hasn't been declared yet, so it was not in scope. When the compiler sees you try to call a function you haven't declared, it gets very confused—poor compiler!

One solution, which I used in earlier examples, is just to put the whole function above the places that use it. Another solution is to **declare** the function before you **define** it.

Although declaring a function and defining a function sound very similar, they have very different meanings, so let's break down the terminology.

Function definitions and declarations

Defining a function means giving the full function, including the body of the function. For example, the way we wrote the add function acted as a definition of the function because it showed what add does. A definition of a function *counts* as a declaration too, since to define the function you need to give all the information that a declaration provides.

Declaring a function *just* gives the basic info about the function that a caller needs: name, return type, and arguments. Functions must be declared before someone else can call them, either by using a declaration or by fully defining the function.

To declare a function, you write a **function prototype**. The declaration tells the compiler what the function will return, what the function will be called, and what arguments the function can be passed. You can think of the function prototype as a blueprint for how to use the function.

```
Return_type function_name (arg_type arg1, ..., arg_type
argN);
```

`arg_type` just means the type for each argument— for instance, an `int`, a `double`, or a `char`. It's exactly the same thing as what you would put if you were declaring a variable.

Let's look at a function prototype:

```
int add (int x, int y);
```

This prototype specifies that the function `add` will accept two arguments, both integers, and that it will return an integer. The semicolon tells the compiler that this is just a prototype and not a full definition of the function; be nice to the compiler and don't forget the trailing semi-colon lest it become confused.

An example of using a function prototype
Let's look at a fixed version of the above code that was missing a function prototype.

```
#include <iostream>

using namespace std;

// function prototype for add
int add (int x, int y);

int main ()
{
    int result = add( 1, 2 );
    cout << "The result is: " << result << '\n';
    cout << "Adding 3 and 4 gives us: " << add( 3, 4 );
}

int add (int x, int y)
{
    return x + y;
}
```
Sample Code 24: function_prototype.cpp

As usual, the program starts with the necessary include files the `using namespace std;` incantation.

Next is the prototype of the function `add`, including the final semicolon. After this point, any code, including `main`, can use the add function even though the `add` function is defined later on, below `main`. Due to its prototype being above `main`, the compiler knows it is declared and can figure out the arguments and return value.

Don't forget that while the function can be called before the definition, eventually a definition must be given for your program to compile.[16]

Breaking down a program into functions

Now that you know how to write a function, you need to know *when* you should write a function.

When you're repeating code again and again

The main use of functions is to make it easy to reuse code. Functions make it much simpler to reuse part of your program's logic later because all you need to do is call the function when you want to use that logic, rather than having to copy and paste the code. Copying and pasting, while it might seem easier, will result in repeating blocks of code dozens of times throughout your program. Using functions will also save you a great deal of space, make the program more readable, and make it easier to make changes. Would you prefer making forty little changes scattered all throughout a large program instead of one change to the function body? Neither would I.

A good rule of thumb is that once you've written the same code three times, turn that code into a function instead of repeating it again.

When you want to make code easier to read

Even if you didn't need to reuse code, sometimes having a long block of code doing something very specific and complicated can make it hard to understand the big picture of what your code is trying to do. Writing a function lets you say, "here's this concept that I want to use" and then you use that concept. For example, it's easy to understand the concept of "read input that the user typed" when you have a single function to do it. The supporting code that implements

---

[16] Technically, it's the linking step that will fail; we'll talk about the distinction between compiling and linking later on.

retrieving key presses, converting them into electric signals, and reading them in to a variable—now that's complicated! Isn't it much nicer to read code that says:

```
int x;
cin >> x;
```

than reading code that implements all the details of the input? If you're working on some code, and you're finding it hard to grasp the big picture—maybe it's time to write some functions just to help keep things organized.

By writing a function, you can focus just on what the function takes as input, and gives as output, rather than needing to remember the details of how it works all the time.

You might be thinking, "But don't I need to know the details?" And it's true, from time to time, you will want to know all the details—but when you do, you can just go look at the function because everything you need to know about the function is there, in one place. If you have all the details mixed in with the larger structure of the program, it becomes very hard to read.

For example, take a menu program that runs complex code when the user selects a menu item. The program should have functions for each of the menu choices. Each individual menu item can be understood by looking at its function, and the main input code also has a structure that is easy to understand quickly. The worst programs usually only have the required function, main, and fill it with pages of jumbled code. In fact, the next chapter, you'll see an example of a program like this.

Naming and overloading functions

Choosing good names for functions, variables and just about anything in your code is important—names help you understand what your code is doing. Function calls don't show the implementation right in front of you, so it's important that you choose a name that describes the important action of the function. Because the name is so important, sometimes you want to use the same name for more than one thing—for example, you might have a function that finds the area of a triangle, where the triangle is specified by three coordinates:

```
int computeTriangleArea (int x1, int y1, int x2, int y2,
int x3, int y3);
```

But what if you want a second function to compute the area of a triangle, this time by taking a width and a height of the triangle? You might want to use the name `computeTriangleArea` again since it really does describe what you are doing. But won't you have a conflict with, well, `computeTriangleArea`? Not in C++! C++ allows function **overloading**; you can use the same name for more than one function, as long as the functions all have different argument lists. So we can write:

```
int computeTriangleArea (int x1, int y1, int x2, int y2,
int x3, int y3);
```

and

```
int computeTriangleArea (int width, int height);
```

The compiler will be able to distinguish the two function calls at the call site since they take different numbers of arguments. (The compiler can also handle functions with the same number of arguments, as long as the arguments are of different types.) So if you write:

```
computeTriangleArea( 1, 1, 1, 4, 1, 9 );
computeTriangleArea( 5, 10 );
```

The compiler will know which of the two functions to call.

You shouldn't abuse the ability to overload functions—just because two things can have the same name doesn't mean that they should—but overloading makes sense if the two functions do the same thing but do it to different arguments.

Summary of functions

Along with variables, loops and if statements, functions are one of the basic tools for C++ programmers. Functions let you hide complex calculations behind a simple interface, and they let you remove repeated uses of the same code, putting it into a function. This makes it far easier to reuse that code later.

Quiz yourself

1. Which is not a proper prototype?
A. `int funct(char x, char y);`
B. `double funct(char x)`
C. `void funct();`
D. `char x();`

2. The function with prototype `int func(char x, double v, float t);` has which of the following as a return type?
A. `char`
B. `int`
C. `float`
D. `double`

3. Which of the following is a valid function call (assuming the function exists)?
A. `funct;`
B. `funct x, y;`
C. `funct();`
D. `int funct();`

4. Which of the following is a complete function?
A. `int funct();`
B. `int funct(int x) {return x=x+1;}`
C. `void funct(int) {cout<<"Hello"}`
D. `void funct(x) {cout<<"Hello";}`

(View solution on page 487)

Practice problems

1. Take the "menu program" you wrote earlier and break it out into a series of calls to functions for each of the menu items. Add the calculator and "99 Bottles of Beer" as two different functions that can be called.

2. Make your calculator program perform computations in a separate function for each type of computation.

3. Modify your password program from before to put all of the password checking logic into a separate function, apart from the rest of the program.

Chapter 7
Switch Case and Enums

Often times, you will write a long series of if-else statements to check many different conditions. For example, if you read in a key from the user, you may check it against five or more possible values; if you were writing a game, you might want to check things like pressing the left arrow, right arrow, up arrow, down arrow, or spacebar. In this chapter, we'll learn how to conveniently write these multi-condition checks using switch case statements, and we'll also learn a little bit about how to create our own simple types that work very well with switch case statements.

Switch case

Switch case statements are a substitute for long if statements that compare a single variable to several **integral** values. An integral value is simply a value that can be expressed as an integer, such as `int` or `char`.

The basic format for using switch case is outlined below. The value of the variable put in the switch is compared to the value following each of the cases, and when one value matches the value of the variable, the computer continues executing the program from that point until either the end of the switch case block, or a break statement is hit.

```
switch ( <variable> )
{
case this-value:
     // Code to execute if <variable> == this-value
     break;
case that-value:
     Code to execute if <variable> == that-value
```

```
        break;
// ...
default:
        // Code to execute if <variable> does not equal the
        // value following any of the cases

        break;
}
```

The first case that has the value associated with the given variable will have the code following the colon executed. The default case will run if no other case does. Using default is optional, but it is wise to include it to handle unexpected cases.

Notice the use of break at the end of each chunk of code. Break prevents the program from **falling through** and executing the code in the following case statement—yes, that's a weird behavior! But that's how it works, so don't forget to put in your break statements unless you actually do want to use the fall through behavior.

The value you give for each case must be a constant integral expression. Sadly, it isn't legal to use case like this:

BAD CODE
```
 int a = 10;
int  b  =  10;

switch ( a )
{
case b:
      // Code
      break;
}
```

If you try to compile this code, you'll see a compiler error that looks like this:

```
badcode.cpp:9: error: 'b' cannot appear in a constant-
expression
```

Below is a sample program you can run that demonstrates the use of switch case in a program.

```
#include <iostream>
```

```
using namespace std;

void playgame ()
{}

void loadgame ()
{}

void playmultiplayer ()
{}

int main ()
{
     int input;

     cout << "1. Play game\n";
     cout << "2. Load game\n";
     cout << "3. Play multiplayer\n";
     cout << "4. Exit\n";
     cout << "Selection: ";
     cin >> input;
     switch ( input )
     {
     case 1:          // Note the colon after each case, not
                      // a semicolon
          playgame();
          break;
     case 2:
          loadgame();
          break;
     case 3:
          playmultiplayer();
          break;
     case 4:
          cout << "Thank you for playing!\n";
          break;
     default:            // Note the colon for default, not
                         // a semicolon
          cout << "Error, bad input, quitting\n";
          break;
     }
}
```
Sample Code 25: switch.cpp

This program will compile and shows you a simple model for how to process user input, although the gameplay might be a bit too much like *Waiting for Godot*.

One issue you might notice is that the user gets only a single choice before the program exits—and if your user types the wrong value, there's no chance for redemption. You can easily fix this by putting a loop around the whole switch case block—but what about those `break` statements? Won't they cause the loop to exit? Nope, good news—the break statement will only jump to the end of the switch statement.

Comparison of switch case with if-else

If you are having trouble following the logic of the switch statement, it is essentially the same as writing an if statement for each case statement:

```
if ( 1 == input )
{
        playgame();
}
else if ( 2 == input )
{
        loadgame();
}
else if ( 3 == input )
{
        playmultiplayer();
}
else if ( 4 == input )
{
        cout << "Thank you for playing!\n";
}
else
{
        cout << "Error, bad input, quitting\n";
}
```

If we can do the same thing with an if/else, why do we need a switch at all? The main advantage of the switch is that it's quite clear how the program flow works: a single variable controls the code path. With a series of if/else conditions, each condition needs to be carefully read.

Creating simple types using enumerations

Sometimes when you're writing programs, you want to have a variable that can take on just a few values, and you know all the possible values ahead of time. For example, you might want to have constants for the available background colors a user can choose. It's very convenient to be able to have both a set of constants, and a variable type that is meant specifically to hold those constants. Moreover, this kind of variable would work great with switch-case because you know every single possible value!

Let's see how to do this using **enums**. An enum, which is short for "enumerated type", is a new variable type you create with a fixed ("enumerated") list of values. Colors of the rainbow might be a good enumerated type:

```
enum RainbowColor {
        RC_RED,
        RC_ORANGE,
        RC_YELLOW,
        RC_GREEN,
        RC_BLUE,
        RC_INDIGO,
        RC_VIOLET
};
```

The important things to notice are:
1) The `enum` keyword is used to introduce a new enum
2) The new type gets its very own name, `RainbowColor`
3) All of the possible values for the type are listed (I used the prefix `RC_` in case someone else wanted to use some of the same color names in a different enum for another reason)
4) And, of course, a semicolon

You can now declare a special variable of the type `RainbowColor` just like this:

```
RainbowColor chosen_color = RC_RED;
```

And you can write code like this:

```
switch (chosen_color)
{
case RC_RED: /* paint screen red */
case RC_ORANGE: /* paint screen orange */
case RC_YELLOW: /* paint screen yellow */
case RC_GREEN: /* paint screen green */
case RC_BLUE: /* paint screen blue */
case RC_INDIGO: /* paint screen indigo */
case RC_VIOLET: /* paint screen violet */
default: /* handle unexpected types */
```

```
}
```

Because we have an enumerated type, we can be pretty sure that we've covered all the possible values for the variable. But an enumerated type is, behind the scenes, just an integer—it can take a value not in the enumeration, but you really shouldn't do that unless you hate maintenance programmers!

You may be wondering: what values do my enums actually have? If you provide no specific value when declaring an enum, then the value is the value of the previous enum plus one. For the first enum, the value is 0. So in this case, RC_RED is 0 and RC_ORANGE is 1.

You can also define your own values; this can be useful if you have code that needs to use specific values from another system—maybe a piece of hardware, or some code you are reusing—and you want to give them nice names.

```
enum RainbowColor {
        RC_RED = 1,
        RC_ORANGE = 3,
        RC_YELLOW = 5,
        RC_GREEN = 7,
        RC_BLUE = 9,
        RC_INDIGO = 11,
        RC_VIOLET = 13
};
```

One major reason that enums are useful is that they allow you to give names to values that you might otherwise hard-code into your program. For example, if you wanted to write a tic-tac-toe game, you need a way to represent the Xs and Os of the board. You might choose to use 0 for a blank square, 1 for O, and 2 for X. If you do this, you'll probably have some code that compares one square of the board with 0, 1 and 2:

```
if ( board_position == 1 )
{
        /* do something because it's an O */
}
```

This is hard to read though—the code has a **magic number** that has some meaning, but whose meaning isn't really obvious from just looking at the code (unless there's a nice comment like the one I added). Enums let you create names for these values:

```
enum TicTacToeSquare { TTTS_BLANK, TTTS_O, TTTS_X };

if ( board_position == TTTS_O )
{
      /* some code */
}
```

Now the poor sap who has to fix bugs in the future (and this poor sap may be you!) can understand just what you mean the program to do.

Enums are good for working with fixed kinds of input, and switch case statements are a great way of working with user input, but neither tool solves the problem of working with more than a few input values at once. For example, you might want to read in a whole bunch of baseball or football statistics and do some processing. In situations like this, what you need is not a switch case block; you need some way to store and manipulate large amounts of data.

That's what Part 2 will be all about. Before we get there, though, we'll learn a little bit more about how to make programs do interesting things and behave differently without requiring big sets of data. Specifically, we'll learn how to add randomness (such as you might want to do to make a game).

Quiz yourself
1. Which follows the case statement?
A. :
B. ;
C. –
D. A newline

2. What is required to avoid falling through from one case to the next?
A. `end;`
B. `break;`
C. `Stop;`
D. You need a semicolon

3. What keyword covers unhandled possibilities?
A. `all`
B. `contingency`

C. `default`

D. `other`

4. What is the result of the following code?

```
int x = 0;
switch( x )
{
        case 1: cout << "One";
        case 0: cout << "Zero";
        case 2: cout << "Hello World";
}
```

A. One

B. Zero

C. Hello World

D. ZeroHello World

(View solution on page 488)

Practice problems

1. Rewrite the menu program you wrote in the practice problems for the Functions chapter on page 103 using switch-case.

2. Write a program that outputs all the lyrics of The Twelve Days of Christmas[17] using switch-case (hint: you might want to take advantage of fall-through cases).

3. Write a two-player tic-tac-toe game, allowing two humans to play against each other; use enums when possible to represent the values of the board.

---

[17] http://en.wikipedia.org/wiki/The_Twelve_Days_of_Christmas_(song)

Chapter 8
Randomizing Your Programs

There are really two ways to make your program behave differently each time it is run:

1) Have the user put in different input (or take different input by reading from files)
2) Have your program behave differently for the same user input

In a lot of cases, the first way is perfectly fine, and users often want their programs to be predictable. For example, if you're writing a text editor or a web browser, you probably want to do exactly the same thing each time the user types in a piece of text or a web address. You don't want your web browser to randomly decide which page you will go to—at least not if you aren't using StumbleUpon.[18]

But in some cases, behaving the same each time is a huge problem. For example, many computer games rely on randomness. Tetris is a great example—if you got the same sequence of blocks falling every game, users would be able to memorize ever-longer sequences and become better and

---

[18] StumbleUpon is a website that lets you 'stumble' across interesting new webpages: http://www.stumbleupon.com/

better just by relying on their ability to know what will come next. This would be about as fun as memorizing pi to a thousand decimal places. In order to make Tetris fun, you need a way of randomly selecting the next tile.

To do this, you need a way for the computer to generate random numbers. Computers, of course, do exactly what you tell them to do, which means that when you ask for something, you always get the same thing back; this makes it hard to generate truly random values. Fortunately, generating truly random numbers isn't always critical. You can do fine with numbers that look random, **pseudo-random numbers**.

To generate pseudo-random numbers, the computer will use a **seed** and apply mathematical transformations to the seed, turning it into another number. This new number becomes the next seed for the random number generator. If your program selects a different seed on each run, you will (for all practical purposes) never get the same sequence of random numbers. The mathematical transformations used are carefully selected so that all numbers generated come up with equal frequency and don't display obvious patterns (for example, it doesn't just add 1 each time to your number).

C++ provides all of this for you—you don't have to worry about doing the math, there are functions you can use. All you need to do is supply the random seed, which is as easy as using the current time. Let's look at the details.

Getting random numbers in C++

C++ has two functions, one for setting a random seed, and another for generating random numbers using the seed:

```
void srand (int seed);
```

`srand` takes a number and sets it as your seed. You should call `srand` once, at the start of your program. The typical way you use `srand` is to give it the result of the `time` function, which returns a number representing the current time:[19]

---

[19] The `time` function actually returns the number of seconds since January 1, 1970. This convention came from the Unix operating system and is sometimes called **Unix time**. In most cases, the time is stored in a signed 32-bit integer. This leads to the interesting possibility of overflowing the size of the integer and ending up with a negative number, representing a time in the past—it turns out that this will happen in the year 2038. This

```
srand( time( NULL20 ) );
```

If you were to keep calling `srand`, you'd seed your random number generation again and again, which would actually make the results less random (since they'd be based on a sequence of closely related time values). To use `srand`, you must include the header file `cstdlib`, and to use the `time` function, you must include the `ctime` header.

```
#include <cstdlib>
#include <ctime>

int main ()
{
    // call just once, at the very start
    srand( time( NULL ) );
}
```
Sample Code 26: srand.cpp

Now let's get our random numbers. To do that, you call the `rand` function, which has the following prototype:

```
int rand ();
```

Notice that `rand` doesn't take any arguments—it just gives you back a number. Let's print the result out:

```
#include <cstdlib>
#include <ctime>
#include <iostream>

using namespace std;

int main ()
{
    // call just once, at the very start
    srand( time( NULL ) );
    cout << rand() << '\n';
```

---

has led to discussions of a possible Year 2038 Problem where computer programs that use Unix time to think the current year is 1901. Read more on Wikipedia: http://en.wikipedia.org/wiki/Year_2038_problem

[20] Don't worry about the `NULL` parameter right now. For now, you can think of it as a formality; it will make more sense when you get to the chapter on pointers.

```
}
```
Sample Code 27: rand.cpp

Yay! This program behaves differently every time you run it, meaning you can use it for hours of exciting entertainment. What number will come up next?!

Okay, maybe it's not really that exciting—after all, the numbers you get have a really wide range. You can do more interesting things if you get the number in a particular range. As it turns out, rand will return a value between 0 and a constant called RAND_MAX (which will be at least 32767). That's pretty large, and you probably only want a small range within that. You could of course call rand in a loop, waiting for it to return a number in your range:

```
int randRange (int low, int high)
{
     while ( 1 )
     {
          int rand_result = rand();
          if ( rand_result >= low
                    &&
               rand_result <= high )
          {
               return rand_result;
          }
     }
}
```

But this is a pretty horrible solution! The first problem is that it's slow—if you want a number between 1 and 4, it's going to take a long time to get one of those values, since rand is returning from a much larger range. The second problem is that it's not guaranteed to terminate—it's possible (though extraordinarily unlikely) that you never get a number in the exact range you're looking for. Why take the chance when you can get guaranteed results?

C++ has an operation that returns the remainder from performing division (for example, 4 / 3 is 1, with a remainder of 1)—the modulus operator. You might remember it from earlier, when we used it to check primality. If you don't, it's ok, math can be a strong sedative. But it turns out that modulus is useful to us here. If you divide any number by 4, the remainder is going to be between 0 and 3. If you divide your random number by the size of the range, you'll end up getting a number between 0 and the size of the range (but never including the size of the range).

For example,

```
#include <ctime>
#include <cstdlib>
#include <iostream>

using namespace std;

int randRange (int low, int high)
{
        // we get a random number, get it to be between 0 and
        // the number of values in our range, then add the
        // lowest possible value
        return rand() % ( high - low + 1 ) + low;
}

int main ()
{
        srand( time( NULL ) );
        for ( int i = 0; i < 1000; ++i )
        {
                cout << randRange( 4, 10 ) << '\n';
        }
}
```
Sample Code 28: modulus.cpp

There are two things you should notice here. First, we must add 1 to `high` − `low`. To see why this is, imagine that our desired range is 0 through 10. In this case, there are 11 possible values. The subtraction gives us the difference between the two values, not the total count of values in our range, so we must add one. Second, notice that we need to add low to the value to get into our desired range. For example, if we want numbers between 10 and 20, we need to get a random number between 0 and 10, and then add 10 to the range.

With the ability to get random numbers in a specific range, you can do all sorts of fun things like create guessing games or simulate dice rolls.

Bugs and randomness
When you are still developing your program, randomness can be a problem. The trouble is that if you want to figure out a bug, it's usually best if your program does exactly the same thing every time. If it doesn't, the bug might not show up all the time, and you could spend a lot of time testing runs of the program that don't fail! Or another bug could happen that you weren't expecting. When first

testing or debugging your program, you may want to comment out the call to srand. Without seeding the random number generator, rand will return the same sequence of values each time your program is run, so you will see the same behavior each time.

What happens when you run into bugs when you've turned on the call to srand? One technique is to save the seed value each time your program is run:

```
int srand_seed = time( NULL );
cout << srand_seed << '\n';
srand( srand_seed );
```

Then if you find a bug, you can change your program so that you debug with the same random seed that allowed you to find the bug in the first place. For example, if the seed is 35434333, you would say:

```
int srand_seed = 35434333; // time( NULL );
cout << srand_seed << '\n';
srand( srand_seed );
```

And now every time the program runs, you will get predictable results.

Quiz yourself

1. What will happen if you don't call srand before calling rand?
A. rand will fail
B. rand will always return 0
C. rand will return the same sequence of numbers every time your program runs
D. Nothing

2. Why would you seed srand with the current time?
A. To ensure your program always runs the same way
B. To generate new random numbers each time your program is run
C. To make sure that the computer generates real random numbers
D. This is done for you, you only need to call srand if you want to set the seed to the same thing each time

3. What range of values does rand return?
A. The range you want
B. 0 to 1000

C. 0 to RAND_MAX
D. 1 to RAND_MAX

4. What does the expression 11 % 3 return?
A. 33
B. 3
C. 8
D. 2

5. When should you use `srand`?
A. Every time you need a random number
B. Never, it's just window dressing
C. Once, at the start of your program
D. Occasionally, after you've used `rand` for a while, to add more randomness

(View solution on page 489)

Practice problems

1. Write a program that simulates a coin flip. Run it many times—do the results look random to you?

2. Write a program that picks a number between 1 and 100, and then lets the user guess what the number is. The program should tell the user if their guess is too high, too low, or just right.

3. Write a program that solves the guessing game from problem 2. How many guesses does your program need?

4. Make a "slot machine" game that randomly displays the results of a slot machine to a player—have three (or more) possible values for each wheel of the slot machine. Don't worry about displaying the text "spinning" by. Just choose the results and display them and print out the winnings (choose your own winning combinations).

5. Write a program to play poker! You can provide 5 cards to the player, let that player choose new cards, and then determine how good the hand is. Think about whether this is easy to do. What problems might you have in terms of keeping track of cards that have been drawn already? Was this easier or harder than the slot machine?

Chapter 9
What If You Can't Figure Out What to Do?

Now that you've learned about a number of different basic language features, maybe you've started to run wild, writing programs all over the place. But wait! How will you know what to write? Even if you know the problem you're solving, you might feel like the underpants gnomes:

Step 1: Collect underpants
Step 2: ??
Step 3: Profit

You know where you want to go, and you know where you're starting, but step 2 isn't so clear.

This can be really masked when you're reading example source code, but you might start running into the problem more clearly when you go to write your own programs (or maybe not—in which case, that's great news, and you're well ahead of schedule; take the night off, have a beer, and I'll see you tomorrow).

Okay, so you're one of the many folks who're stuck on step 2—that's ok! This is actually the fun part (don't tell your buddy popping open the beer; he'll be sad).

Now I'll be the first to admit that this is also one of the most challenging parts of programming—more difficult than the language syntax, for example, but it's also one of the most satisfying. When you design a new program, from scratch, that does something that sounds difficult, it's magical; there's nothing like seeing your program come to life, making a difficult problem seem easy. The more you practice, the better you'll get, but you need to know a little bit about what to practice. That's what this chapter is all about. The one bit of bad news is that step 2 is probably going to become more like steps 2 through 22 because the trick to solving the problem is to break things down into finger sandwich sized chunks.

So let's get out the knives, the deli meats, some mayo and make appetizers. Okay, actually, let's start off with how to deal with situations where you have a basic understanding of how to solve the problem. When you have a pretty good idea of what's going on, and you're just not sure how to turn it into code, that's when you have a basic sense for the **algorithm**. The algorithm is the series of steps required to solve a problem. Even when you have the algorithm, it's not always easy to turn the logic into code. Perhaps the amount of stuff your program must do is overwhelming. Fortunately, there are tools to solve this problem.

Breaking a problem into chunks

Remember how I said earlier that programming is all about breaking things down into little pieces that the computer can understand? Well, the great thing about functions is that they let you create building blocks that the computer can understand, rather than always working from raw materials. What do I mean? Let's say that you want to print the prime numbers from 1 to 100. This is clearly more than a single operation, so we need to break it down into something the computer can understand.

The trouble is that there's a lot going on to accomplish this task! It would be pretty daunting to think about how to do the whole thing all at the same time.

What if we think about it in another way: how can we break it down into smaller parts? These steps don't have to be individual instructions; let's just try to come up with steps that are simpler than the ones we already have. A couple of reasonable steps are:

1) Go over all numbers from 1 to 100
2) For each number, test whether it is prime
3) If the number is prime, print it

Ok, that's great, we've divided this into a few different, smaller problems—but clearly we can't translate this into a program yet. What do we need to do? Can you think of a way to go through the numbers from 1 to 100? That sounds an awful lot like a loop. In fact, we can practically write the code for that already:

```
for ( int i = 0; i < 100; i++ )
{
    // check whether i is prime? If it is, print it
}
```

Let's put in a little bit of a placeholder function—call it isPrime. This function should return true if its argument is prime, or false otherwise. We'll need to figure out how to implement isPrime, but if we imagine it exists, we can at least fill in a little more code. Most functions we can imagine, we can write, and we've made the problem a little bit smaller—checking one number for primality is a smaller problem than checking 100—so we're on track.

```
for ( int i = 0; i < 100; i++ )
{
    if ( isPrime( i ) )
    {
        cout << i << endl;
    }
}
```

Isn't that nice? We have a basic structure to work with. Now all we need to do is write isPrime. Let's think about how to check if a number is prime or not. A number is prime if it has no divisors other than 1 and itself. Does that definition give us enough information to break this down into smaller sub-problems? I think it does. To check if a number has a divisor, we need to see if there's any number (other than 1 and itself) that divides it evenly. Since we need to check division by multiple different numbers, that suggests we need another loop. Here are the specific steps for this part of the algorithm:

1) For each number between 1 and the number being tested
2) Check if the number is divisible by the loop variable
        If it is, return false
3) If it's not divisible by any of these values, return true

Let's see if we can translate this into some source code. We don't yet know how to check if a number is divisible by another number of not—let's take a leap of faith and assume we can figure that out, and for now we'll just use a function, isDivisible, as a placeholder for that logic.

```
bool isPrime (int num)
{
    for ( int i = 2; i < num; i++)
    {
        if ( isDivisible( num, i ) )
        {
            return false;
        }
    }
    return true;
}
```

Once again we translated checking a range of values into a loop. We also easily translated the if statement in our logic into an if statement in the code.

Now how do we implement isDivisible? One way is to use a special operator, called the modulus operator and represented as a % sign, that returns the remainder when dividing one number by another:[21]

```
10 % 2 == 0 // 10 / 2 = 5 with no remainder
```

All we need to do is check if the number has no remainder when divided by the divisor:

```
bool isDivisible (int number, int divisor)
{
    return num % divisor == 0;
}
```

Hey, and look at that! We've reduced the problem down to only things the computer understands. There aren't any more functions we need to write; everything in our program is an instruction that is either already defined, or a

---

[21] It might seem a little bit magical that I just pulled out this new operator, but the truth is that there are other ways to check if one number is divisible by another; I just used modulus because it's the most straight-forward. If you want an exercise, try coming up with other approaches to the same problem.

function that we were able to define. Let's put it all together to see the big picture.

```cpp
#include <iostream>

// note the use of function prototypes
bool isDivisible (int number, int divisor);
bool isPrime (int number);

using namespace std;

int main ()
{
    for ( int i = 0; i < 100; i++ )
    {
        if ( isPrime( i ) )
        {
            cout << i << endl;
        }
    }
}

bool isPrime (int number)
{
    for ( int i = 2; i < number; i++)
    {
        if ( isDivisible( number, i  ) )
        {
            return false;
        }
    }
    return true;
}

bool isDivisible (int number, int divisor)
{
    return number % divisor == 0;
}
```

By using function prototypes, we can even order the code in exactly the same way that we thought about the design in the first place! Moreover, we can easily read through the code, starting at the big picture, just like in our design, and then reading the details of how the **helper functions** are implemented.

A brief aside about efficiency and security

By the way, we could improve this code a little bit—to make it more efficient—because we really don't need to go all the way from 2 to num in our loop in isPrime; just because we can think of an algorithm quickly, that doesn't mean it's the best, most efficient algorithm. In this case, we could go from 2 to the square root of num. However, since we are only checking a few very small numbers for primality, it's not that important that we be efficient. On the other hand, some important algorithms such as the RSA algorithm for public key cryptography, which is used on most bank and ecommerce websites as well as to secure sensitive data, relies on being able to generate large prime numbers to create encryption keys.[22] Generating a large prime number, of course, requires checking if a number is prime or not. If you were going to generate many RSA encryption keys, you'd really want to use a fast, efficient prime number generator!

Whenever you are working on a problem that seems too big to figure out, try to break it down into smaller problems that are a little bit more manageable. You don't need to immediately know how to solve those smaller problems (it doesn't hurt to have an idea for how to do it, of course). What matters is that you understand what inputs are needed, and what the result is, from the smaller problem. If you're able to write your program with functions that solve those problems, then you can tackle the next challenge: solving those smaller problems. You keep doing that for long enough, and you'll end up with some source code.

Sometimes you'll find that solving the sub-problems are impossible for some reason; designing a program is not always easy (if it were, there'd be a lot more bored software engineers). If you find that you're having trouble breaking the problem down, try taking a step back and coming up with another way of breaking down your problem to see if you can find more tractable sub-problems.

This approach to breaking down programs is called **top-down design**. It is a powerful approach to thinking about programming. Another approach, **bottom-up design**, focuses on trying to figure out the helper functions first, and then trying to use them to solve the larger problem. A bottom-up design can lead to

---

[22] You can read more about the RSA algorithm on Wikipedia:
http://en.wikipedia.org/wiki/RSA_(algorithm)

situations where you build helper functions that you don't need at all, but it can be a little bit easier to get started with because you start out by having working functions. For a beginner, though, it's often better to use a top-down design approach because it will focus you on writing the functions that solve the problem that you want to solve. Rather than trying to guess what functions might be useful to help solve the problem, your design is optimized for finding exactly what helper functions you need.[23]

You don't have to do all of your design with source code either. Writing down the design on paper, or a whiteboard, gives you a chance to see how everything fits together without having to fuss with C++ syntax and compiler errors. Doing your design directly with code can sometimes obscure the big picture as you work on sorting out each tiny little piece of the syntax that you need. So it's ok if you decide to try to write down each step of the process and break down each step into a smaller series of steps, without immediately turning it into code. This is a legitimate and very natural design approach.

If there's one thing to know, it's that designing a problem won't always be easy; what I've told you will help, but it won't be a magic bullet. What does help is practice—you will get it, and you'll get better at it. It just might take some time; don't give up.

What if you don't know the algorithm?

In the case of finding prime numbers, our task was ultimately pretty easy because the definition of a prime number is practically an algorithm for how to check if a number is prime. The problem was "just" a question of translating the algorithm into code. Most of the time, it won't be quite this easy—you'll have to come up with an algorithm to solve the problem.

For example, imagine trying to come up with an algorithm for a program that displayed the English name for a number (example: 1204, one thousand, two hundred four). When you're speaking, this translation is so natural that you probably don't even think about the structure of the algorithm; you just do it (assuming English is your native language; if it isn't, you might just have an advantage over native speakers in solving this problem!). In order to approach

---

[23] Don't let me stop you from trying bottom-up design though; it works for some folks, and it might work for you. If you just can't get your head around top-down design, flip it over before giving up.

this kind of problem, what you need to do is understand the pattern in the data so that you can come up with the algorithm.

A good starting point is to write out a couple of examples and try to think about the similarities and the differences between them until you find some patterns. Let's do that:

1	one
10	ten
101	one hundred one
1,001	one thousand one
10,001	ten thousand one
100,001	one hundred thousand one
1,000,001	one million one
10,000,001	ten million one
100,000,001	one hundred million one

Do you see the pattern forming?

1	**One**
10	**Ten**
101	**one hundred** one
1,001	**one** thousand one
10,001	**ten** thousand one
100,001	**one hundred** thousand one
1,000,001	**one** million one
10,000,001	**ten** million one
100,000,001	**one hundred** million one

Every three digits, we go up a level—from nothing, to thousand, to million. Moreover, for each three-digit chunk, we have a pattern: "one, ten, one hundred". We then combine them back together with the "higher level" chunks: "one thousand", "ten thousand", "one hundred thousand".

Our algorithm, then, needs to start by breaking down the number into chunks of three digits, figure out what the "magnitude" is for the current chunk (thousand, million, billion) and then translate that chunk into text to combine with the magnitude. Each three-digit chunk is less than one thousand, so we have a much smaller problem to solve—always a good thing. Let's look for more patterns:

5	Five
15	Fifteen
25	twenty five
35	thirty five
45	forty five
105	one hundred five
115	one hundred fifteen
125	one hundred twenty five
135	one hundred thirty five
145	one hundred forty five

We have a similar pattern here: if we have a number greater than 100, the text is "X hundred", and then we have the text for the two-digit chunk. If we don't have a hundreds value, it's just the text of the two-digit chunk.

Now all we need to do is decide how to handle the two-digit chunks. Do you see that there is again a pattern? Except for the numbers less than 20, the pattern is always "name of the tens" "name of the ones", which we could code with a simple series of if/else statements.

To deal with the numbers from 1 to 19, well, we'll just have to hard-code those directly into the program—there's no algorithm to solve that. Not that I can see anyway!

So our algorithm will look something like this:
1) Break the number up into chunks of three digits

2) For each three-digit chunk, compute the text; append the magnitude of that chunk; append the chunks together

3) To compute the text of a three-digit chunk, compute the number of hundreds, and convert that one-digit number to text, and add "hundreds", appending the text of the two-digit chunk

4) To compute the text of a two-digit chunk, if it's less than 20, look it up; if it's greater than 20, compute the number of tens, and look up the word, and append the text of the one-digit number

We would need another pass to convert this algorithm into source code, as not all of the details are fully specified, but now you have enough of an outline that you can use the previous approach of taking a top-down design in order to implement the algorithm.

Do you see how this process worked? By working through the examples of the different numbers, we were able to find a certain pattern to the way the numbers are structured. We found a seed of the algorithm—not all of the details were completely specified, but that's ok; at each step in the process, we'll keep making things a little bit more refined, until it all comes out in the end.

Practice Problems

1. Implement the source code that turns numbers into English text for numbers between -999,999 and 999,999. (Hint: You might also be able to take advantage of the fact that the integer data type will truncate decimal points. Also, remember that your algorithm doesn't have to work for all numbers—only numbers with six digits or less.)

2. Think about how you would go in the opposite direction, reading English text and translating it into source code. Is this easier or harder than the earlier algorithm? How would you handle bad input?

3. Design a program that finds all numbers from 1 to 1000 whose prime factors, when added together, sum up to a prime number (for example, 12 has prime factors of 2, 2, and 3, which sum to 7, which is prime). Implement the code for that algorithm. (Hint: If you don't know the algorithm to find the prime factors of a number and have trouble figuring it out, it's OK to look it up on Google! I meant it when I told you that you don't need to know math to be a programmer.)

Part 2: Working with Data

You've learned a lot about how to make basic programs that can do interesting things—display output (like your name), interact with the user, make decisions based on the input provided by the user, repeatedly perform simple operations and even create games of chance.

That's all good stuff, but after a while, you might find that your programs get dull; it is tough to do interesting things with small amounts of data. But so far, you haven't really learned enough to work with large amounts of data. Think back to the poker exercise from the end of the past chapter—how easy was it to keep track of the cards that had been played? How hard it would be if you wanted to shuffle an entire deck of cards and display the deck in shuffled order?

[Brief interlude]

It'll be hard. First, you'd need some way of storing the 52 different values— you'd need 52 different variables. Each time you set the value for a new card, you have to check every single one of the variables to see if you'd already drawn the card that variable represents. By the time you got to the 52nd card, you'd have an awful lot of code and very little desire to do any more programming. Fortunately , programmers are lazy—they don't like doing work they don't have to—and they've come up with nicer ways of solving this problem.

This section of the book is all about solving these problems, allowing you to work with large amounts of data: reading it in, storing it in memory, and manipulating it. We'll start off with a technique for holding lots of data without creating many different variables, which will solve the poker problem.

Chapter 10
Arrays

Arrays are the answer to the question of "how do I easily store a lot of data?" An **array** is, essentially, a variable with a single name that can store multiple values, but with each value indexed by a number. You can think of an array as a numbered list where you can access elements by number.

Arrays are fairly easy to visualize:

I always think of arrays as a big chain of boxes lined up next to each other; each box is an **element** of the array. Getting a value out of an array is like asking for a particular box by number: "box number 5 please!" And that's the magic—because an array stores all of its values with a single name, it is possible to **programmatically** select which element of the array you want at run time. By programmatically, I mean that you don't have to actually type in the name of the variable—your program can figure out which variable it wants by figuring out the right number. If you want to draw a poker hand of five cards, you could store all five cards in an array of size five. Then picking a new card for a hand requires changing which array index you are setting, rather than using a new variable. Consequently, by using a variable to store the index you can use the same code to draw each separate card, rather than having to write different code for every single variable. It's the difference between writing:

```
Card1 = getRandomCard();
Card2 = getRandomCard();
Card3 = getRandomCard();
Card4 = getRandomCard();
Card5 = getRandomCard();
```

and

```
for ( int i = 0; i < 5; i++ )
{
      card[ i ] = getRandomCard();
}
```

Now imagine the difference for 100 cards!

Some basic array syntax

To declare an array, you specify two things (besides the name): the type and the size.

```
int my_array[ 6 ];
```

This declares an array with six integer elements. Notice that the size goes between the square brackets, and the brackets go after the name of the variable.

To access the elements of the array, you use brackets, but this time, instead of the size, you give the index of the element you want to access:

```
my_array[ 3 ];
```

We can visualize it like this:

my_array

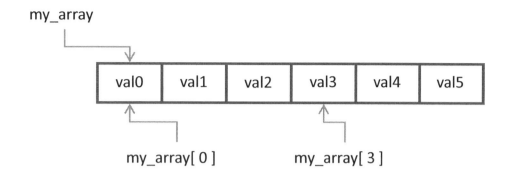

my_array[0]   my_array[3]

my_array refers to the array as a whole, whereas my_array[0] refers to the first element, and my_array[3] to the fourth. If you just did a double-take, well, it's good that you're paying attention. But that's not a typo; array **indexing** starts at 0. By indexing, I mean the number that you plug in to get a particular value out of an array. This is probably not what you're used to, unless your parents (or whoever taught you to count) were computer programmers.

Here's an easy way to think about it: the index is how far you need to go down the list before you reach your box. You'll probably run into the term **offset** at some point; offset is just a fancy way of saying the same thing—the value in the array is offset from the beginning of the array by its index. Since the first element of the array is already at the beginning, the offset, and consequently the index, is 0.

Once you've chosen a particular element in the array, you treat it like any other variable. You can modify an element of the array like so:

```
int my_array[ 4 ]; // declare the array
my_array[ 2 ] = 2; // set the third element (yes, really!)
                   // of the array to 2
```

Example uses for arrays

Using arrays to store orderings

Remember the question I posed earlier: "how would you shuffle a 52 card deck?" Part of the problem is that you need some way of representing 52 cards—now you have it, you can use an array. The other part of the problem is, how do show the order of the cards in the deck? The good news is that since arrays are accessed numerically, you can simply treat the order of the elements in the array as the natural order of the cards in the deck. So if you randomly assigned 52 unique values to an array, you can say that the first element (index 0) in the array is the top of the deck, and the last element (index 51) is the bottom.

Another common use of arrays is to store sorted values. For example, what if you wanted to read in 100 values and show them in sorted order? Ignoring the issue of sorting, the way you'd represent the order of the values is by putting them into the array—again taking advantage of the natural ordering of arrays.

Representing grids with multidimensional arrays

Arrays can also be used to represent **multidimensional** data, like a chess or checkers board (or, if you prefer something a bit simpler, a tic-tac-toe board). Multidimensional data just means that you have more than one index for it.

To declare a two-dimensional array you provide each of the dimensions:

```
int tic_tac_toe_board[ 3 ][ 3 ];
```

Here's a simple visualization for `tic_tac_toe_board`:

[0][0]	[0][1]	[0][2]
[1][0]	[1][1]	[1][2]
[2][0]	[2][1]	[2][2]

Since a two-dimensional array is rectangular, there are two indices that you must use to access it—one for the row, and one for the column. In the diagram, I've put the exact indices you'd need to use to access each element. All you need are two values, one that goes in the first slot and one that goes in the second slot.

You can make a three-dimensional array, though you probably won't need to. In fact, you could make a four- five- or more dimensional array. It would be become pretty hard to visualize, and you won't use them much in practice, so I'm not going to draw you a diagram.

Having a grid-shaped array means that you can organize data better; if you have a tic-tac-toe board, you can set the value of each element of the array to match the current board position. You can also use an array to represent a maze or the layout of a level in an RPG.

Using arrays

Arrays and for loops

Arrays and for loops work extremely well together; an array can be accessed by initializing a variable to 0 and incrementing that variable until that variable is as big as the length of the array—a pattern that exactly fits the model of a for loop.

Here's a small program that demonstrates using for loops to create multiplication tables and store the results in a two-dimensional array.

```cpp
#include <iostream>

using namespace std;

int main ()
{
        int array[ 8 ][ 8 ]; // Declares an array that looks
                             // like a chessboard

        for ( int i = 0; i < 8; i++ )
        {
                for ( int j = 0; j < 8; j++ )
                {
                        // Set each element to a value
                        array[ i ][ j ] = i * j;

                }
        }
        cout << "Multiplication table:\n";
        for ( int i = 0; i < 8; i++ )
        {
                for ( int j = 0; j < 8; j++ )
                {
                        cout << "[ "<< i <<" ][ "<< j <<" ] = ";
                        cout << array[ i ][ j ] <<" ";
                        cout << "\n";
                }
```

```
        }
}
```
Sample Code 29: multidimensional_array.cpp

Passing arrays to functions

You'll quickly learn that language features interact with each other.   For example, now that you know about arrays, you'd be well within reason to ask, "How can I pass an array to a function?"   Fortunately, there isn't much to it syntactically.

When calling a function, you just use the name of the array:

```
int values[ 10 ];
sum_array( values );
```

When declaring the function, you put the name of the array like this:

```
int sum_array (int values[]);
```

"Wait," you ask, "what's the deal? There's no size given!" That's right, for a single-dimensional array, you do not need to specify a size. The size is necessary if you are defining an array, since the compiler needs to create space for it; when you pass an array into a function, it just passes in the original array, so there's no need to give it the size because it isn't making a new array. The fact that the original array is passed to the function means that if you *modify* an array within a function, that change will stick after the function returns. Normal variables, as we saw earlier, are copied; when a function takes an argument and then modifies the variable holding that value, it doesn't affect the original value.

Of course, unless the function knows how big the array is, to use the array, that function needs to take the size of the array as a second parameter:

```
int sumArray (int values[], int size)
{
        int sum = 0;
        for ( int i = 0; i < size; i++ )
        {
                sum += values[ i ];
        }
        return sum;
}
```

On the other hand, if you pass in a multidimensional array, you need to give every size except the first

```
int check_tic_tac_toe (int board[][ 3 ]);
```

This is definitely weird! For now, just remember you don't need to include the first dimension (although you can, if you wish; it will be ignored).

I'll talk more about passing arrays into functions when we get to Introduction to Pointers on page 157. At that time, I'll explain the calculations that are going on behind the scenes. For now, you can just treat this as a syntactic quirk of the language.

Let's write out a full program that demonstrates the sum_array function:

```
#include <iostream>

using namespace std;

int sumArray (int values[], int size)
{
        int sum = 0;
        // this array stops when i == size. Why? The last
        // element is size - 1
        for ( int i = 0; i < size; i++ )
        {
                sum += values[ i ];
        }
        return sum;
}

int main ()
{
        int values[ 10 ];
        for ( int i = 0; i < 10; i++ )
        {
                cout << "Enter value " << i << ": ";
                cin >> values[ i ];
        }
        cout << sumArray( values, 10 ) << endl;
}
```
Sample Code 30: sum_array.cpp

Think about how you would write this kind of program without an array. You'd have no way of storing all of the values, so you'd have to keep a running sum—

every time the user entered an input, you'd have to immediately add it. You couldn't easily keep track of all the numbers if you wanted to use them later (for example, to show the numbers that were added).

Writing off the end of an array
While you have free rein over the elements of the array, you should never attempt to write data past the last element of the array, such as when you have a 10 element array, and you try to write to offset 10:

BAD CODE
```
int my_array[ 10 ];
my_array[ 10 ] = 4;   // tries to write an eleventh element
```

The array is only ten elements large, so the last valid array index is nine. Using an index of 10 isn't valid and may in fact cause your program to crash! (I'll explain why once we talk about how memory works.) The most common scenario where this will happen is if you are writing a loop over an array:

BAD CODE
```
int vals[ 10 ];
for ( int i = 0; i <= 10; i++ )
{
      cin >> vals[ i ];
}
```

Here, the array has ten elements, but the loop condition is checking whether i is less than or equal to 10; this meaning it will write data into vals[10], which it ought not do. Unfortunately, despite its normal fastidiousness, the compiler will not tell you about these bugs. You will only know you have a problem when your program crashes or behaves very strangely because the changed value is used by some other code.

Sorting arrays
Let's take a stab at answering the question I raised earlier: "How would you take 100 values and sort them?" The basic skeleton of the code should now be fairly clear; you need a loop that reads in 100 integers from the user:

```
#include <iostream>

using namespace std;
```

```
int main ()
{
      int values[ 100 ];
      for ( int i = 0; i < 100; i++ )
      {
            cout << "Enter value " << i << ": ";
            cin >> values[ i ];
      }
}
```
Sample Code 31: read_ints.cpp

That's the easy part—now that you've got the data read in, how do you sort it? The way most people naturally sort things is that they find the lowest value in a list, and move it to the beginning. Then they find the second lowest value in the list, and move it right after the first. Then you find the third lowest value in the list, and move it after the second.

Visually, if you were sorting the list

```
3, 1, 2
```

You'd first move 1 to the beginning of the list

```
1, 3, 2
```

Then you'd move 2 to the second spot in the list

```
1, 2, 3
```

Does that sound like you could write code to do that using the C++ features you have seen? It looks a lot like a loop to me. You're looping over the array, starting at the first element, and deciding which value to put there by finding the smallest element left in the rest of the array (the unsorted portion of the array). Then we swap that value with the value of the element at the current index (that value has to go somewhere). We can start off writing a little bit of code for this, using the top-down approach to design:

```
void sort (int array[])
{
      for ( int i = 0; i < 100; i++ )
      {
            int index =
                  findSmallestRemainingElement( array, i );
```

```
                    swap( array, i, index );
            }
    }
```

Now we can think about implementing the two helper functions, findSmallestRemainingElement and swap. Let's start thinking about findSmallestRemainingElement; this function needs to go through the array, and find the smallest element in the array, starting from index i. That sounds like another loop, doesn't it? We will look at each element of the array and, if it's smaller than the smallest element we've seen so far, we'll take the index of that element as the current index for the smallest element.

```
int findSmallestRemainingElement (int array[], int index)
{
        int index_of_smallest_value = index;
        for (int i = index + 1; i < ???; i++)
        {
                if ( array[ i ]
                            <
                        array[ index_of_smallest_value ]  )
                {
                        index_of_smallest_value = i;
                }
        }
        return index_of_smallest_value;
}
```

That looks pretty reasonable, doesn't it? There's just one small problem—how do we know when our loop should stop? There's no information in the function arguments to indicate how large the array is! We need to add it, and we also need to add the size to the call to the findSmallestRemainingElement function. Notice that this is a situation where the top-down design approach requires going back to the original code and making some changes—that's ok, and it's a natural part of the design process, so don't worry about doing it. Let's also fix things up so that our sorting code doesn't have a hard-coded value of 100 for the size of the array either.

```
int findSmallestRemainingElement (
            int array[],
            int size,
            int index
        )
{
        int index_of_smallest_value = index;
```

```
        for (int i = index + 1; i < size; i++)
        {
            if ( array[ i ]
                   <
                array[ index_of_smallest_value ]  )
            {
                index_of_smallest_value = i;
            }
        }
        return index_of_smallest_value;
}

void sort (int array[], int size)
{
        for ( int i = 0; i < size; i++ )
        {
            int index =
                findSmallestRemainingElement(
                    array,
                    size,
                    i
                );
            swap( array, i, index );
        }
}
```

Finally, we need to implement the `swap` function. Since a function can modify the original array that is passed to it, we can do this simply by exchanging the two values, using a temporary variable to hold the first value that is overwritten:

```
void swap (int array[], int first_index, int second_index)
{
        int temp = array[ first_index ];
        array[ first_index ] = array[ second_index ];
        array[ second_index ] = temp;
}
```

Since the original array passed into the `swap` function can be modified directly, that's all there is to it.

To prove that this sort algorithm works, you can fill an array with randomly generated data and then sort it. Here's the full listing:

```
#include <cstdlib>
#include <ctime>
#include <iostream>
```

```cpp
using namespace std;

int findSmallestRemainingElement (
int array[], int size, int index);
void swap (int array[], int first_index, int second_index);

void sort (int array[], int size)
{
    for ( int i = 0; i < size; i++ )
    {
        int index =
            findSmallestRemainingElement(
                array,
                size,
                i
            );
        swap( array, i, index );
    }
}

int findSmallestRemainingElement (
    int array[],
    int size,
    int index
)

{
    int index_of_smallest_value = index;
    for (int i = index + 1; i < size; i++)
    {
        if ( array[ i ]
                <
            array[ index_of_smallest_value ]   )
        {
            index_of_smallest_value = i;
        }
    }
    return index_of_smallest_value;
}


void swap (int array[], int first_index, int second_index)
{
    int temp = array[ first_index ];
    array[ first_index ] = array[ second_index ];
    array[ second_index ] = temp;
}
```

```cpp
// small helper function to display the before and after
// arrays
void displayArray (int array[], int size)
{
      cout << "{";
      for ( int i = 0; i < size; i++ )
      {
            // you'll see this pattern a lot for nicely
            // formatting lists--check if we're past the
            // first element, and if so, append a comma
            if ( i != 0 )
            {
                  cout << ", ";
            }
            cout << array[ i ];
      }
      cout << "}";
}

int main ()
{
      int array[ 10 ];
      srand( time( NULL ) );
      for ( int i = 0; i < 10; i++ )
      {
            // keep the numbers small so they're easy to
            // read
            array[ i ] = rand() % 100;
      }
      cout << "Original array: ";
      displayArray( array, 10 );
      cout << '\n';

      sort( array, 10 );

      cout << "Sorted array: ";
      displayArray( array, 10 );
      cout << '\n';
}
```
Sample Code 32: insertion_sort.cpp

The sorting algorithm you just learned, called **insertion sort**, is not the fastest algorithm for sorting numbers, but it has one advantage: it's pretty simple to understand and to implement. If you were going to use your sorting algorithm on a very large data set, you might choose an algorithm that was a faster but more difficult to implement and understand. These are the kinds of tradeoffs you will face as a programmer. In many cases, the answer is that the easiest algorithm to implement is also the best, but if you are serving millions of visitors to a website every day, the easiest algorithm isn't going to cut it. It's up to you to make informed decision about which algorithm to use, based on the amount of data you expect to see, and the importance of the algorithm completing quickly. If you can run a batch job overnight, it's ok to be a bit slower, but if you need to respond in real time to a user's search (like Google) it's not ok.

As you can see, arrays provide us with a lot of power—we can work with and organize lots more data than we had in the past. There are still a few problems for us to solve though. What if we want to associate multiple different but related values together, rather than storing just a single value? Arrays help us organize distinct pieces of data, but they don't help us organize data that belongs together. We'll see the way to solve this problem in the next chapter, on structures.

A second problem is that arrays provide a fixed amount of memory—lots of it, if we need it—but it's determined once, when you're writing the program. If you want to write a program that can store and work with unlimited amounts of data, a fixed size array won't cut it. We'll soon talk about solutions to this problem as well.

Despite these limitations, arrays are a tremendous improvement, and the idea of using indices to access data will show up all the time.

Quiz yourself

1. Which of the following correctly declares an array?
A. `int anarray[ 10 ];`
B. `int anarray;`
C. `anarray{ 10 };`
D. `array anarray[ 10 ];`

2. What is the index number of the last element of an array with 29 elements?
A. 29
B. 28
C. 0
D. Programmer-defined

3. Which of the following is a two-dimensional array?
A. `array anarray[ 20 ][ 20 ];`

```
B. int anarray[ 20 ][ 20 ];
C. int array[ 20, 20 ];
D. char array[ 20 ];
```

4. Which of the following correctly accesses the seventh element stored in foo, an array with 100 elements?
A. `foo[ 6 ];`
B. `foo[ 7 ];`
C. `foo( 7 );`
D. `foo;`

5. Which of the following properly declares a function that takes a two-dimensional array?
A. `int func ( int x[][] );`
B. `int func ( int x[ 10 ][] );`
C. `int func ( int x[] );`
D. `int func ( int x[][ 10 ] );`

(View solution on page 490)

Practice problems

1. Turn the code that we wrote for insertion sort into an insertion_sort function that works for any size of array.

2. Write a program that takes in 50 values and prints out the highest, the lowest, the average and then all 50 input values, one per line.

3. Write a program that detects whether an array is sorted or not, and if it is not sorted, sort it.

4. Write a small tic-tac-toe program that allows two players to play tic-tac-toe competitively. Your program should check to see if either player has won, or if the board is filled completely (with the game ending in a tie). Bonus: can you make your program detect if the game cannot be won by either side before the entire grid is filled?

5. Make your tic-tac-toe game into a game that allows boards bigger than 3x3 but requires four-in-a-row to win. Allow the players to specify the size of the board while the program is running. (Hint: right now, you have to define your

board to be a fixed size at compile time, so you may need to limit the maximum size of the board.)

6. Make a two-player checkers program that allows each player to make a move, and checks for legal moves and whether the game is over. Be sure to support kinging! Feel free to add support for any house rules that you use when you play. Consider allowing the user to choose the type of rules at program startup.

Chapter 11
Structures

Associating multiple values together

Now that you can store a single value in an array, it's possible for you to write programs that deal with a lot of data. As you work with more data, there will be times that you have several pieces of data that are all associated together. For example, you might want to store screen coordinates (x and y values) for players in a video game along with their names. Right now, you could do that with three separate arrays:

```
int x_coordinates[ 10 ];
int y_coordinates[ 10 ];
string names[ 10 ];
```

But you'd have to remember that each array is matched up with another, so if you moved the position of an element in one of the arrays, you would have to move the associated element in the other two arrays.

This would also get pretty unwieldy when you need to keep track of a fourth value. You'd have add another array and keep it in sync with the original three. Fortunately, the people who design programming languages are not masochists, so there is a better way of associating values together: structures. Structures allow you to store different values in variables under the same variable name. Structures are useful whenever several pieces of data need to be grouped together.

Syntax
The format for defining a structure is

```
struct SpaceShip
{
        int x_coordinate;
        int y_coordinate;
        string name;
}; // <- Notice that pesky semicolon; you must include it
```

Here, `SpaceShip` is the name of the particular type of structure that we are defining. In other words, you have created your own type, just like `double` or `int`, which you can use to declare a variable, like so:

```
SpaceShip my_ship;
```

The names `x_coordinate`, `y_coordinate` and `name` are the **fields** of our new type. Wait, fields, what does that mean exactly?

Here's the story: we've just created a compound type—a variable that stores multiple values that are all associated with each other (like two screen coordinates, or a first and last name). The way you tell the variable which one of those values you want is by naming the field you want to access. It's like having two separate variables with different names, except that the two variables are grouped together and you have a consistent way of naming them. You can think of a structure as a form (think driver's license application) with fields—the form stores a lot of data, and each field of the form is a particular piece of that related data. Declaring a structure is the way to define the form, and declaring a variable of that structure's type creates a copy of that form that you can fill out and use to store a bunch of data.

To access fields, you put in the name of the variable (not the name of the structure—each variable has its own separate values for its fields) followed by a dot '.', followed by the name of the field:

```
// declare the variable
SpaceShip my_ship;

// use it
my_ship.x_coordinate = 40;
my_ship.y_coordinate = 40;
```

```
my_ship.name = "USS Enterprise (NCC-1701-D)";
```

As you can see, you can have many fields in a structure, practically as many as you want, and they do not all have to be the same type.

Let's now look at an example program that demonstrates reading in the names of five players in a game (game not included), which will combine arrays and structures:

```cpp
#include <iostream>

using namespace std;

struct PlayerInfo
{
      int skill_level;
      string name;
};

using namespace std;

int main ()
{
      // like normal variable types, you can make arrays of
      // structures
      PlayerInfo players[ 5 ];
      for ( int i = 0; i < 5; i++ )
      {
            cout << "Please enter the name for player : "
                << i << '\n';
            // first access the element of the array, using
            // normal array syntax; then access the field
            // of the structure using the '.' syntax
            cin >> players[ i ].name;
            cout << "Please enter the skill level for "
                << players[ i ].name << '\n';
            cin >> players[ i ].skill_level;
      }
      for ( int i = 0; i < 5; ++i )
      {
            cout << players[ i ].name
                << " is at skill level "
                << players[ i ].skill_level << '\n';
      }
}
```

The struct `PlayerInfo` declares that it has two fields: the name of a player, and the player's `skill_level`. Since you can use `PlayerInfo` like any other variable type (e.g. `int`), you can create an array of players. When you create an array of structures, you treat each element of the array like you would treat a single structure instance—to access a field of the first structure in the array, you would just write `players[ 0 ].name` to access to the name of the player in the first element of the array.

This program takes advantage of the ability to combine arrays and structures to read in the information for five different players, with two different pieces of data, in a single for loop, and then display that information in a second loop. There's no need to have multiple related arrays for each individual piece of data. You don't need separate `player_names` and `player_skill_level` arrays.

Passing structures around

You will often want to write a function that either receives a structure as an argument or that returns a structure. For example, if you had a small game with spaceships moving around, you might want a function to initialize a structure for a new enemy.

```
struct EnemySpaceShip
{
        int x_coordinate;
        int y_coordinate;
        int weapon_power;
};

EnemySpaceShip getNewEnemy ();
```

In this case, calling `getNewEnemy` should return a value with all of the values in the structure initialized. Here's how you could write it:

```
EnemySpaceShip getNewEnemy ()
{
        EnemySpaceShip ship;
        ship.x_coordinate = 0;
        ship.y_coordinate = 0;
        ship.weapon_power = 20;
        return ship;
}
```

This function will actually make a copy of the `ship` local variable that it returns. This means that it will copy every field of the structure into a new variable, one by one. Although copying many fields may seem slow, most of the time the computer is fast enough that it doesn't matter. However, once you start working with large numbers of structures, it does start to matter, so we'll talk about how to avoid those extra copies in the next chapter, on pointers.

To actually receive the variable that is returned, you'd write code like this:

```
EnemySpaceShip ship = getNewEnemy();
```

You can now use the ship variable just like any other structure variable.

Passing in a structure would look like this:

```
EnemySpaceShip upgradeWeapons (EnemySpaceShip ship)
{
        ship.weapon_power += 10;
        return ship;
}
```

When a structure is passed into a function, it will be copied (just like when we returned a structure), so any changes made to the structure in the function will be lost! That's why this function needs to return a copy of the structure after modifying it—the original structure has not been changed.

In order to use `upgradeWeapons` to modify an `EnemySpaceShip` we would have to write:

```
ship = upgradeWeapons( ship );
```

When the function is called, the ship variable is copied into the argument to the function; when the function returns, the `EnemySpaceShip` variable that was returned is copied back into `ship`, overwriting the original fields.

Here's a simple program that demonstrates creating and upgrading a single enemy ship:

```
struct EnemySpaceShip
{
        int x_coordinate;
```

```
        int y_coordinate;
        int weapon_power;
};

EnemySpaceShip getNewEnemy ()
{
        EnemySpaceShip ship;
        ship.x_coordinate = 0;
        ship.y_coordinate = 0;
        ship.weapon_power = 20;
        return ship;
}

EnemySpaceShip upgradeWeapons (EnemySpaceShip ship)
{
        ship.weapon_power += 10;
        return ship;
}

int main ()
{
        EnemySpaceShip enemy = getNewEnemy();
        enemy = upgradeWeapons( enemy );
}
```
Sample Code 33: upgrade.cpp

You might be wondering, what if you wanted to create an unlimited supply of enemy ships and keep track of all of them as the game progressed? How would make enemy ships? You'd call `getNewEnemy`. But where would you keep track of them—where would you store them? Right now, we only have access to fixed-size arrays. We could create an array of `EnemySpaceShip` values:

```
EnemySpaceShip my_enemy_ships[ 10 ];
```

But that still gives you no more than ten enemies at once. That might be enough, but it might not. The solution to this problem is again in the next few chapters, starting in   Introduction to Pointers.

Quiz yourself

1. Which of the following accesses a variable in structure b?

A. `b->var;`

B. `b.var;`

C. `b-var;`

D. `b>var;`

2. Which of the following is a properly defined structure?

A. `struct {int a;}`
B. `struct a_struct {int a};`
C. `struct a_struct int a;`
D. `struct a_struct {int a;};`

3. Which properly declares a structure variable of type `foo` with the name `my_foo`?

A. `my_foo as struct foo`
B. `foo my_foo;`
C. `my_foo;`
D. `int my_foo;`

4. What is the final value output by this code?

```
#include <iostream>

using namespace std;

struct MyStruct
{
      int x;
};

void updateStruct (MyStruct my_struct)
{
      my_struct.x = 10;
}

int main ()
{
      MyStruct my_struct;
      my_struct.x = 5;
      updateStruct( my_struct );
      cout << my_struct.x << '\n';
}
```

A. 5
B. 10
C. This code will not compile

(View solution on page 491)

Practice problems

1. Write a program that lets the user fill in a single structure with the name, address, and phone number of a single person.

2. Create an array of space ship objects and write a program that continually updates their positions until they all go off the screen. Assume that the size of the screen is 1024 pixels by 768 pixels.

3. Create an address book program that builds on problem #1—this time, the user should be able to not just fill out a single structure, but should be able to add new entries, each with a separate name and phone number. Let the user add as many entries as he or she wants—is this easy to do? Is it even possible? Add the ability to display all, or some of the entries, letting the user browse the list of entries.

4. Write a program that allows a user to enter high scores of a game, keeping tracking of the name of the user and the score. Add the ability to show the highest score for each user, all scores for a particular user, all scores from all users, and the list of users.

Chapter 12
Introduction to Pointers

Forget everything you've ever heard

Unfortunately, the concept of pointers has acquired something of a mystique amongst beginners (and even professional programmers). If you're heard that pointers are hard to learn, confusing, or too difficult to understand—forget it and ignore it.

The reality is that when I taught programming, pretty much everyone who got *to* pointers got *through* pointers. You're reading **my** book, and **my promise** is that you're going to understand how pointers work, why you want to use them, and how to use them—if you take the time to do so.

They might bend your brain for a few days, but a little mental flexibility is a good thing. I'll make sure to write the next few chapters in small chunks, so that you can take lots of mental breaks. I'll start off explaining the concept of pointers and why you'd want them before getting into the details of the syntax.

Ok, then—what are pointers? Why should you care?

Up until now, we've only been able to work with a fixed amount of memory, an amount decided up-front before the program has even started. Whenever you declare a variable, it causes some amount of memory to be allocated behind the scenes to hold the information stored in that variable. When you declare a variable, the amount of memory allocated is chosen at compile time—you can't change it or add to it while the program is running. We've been able to create arrays of data to get a lot of variables—a big chunk of memory—but the array can hold no more elements than the number that you specified when writing the program. In the next few chapters, we'll learn about how to get access to more memory than we started our program with. You'll learn how to create an unlimited number of enemy spaceships all flying around at once (minus the flying around...).

In order to get access to (nearly) unlimited amounts of memory, we need a kind of variable that can refer directly to the memory that stores variables. This type of variable is called a **pointer**.

Pointers are aptly named: they are variables that "point" to locations in memory. A pointer is very similar to a hyperlink. A webpage is located in one place—on some person's web server. If you want to send someone a copy of that web page, do you download the entire page and email it to them? No, you just email a link. Similarly, a pointer allows you to store or send a "link" to a variable, array or structure, rather than making a copy.

A pointer, like a hyperlink, stores the location of some other data. Because a pointer can store the location (the **address**) of other data, you can use it to hold on to memory that you get from the operating system. In other words, your program can ask for more memory and can access that memory using pointers.

You've actually already seen one example of a pointer—when we passed an array into a function it didn't get copied, did it? Instead, the original array was passed to that function. The way that works is by using pointers. See, they aren't so bad!

But before we go any further, let's talk more about memory.

What is memory?

An easy way to visualize computer memory is to think of an Excel spreadsheet. Spreadsheets are basically a large number of "cells" that can each store a piece of data. This, too, is what computer memory is: a large number of sequential pieces of data. Unlike Excel, in memory, each "cell" can store only a very small amount of data—1 byte, which can itself only store 256 possible values (0-255). Also unlike Excel, memory is organized "linearly" rather than in a grid. In fact, you can even think about memory as being a very long array of chars.

Just as each cell in an Excel spreadsheet has a way to locate it (using its row number and column letter), each cell in memory has an address. This address is the value that a pointer stores, when it holds the location of memory. (In Excel, a pointer would be a cell that holds the name of another cell—for example, if cell C1 held the string A1).

Here's a diagram that shows how you can think about a small chunk of memory. Notice that the diagram is a lot like an array; an array is just a bunch of sequential memory:

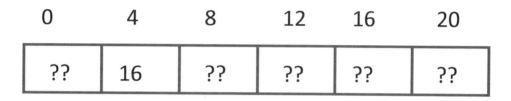

The boxes here represent locations in memory where data can be stored; the numbers are the **memory addresses**, which are the way to identify a location in memory. They're marked in steps of four because most variables in memory take up four bytes, so we're looking at the memory associated with six different variables of four bytes each.[24] (By the way, you'll often see memory addresses written in hexadecimal form, which look quite a bit like gibberish if you've never seen them before; I'll use normal numbers.[25])

Here, you can see the memory at address 4 stores a value that could be another memory address, 16. The memory at address 4 belongs to a pointer variable. The other values are marked as ?? to indicate that they don't have any particular known value, but of course there is something in each memory address at all times. Until that memory is initialized, the value is not useful—it could be anything.

---

[24] Actually, this is only true on 32-bit machines (32 bits make four bytes) where most of the native CPU operations take values that are four bytes in size. And even then, it's only partially true—there are some variables that are bigger than four bytes (like doubles). But it's an easy way to think about it, so we won't worry about the details right now.

[25] If you're curious, hexadecimal numbers use base sixteen and are usually written in a form that looks like this: 0x10ab0200 The 0x tells you that the format is hexadecimal, and the rest of the number uses the letters A-F to denote the digits from 10 to 15.

Variables vs. addresses

You might be confused by the distinction between a variable and an address. A variable is a representation of a value; that value is actually stored at a particular location in memory, at a particular memory address. In other words, the compiler uses memory addresses to implement the variables in your program. Pointers are a special kind of variable that lets you store the address that "backs" another variable.

The cool thing is that once you can talk about the address of a variable, you'll then be able to go to that address and retrieve the data stored in it. If you happen to have a huge piece of data that you want to pass into a function, it's a lot more efficient (when your program is running) to pass its location to the function than it is to copy every element of the data—just as we saw with arrays. We can also use this approach to avoid copying structures when passing them into functions. The idea is to take the address that stores the data associated with the structure variable and pass that address to the function instead of making a copy of the data stored in the structure.

The most important function of pointers is to enable you to get more memory at any time from the operating system. How do you get that memory from the operating system?[26] The operating system tells you the address of the memory. You need pointers to store the memory address. If you need more memory later, you can just ask for more memory and change the value that you are pointing to. Consequently, pointers let us go beyond a fixed amount of data, letting us choose at run time how much memory we will need.

A note about terms

The word pointer can refer either to

  1) A memory address itself
  2) A variable that stores a memory address

---

[26] The operating system does manage memory, so this statement is mostly true, but the real story is that there are usually several different "layers" of code that handle memory allocation—the operating system is one layer, but there are other layers on top. I'm going to ignore this distinction for now because it's confusing. If you didn't get all that, please don't worry—if it were important, I wouldn't have used a footnote. It really shouldn't matter now, and it will make sense later.

Usually, the distinction isn't really that important: if you pass a pointer variable into a function, you're passing the value stored in the pointer—the memory address.

When I want to talk about a memory address, I'll refer to it as a memory address or just an address; when I want a variable that stores a memory address, I'll call it a pointer.

When a variable stores the address of another variable, I'll say that it is **pointing to** that variable.

Memory layout

Where exactly does that memory come from? Why do you need to request it from the operating system, anyway?

In Excel, you have one very large group of cells that you can access. In computer memory, you also have a great deal of memory available. But that memory is more structured. Some parts of the memory available to your program are already in use. One part of memory is used to store the variables that you declare in the functions that are currently being executed—this part of memory is called the **stack**. Its name comes from the fact that if you make several function calls, the local variables for each function "stack up" on top of each other in this part of memory. All of the variables we've worked with so far have been stored on the stack.

A second part of memory is the **free store** (sometimes known as the **heap**), which is unallocated memory that you can request in chunks. This part of memory is managed by the operating system; once a piece of memory is given out, it should only be used by the original code that allocated the memory—or by code to which that address is provided by the memory allocator. Using pointers will allow us to gain access to this memory.

Being able to access this memory is powerful, but with great power comes great responsibility. Memory is a scarce resource. Not as scarce as it used to be before multiple gigabytes of RAM became standard, but it's still limited. Each piece of memory you have allocated from the free store should eventually be released back to the free store when your program no longer needs it. The part of the code responsible for releasing a particular piece of memory is called the **owner** of that memory. When the owner of memory no longer needs it—for example, in a space shooter game, if a ship is destroyed—the code that owns the memory should return it to the free store so that it can be given out to other code. If you don't return the memory, eventually your program will start to run out of memory, causing slowdowns or even crashes. You may have heard people complain (or seen yourself) that the Firefox web browser used too much memory, causing the browser to slow down to a crawl. That's because someone didn't free memory that they should have, causing what's known as a **memory leak**.[27]

The concept of ownership is part of the interface between a function and its users—it is not explicitly part of the language. When you write a function that takes a pointer, you should document whether the function takes ownership of the memory or not. C++ will not track this for you, and it will never free memory that you have explicitly allocated while your program is still running unless you explicitly request it.

The fact that only certain code should use certain memory explains why you can't just go grab some of it—what if you just generated a random number and treated that as a memory address? You could technically do that, but it would be a bad idea. You don't know who allocated that memory—it might even be the stack itself. So if you then modified that memory, you'd ruin data that was in use! In order to help detect this kind of thing, the operating system protects memory that has not been handed out for you to use—the memory is **invalid** and accessing it will cause your program to crash so that you can detect the problem.[28]

Wait, did I just suggest that a crash is a good thing? Well, indeed it is! Crashes caused by accessing invalid memory are almost always easier to diagnose than the bugs that would happen if you write bad data into valid memory. You'll usually find these kinds of crashes pretty quickly because the problem happens

---

[27] In defense of Firefox, some of these complaints were likely due to poorly written extensions—add-ons written by users—rather than by the core Firefox code. Still, the end result is the same: running low on memory caused serious consequences for users!

[28] By the way, there's another small problem with randomly generating memory addresses—memory addresses generally need to be properly aligned. To access an integer, you need to use a memory address that is a multiple of four (4, 8, 12, 16, etc.). If you randomly generate a memory address, you'd have to correctly align it. Memory alignment requirements differ from architecture to architecture, but generally they exist for performance reasons.

immediately. If you change valid memory that you don't own, the bug won't show up until the code that *does* own that memory tries to use it. This could be much later, long after the memory was written. A coworker of mine liked to explain it as: "the tire just fell off, but the lug nut fell out a mile back." Good luck finding that lug nut!

By the way, some people will tell you that crashes caused by invalid memory are really hard to diagnose—those people didn't read this book. In the chapter Debugging with Code::Blocks we'll talk about how to debug crashes caused by bad memory almost instantly.

Invalid pointers

One way that you can accidentally use invalid memory is to use a pointer without initializing it. When you declare a pointer, it will initially have effectively random data inside it—it will point to some place in memory that may or may not be valid, but it's certainly quite dangerous to use. In fact, it's almost as though you had generated a random number! Using this value will result in either a crash or data corruption. You must always initialize pointers before you use them!

Memory and arrays

Remember how I said that writing past the end of an array was a problem? Now that we know a bit more about memory, you can see why this would be. An array has a specific amount of memory associated with it, based on the size of the array. If you access an element past the end of the array, it's accessing memory that isn't associated with the array—that memory is, well, it's just not the array; exactly it is what will depend on the exact code and how the compiler is implemented. But it won't be part of the array, so using it will almost definitely cause problems.

Other advantages (and disadvantages) of pointers

Now that you've learned a bit about the details of pointers, let's go back to our previous analogy and look at some of the tradeoffs of using pointers. Hyperlinks and pointers have a lot of the same advantages and disadvantages.

1) You don't have to make a copy—if the web page is quite large or complicated, this could be hard (imagine trying to send someone a copy of all of Wikipedia!). Similarly, data in memory might be quite

complicated, and it might be hard to copy correctly (more on this later) or just slow (copying a lot of memory may be time consuming).

2) You don't have to worry about whether you've got the latest version of the webpage. If the author updates the page, then you get the changes as soon as you revisit the link. If you have a pointer to memory, you are always able to access the latest value at that memory address.

Of course, there are also disadvantages to sending a link rather than a copy:

1) The page might be moved, or deleted. Similarly, memory can be returned to the operating system, even if someone still has pointer to it. To avoid these issues, the code that owns the memory must keep track of whether anyone else might be using it.

2) You have to be online to access it. This one generally doesn't affect pointers.

Thinking about a pointer as a link on the web should help you understand why you want to use pointers, but there are a few issues with the analogy. One problem is that hyperlinks and web pages are different things, whereas pointers and variables aren't. What do I mean? A pointer is just another kind of variable (albeit one with special properties), whereas a hyperlink just isn't a webpage, no matter how you try. On the other hand, a pointer is a different *type* of variable, just as a hyperlink is a different thing than a webpage.

Did you get everything so far? I promised earlier to split this stuff up across lots of short chapters to give your brain a break. So that's the end of this chapter; the next chapter will talk about the nuts and bolts of using pointers, now that you have some of the core ideas that you'll need.

Quiz yourself
1. Which of these is NOT a good reason to use a pointer?
A. You want to allow a function to modify an argument passed to it
B. You want to save space and avoid copying a large variable
C. You want to be able to get more memory from the operating system
D. You want to be able to access variables more quickly

2. What does a pointer store?

A. The name of another variable
B. An integer value
C. The address of another variable in memory
D. A memory address, but not necessarily another variable

3. Where can you get more memory from during your program's execution?
A. You can't get any more memory
B. The stack
C. The free store
D. By declaring another variable

4. What can go wrong when using pointers?
A. You could access memory that you cannot use, causing a crash
B. You could access the wrong memory address, corrupting data
C. You could forget to return memory to the OS, causing the program to run out of memory
D. All of the above

5. Where does memory for a normal variable declared in a function come from?
A. The free store
B. The stack
C. Normal variables do not use memory
D. The program's binary itself (that's why EXEs are so large!)

6. Once you allocate memory, what do you need to do with it?
A. Nothing, it is yours forever
B. Return it to the operating system when you're done using it
C. Set the value pointed to to 0
D. Store the value 0 in the pointer

(View solution on page 493)

Practice problems

1. Take a small program that you've written before, perhaps as one of the practice problems from earlier in the book. Look for all of the variables, and imagine each variable as having some memory associated with it. Try drawing out a box diagram like the ones I've used that would show each variable associated with some memory. Think of how you might represent a series of

variables that are not part of a single array—but that are lined up in memory one after another.

2. Think about how many slots of memory are needed for this program:

```
int main ()
{
        int i;
        int votes[ 10 ];
}
```

Is there anything you can say for sure about the positions in memory of the variables votes[0], votes[9], and i? (Hint: you might not be able to know where i is, but you do know where it is not.) Try drawing out the possible configurations of memory for this program.

Chapter 13
Using Pointers

So now that we've learned about what memory is and how you should think about it: how do you write code that can use this memory? In this chapter, you'll learn about the syntax needed to work with pointers—with plenty of diagrams—and then we'll see some basic examples of how to use pointers in real programs. We won't quite get to accessing memory from the free store—that'll be the next chapter—but we'll have all the tools to do it.

Pointer syntax

Declaring a pointer
C++ has special syntax for declaring that a variable is a pointer, which indicates both that a value is a pointer and what type of memory is pointed to.

The pointer declaration looks like this:

```
<type> *<ptr_name>;
```

For example, you could declare a pointer that stores the address of an integer with the following syntax:

```
int *p_points_to_integer;
```

Notice the use of the *. This is the key to declaring a pointer; if you add it before the variable name, it will declare the variable to be a pointer. You can put the space on either side of the *. these two declarations are equivalent:

```
int *p_points_to_integer;
```

and

```
int* p_points_to_integer;
```

The prefix p_ is not required by the language, but I always use it to make it clear when a variable is a pointer. Minor gotcha: if you declare multiple pointers on the same line, you must precede each variable name with an asterisk:

```
// one pointer, one regular int
int *p_pointer1, nonpointer1;
```

```
// two pointers
int *p_pointer1, *p_pointer2;
```

You might wonder why there isn't a simpler way to do this, like writing pointer p_pointer. The reason is that in order to use the memory address, the compiler needs to know what kind of data is at that address or it won't be able to interpret it correctly (for example, the same bytes in memory mean different things for a double and for an int.) . Rather than have a separate name for a pointer for each type (int_ptr, char_ptr, etc.) you always use a * with the type name to get a pointer.

Pointing to something: getting the address of a variable

Although we can use pointers to hold on to new memory, let's start off seeing how to make pointers work with existing variables. To get the memory address of a variable (its location in memory), put the & sign in front of the variable name. & is called the **address-of** operator because it returns the memory address of a variable:

```
int x;
int *p_x = & x;
*p_x = 2; // initialize x to 2
```

Conveniently, both ampersand and address-of start with 'a'; that's a useful way to remember that you use & to get the address of a variable. Using the ampersand is like looking in the address bar of a website to get the URL, rather than looking at the contents of the page itself.

It should make perfect sense that you need to do something special to ask for the place where a variable is stored in memory—most of the time, all you want from a variable is its actual value.

Using a pointer

Using a pointer also requires some new syntax because when you have a pointer, you need the ability to do two separate things:

1) request the memory location the pointer stores
2) request the value stored at that memory location

When you use a pointer like a normal variable, you get the memory location stored in the pointer.

This snippet prints out the address of the variable x, pointed to by (stored in) p_pointer_to_integer

```
int x = 5;
int *p_pointer_to_integer = & x;
cout << p_pointer_to_integer; // prints the address of x
// this is equivalent of cout << & x;
```

To access the value at that memory location, you use the *. Here's a small example that initializes a pointer that points to another variable:

```
int x = 5;
int *p_pointer_to_integer = & x;
cout << *p_pointer_to_integer; // prints 5
// this is the equivalent of cout << x;
```

The code *p_pointer_to_integer says, "follow the pointer and get the value stored in the memory that is pointed to". In this case, since p_pointer_to_integer points to x, and x has the value 5, we print the value 5.

An easy way to remember that the * is used to get the value pointed to is that the pointer variable is just like a normal variable—to get the value it holds, you use the name of the variable. The value it holds is a memory address. If you want to do something special and unusual—get the value stored at that memory address—then you have to use special syntax. Just think of the star as a little asterisk indicating a special behavior, just like someone might put an asterisk next to Barry Bonds's home run record in baseball.

Using * to get the value at a pointed-to address is called **dereferencing the pointer**; the name comes from fact that to retrieve the value, you are taking a reference to some memory address and following it.

Dereferencing a variable also lets you set a value into a memory address.

```
int x;
int *p_pointer_to_integer = & x;
*p_pointer_to_integer = 5;   // x is now 5!
cout << x;
```

It can be tricky to keep track of when you should add the asterisk (or the ampersand). Here's a chart you can use for reference:

Action	Punctuation needed	Example
Declare a pointer	*	`int *p_x;`
Get address held by pointer	Nothing	`cout << p_x;`
Set address stored in pointer	Nothing	`int *p_x; p_x = /*address*/;`
Get value at that address	*	`cout << *p_x;`
Set new value to that address	*	`*p_x = 5;`
Declare a variable	Nothing	`int y;`
Get value stored in a variable	Nothing	`int y;   cout << y;`
Set value stored in a variable	Nothing	`int y; y = 5`
Get address of a variable	&	`int y; int *p_x; p_x = & y;`
Set address of variable	NA	Not possible—a variable cannot change addresses

An easy pair of rules is that:

A pointer stores an address, so when you use the bare pointer, you get that address back. You have to add something extra, the asterisk, in order to retrieve or modify the value stored at the address.

A variable stores a value, so when you use the variable, you get its value. You have to add some extra, the ampersand, in order to retrieve the address of that variable.

Now let's look at a brief program that illustrates these features and look at a useful technique for analyzing what happens in memory:

```cpp
#include <iostream>

using namespace std;

int main ()
{
    int x;          // A normal integer
    int *p_int;     // A pointer to an integer

    p_int = & x;    // Read it, "assign the address of x
                    // to p_int"
    cout << "Please enter a number: ";
    cin >> x;       // Put a value in x, we could also use
                    // *p_int here
    cout << *p_int << '\n'; // Note the use of the * to
                            // get the value
    *p_int = 10;
    cout << x;      // outputs 10 again!
}
```
Sample Code 34: pointer.cpp

The first `cout` outputs the value stored in x. Why is that? Let's step through the program and watch how it affects memory, using arrows to indicate where a pointer points to, and putting in values into memory for non-pointer values.

We start off with an integer called x and a pointer to an integer named p_int.

Visually, you can think of it as though we have two variables (probably next to each other) that have unknown values.

Then the code stores the memory location of x into the pointer p_int by using the address-of operator (&) to get the address of the variable.

```
p_int = & x;    // Read it, "assign the address of x
                // to p_int"
```

Now we can draw a line from the p_int variable to the x variable to indicate that p_int points to x.

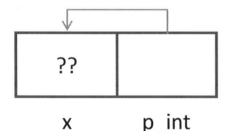

The user then inputs a number that is stored in the variable x; this is the same location pointed to by p_int.

```
cin >> x;    // Put a value in x, we could also use
             // *p_int here
```

Let's imagine that the user types five—visually, we now have the following situation:

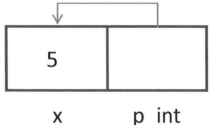

The next line then passes *p_int into cout. *p_int dereferences p_int; it looks at the address stored in p_int, and goes to that address and returns the value. You can think of it as though the program is following the arrow in the memory diagram.

```
cout << *p_int << '\n'; // Note the use of the * to
                        // get the value
```

Finally, the last couple of lines demonstrate that modifying a pointer also modifies the original variable. This line stores the value 10 in the memory pointed to by p_int (which is also the memory storing the value of x):

```
*p_int = 10;
```

Now the state of memory is:

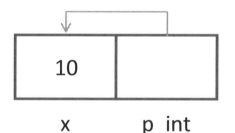

x   p_int

As I hope you have seen, using box-and-arrows diagrams can make it easy to follow what happens when you work with pointers. Whenever you get confused about what is happening, draw out the initial state of the memory, and then walk line-by-line through the program, showing how the memory changes. When a pointer changes where it points, draw a new line; when a variable changes a value, update its value. By doing this, you will be able to see and understand even complex systems.

Uninitialized pointers and NULL

Notice that in the above example, the pointer (p_int) is initialized to point to a specific memory address before it is used. If this were not the case, it could be pointing to anything. This can lead to extremely unpleasant consequences like overwriting memory held in some other variable or your program crashing. To avoid these crashes and other bad behavior, you should always initialize pointers before you use them.

Sometimes, though, you need to be able to say, "this pointer is explicitly NOT initialized yet." C++ has a special value that you can use to mark a pointer as explicitly uninitialized: the value **NULL**. If you make a pointer point to NULL (store the value NULL), you know that it is uninitialized. Whenever you create a new pointer, first set it to NULL so that you can later check and see if it has been set to something usable or not. Otherwise, there is no way to test if the pointer is usable without risking a crash:

```
int *p_int = NULL;

// code that might or might not set p_int
if ( p_int != NULL )
{
     *p_int = 2;
}
```

To add a NULL pointer into your memory diagram you can simply write in NULL rather than drawing an arrow to point to NULL:

```
┌─────────────────┐
│                 │
│   NULL          │
│                 │
└─────────────────┘
     p_int
```

Pointers and functions

Pointers allow you to pass the address of a local variable into a function, which can then modify the local variable. Pretty much everyone illustrates this with a simple pair of functions that attempt to swap the values stored in two variables:

```
#include <iostream>

using namespace std;

void swap1 (int left, int right)
{
     int temp = left;
     left = right;
     right = temp;
}

void swap2 (int *p_left, int *p_right)
{
     int temp = *p_left;
     *p_left = *p_right;
```

```
        *p_right = temp;
}

int main ()
{
        int x = 1, y = 2;
        swap1 ( x, y );
        cout << x << " " << y << '\n';
        swap2 ( & x, & y );
        cout << x << " " << y << '\n';
}
```
Sample Code 35: swap.cpp

Take a minute to see if you can guess which function correctly swaps the two values.

That's right—function `swap1` just switches the values of two variables local to the swap function; it can't touch the values passed into it because they just store copies of the original values (the values stored in variables x and y) passed into them. Visually, you can see that the function call copies the values of x and y into the variables `left` and `right`:

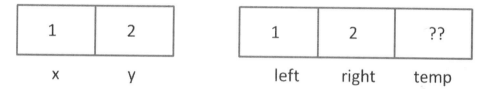

Then the value in `left` is put into `temp`, and `left` is assigned the value in `right`:

Finally, the value in `temp` is put into `right`, swapping `left` and `right`—but leaving x and y completely unchanged:

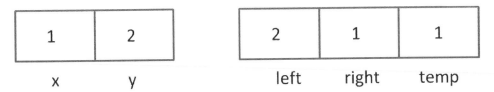

Function `swap2`, more interestingly, takes in the addresses of the local variables x and y. The variables p_left and p_right now point to x and y:

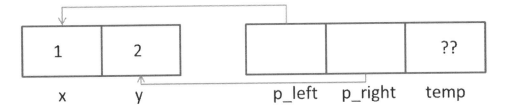

Now the function has access to the memory that backs those two variables, so when it performs its switch, it writes into the memory of variables x and y. First, it copies the value pointed to by p_left into the temp variable, and then it copies the value pointed to by p_right into p_left:

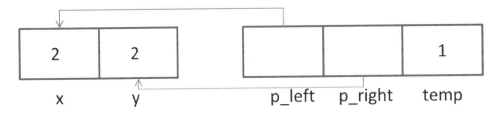

Notice that the memory that holds the x variable has been modified this time. Finally, the value in temp is assigned to the memory pointed to by p_right, completing the swap:

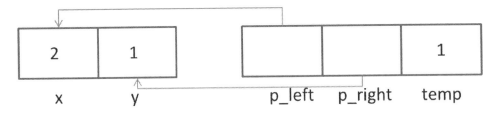

The ability to swap two variables like this isn't the main value of pointers, however; there is another C++ language feature that makes it easy to write this kind of swap function without having to get the full pointer of pointers, using references.

References

Sometimes you need some of the features pointers provide, such as avoiding extra copies of large pieces of data, but don't need the full power of pointers. In these situations, you could use a **reference**. A reference is a variable that refers to another variable, sharing the same backing memory. References, however, are used just like regular variables. You can think of a reference as a stripped-down pointer without needing to use special asterisk and ampersand syntax to use the referred-to value or when assigning to the reference. A reference, unlike a pointer, must always refer to valid memory. References are declared with the ampersand:

```
int &ref;
```

This declaration, however, is illegal because references must always be initialized. (A reference must always refer to a valid address.)

```
int x = 5;
// notice that you do not need an ampersand before x!
int &ref = x;
```

You can visualize a reference the same way that you visualize a pointer; the difference is that when you use a reference, you get the value of the referenced memory rather than the address of that memory:

```
int x = 5;
int &ref = x;
```

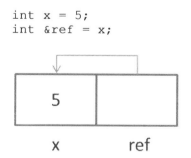

Here, the actual memory of the `ref` variable holds a pointer to the memory of the `x` variable. The compiler knows that when you write plain old `ref`, you want the actual value pointed to. In a sense, references are pointers with a reversed "default" behavior for what happens you write the name of the variable.

References can be used to pass structures into functions without having to pass the whole structure, and without having to worry about NULL pointers.

```
struct myBigStruct
{
        int x[ 100 ]; // big struct with lots of memory!
};

void takeStruct (myBigStruct& my_struct)
{
        my_struct.x[ 0 ] = 23;
}
```

Since a reference refers to the original object at all times, you both avoid copying and can modify the original object passed in to the function. The above example demonstrates setting my_struct.x[0] so that the original structure that was passed in will contain 23 once the function returns.

We just saw a way of writing a swap function with pointers, now let's see an even easier way of writing it with references:

```
void swap (int& left, int& right)
{
        int temp = right;
        right = left;
        left = temp;
}
```

Notice that this is far simpler than the equivalent with pointers. You can really think of a reference as just a stand-in for the original variable. Of course, the implementation of a reference by the compiler is to use pointers to store references; the actual getting of the data, the dereferencing, is done for you.

References vs. pointers
References are a replacement for pointers when you need to refer to a variable by multiple names—such as when you want to pass arguments to a function without copying them, or when you want the function to be able to modify its parameters in a way that is visible to the caller.

References don't provide as much flexibility as pointers because they must always be valid. There is no way of indicating NULL; you cannot, using a reference, say that you don't have something valid. That's just not what references were designed for. Because references cannot represent NULL, you cannot build sophisticated data structures using references. We'll talk lots more about building data structures in the next few chapters; ask yourself each time if you could do the same thing with a reference.

One other difference is that once a reference is initialized, you cannot change the memory it refers to. A reference permanently refers to the same variable, which also limits their flexibility in building sophisticated data structures.

Throughout the rest of this book, I will use references where appropriate— almost always when taking an instance of a structure (or class, when we get to them) as an argument to a function. This pattern almost always looks like similar to this:

```
void (myStructType& arg);
```

Quiz yourself

1. Which of the following is the proper declaration of a pointer?

A. `int x;`

B. `int &x;`

C. `ptr x;`

D. `int *x;`

2. Which of the following gives the memory address of integer variable a?

A. `*a;`

B. `a;`

C. `&a;`

D. `address( a );`

3. Which of the following gives the memory address of a variable pointed to by pointer p_a?

A. `p_a;`

B. `*p_a;`

C. `&p_a;`

D. `address( p_a );`

4. Which of the following gives the value stored at the address pointed to by the pointer p_a?
A. p_a;
B. val (p_a);
C. *p_a;
D. &p_a;

5. Which of the following properly declares a reference?
A. int *p_int;
B. int &my_ref;
C. int &my_ref = & my_orig_val;
D. int &my_ref = my_orig_val;

6. Which of the following is not a good time to use a reference?
A. To store an address that was dynamically allocated from the free store
B. To avoid copying a large value when passing it into a function
C. To force that a parameter to a function is never NULL
D. To allow a function to access the original variable passed to it, without using pointers

(View solution on page 494)

Practice problems

1. Write a function that prompts the user to enter his or her first name and last name, as two separate values. This function should return both values to the caller via additional pointer (or reference) parameters that are passed to the function. Try doing this first with pointers and then with references. (Hint: the function signature will look similar to the swap function from earlier!)

2. Draw a diagram similar to the ones I drew to demonstrate the swap function, but for the function you wrote in exercise 1.

3. Modify the program you wrote for exercise 1 so that instead of always prompting the user for a last name, it does so only if the caller passes in a NULL pointer for the last name.

4. Write a function that takes two input arguments and provides two separate results to the caller, one that is the result of multiplying the two arguments, the

other the result of adding them. Since you can directly return only one value from a function, you'll need the second value to be returned through a pointer or reference parameter.

5. Write a program that compares the memory addresses of two different variables on the stack and prints out the order of the variables by numerical order of their addresses. Does the order surprise you?

Chapter 14
Dynamic Memory Allocation

If you've made it through the last few chapters, you're doing great. Now we get to the fun part of pointers: using them to solve real problems. As I've been hinting, we're finally ready to learn how to get as much memory as we want while our programs are running. Yes, we can corner the memory market! Although we probably shouldn't.

Getting more memory with new

Dynamic allocation means requesting as much (or as little) memory as you need, while your program is running. You program will calculate the amount of memory it needs instead of working with a fixed set of variables with a particular size. This section will provide the foundation of how to allocate memory, and subsequent sections will explain how to fully take advantage of having dynamic allocation.

First let's see how to get more memory. The keyword **new** is used to initialize pointers with memory from the free store. Remember that the free store is a chunk of unused memory that your program can request access to. Here's the basic syntax:

```
int *p_int = new int;
```

The `new` operator takes an "example" variable from which it computes the size of the memory requested. In this case, it takes an integer, and it returns enough memory to hold an integer value.

`p_int` is set to point to that memory, and now `p_int` and the associated code that uses it become the owner of that memory—in other words, the code that uses `p_int` must eventually return this memory back to the free store, an operation called **freeing** the memory. Until `p_int` is freed, the memory that is pointed to will be marked as in-use and will not be given out again. If you keep allocating memory and never free it, you will run out of memory.

To return the memory to the free store, you use the **delete** keyword. The delete operation frees up the memory allocated through new. Here's how you'd free `p_int`:

```
delete p_int;
```

After deleting a pointer, it is a good idea to reset it to point to NULL again:

```
delete p_int;
p_int = NULL;
```

It isn't necessary that you do this, but once a pointer is deleted, you can't read or write to the memory it was pointing to because it's been returned to the free store (and might get handed out again later). By setting the pointer to NULL, if your code does try to dereference the pointer after it is freed (it happens a lot, even to experienced programmers), you will find out immediately because the program will crash. This is much better than finding out later, when your program crashes or corrupts some user's data.

Running out of memory

Memory is not an infinite resource—you can literally corner the market on memory. If you do, you will not be able to get any more memory. In C++, if a call to new fails because the system is out of memory, then it will "throw an exception". In general, you need not worry too much about this case; it is so rare on modern operating systems that many programs decide to ignore the possibility (it is especially unlikely to happen if the program is well-written and properly frees memory—a program that never frees its memory is much more likely to run out of memory). Exceptions are an advanced topic covered near the end of the book. In general, the best guidance is simply to always free the memory that you allocate, and don't worry about the fact that new might fail.

References and dynamic allocation

In general, you should not store memory that you just allocated in a reference:

```
int &val = *(new int);
```

The reason is that a reference does not provide immediate access to the raw memory address. You can get it using &, but generally references should provide an additional name for a variable, not storage for dynamically allocated memory.

Pointers and arrays

Okay, so you might be wondering, how do you actually use new to get more memory than you started with if all you can do with it is initialize a single pointer? The answer is that pointers can also point to a sequence of values. In other words, a pointer can be treated like an array. An array is, after all, a series of values laid out sequentially in memory. Since a pointer stores a memory address, it can store the address of the first element of an array. To access each individual element of the array you simply take a value that is a fixed distance away from the start of the array.

Why might this be useful? Because you can actually create a new array dynamically from the free store, allowing you to determine the amount of memory that you need at runtime. I'll show an example in a few moments, but first some basics.

You can assign an array to a pointer, like this, without using the address-of operator:

```
int numbers[ 8 ];
int* p_numbers = numbers;
```

And you now use p_numbers just like an array:

```
for ( int i = 0; i < 8; ++i )
{
     p_numbers[ i ] = i;
}
```

The array `numbers`, when assigned to a pointer, acts as though it is just a pointer. **It is important to understand that arrays are not pointers, but that arrays can be assigned to pointers.** The C++ compiler understands how to convert an array into a pointer that points to the first element of the array. (This kind of conversion happens a lot in C++. For example, you can assign a variable of type `char` to a variable of type `int`; a `char` is not an `int`, but the compiler knows how to do the conversion.)

You can dynamically allocate an array of memory using `new` and assign that memory to a pointer:

```
int *p_numbers = new int[ 8 ];
```

Using the array syntax as the argument to `new` tells the compiler how much memory it needs—enough for an 8-element integer array. Now you can use `p_numbers` just as if it pointed to an array. Unlike arrays, though, you need to free the memory pointed to by `p_numbers` whereas you never want to free a pointer pointing to a statically declared array. To free the memory, there is a special syntax for the delete operator:

```
delete[] p_numbers;
```

The brackets tell the compiler that the pointer points to an array of values, rather than a single value.

Now for the example you've been waiting for—dynamically determining how much memory you need:

```
int count_of_numbers;
cin >> count_of_numbers;
int *p_numbers = new int[ count_of_numbers ];
```

This code asks the user how many numbers are needed and then uses that variable to determine the size of the dynamically allocated array. In fact, we don't even need to know up-front the exact number—we can just reallocate the memory as the values grow. This means we'll be doing some extra copying, but it's possible. Let's look at a program that demonstrates this technique. Let's have this program read in numbers from the user, and if the user enters more numbers than can fit in the array, we'll resize it.

```
#include <iostream>

using namespace std;

int *growArray (int* p_values, int *size);
void printArray (
        int* p_values,
        int size,
        int elements_set
);

int main ()
{
        int next_element = 0;
        int size = 10;
        int *p_values = new int[ size ];
        int val;
        cout << "Please enter a number: ";
        cin >> val;
        while ( val > 0 )
        {
                if ( size == next_element + 1 )
                {
                        // now all we need to do is implement
                        // growArray. Notice that we need to pass
                        // in size as a pointer since we need to
                        // keep track of the size of the array as
                        // it grows!
                        p_values = growArray( p_values, & size );
                }
                p_values[ next_element ] = val;
                next_element++;
                cout << "Current array values are: " << endl;
                printArray( p_values, size, next_element );
                cout << "Please enter a number (or 0 to exit):
";
                cin >> val;
        }
        delete [] p_values;
}

void printArray (int *p_values, int size, int elements_set)
{
        cout << "The total size of the array is: " << size
            << endl;
```

```
cout << "Number of slots set so far: "
     << elements_set << endl;
cout << "Values in the array: " << endl;
for ( int i = 0; i < elements_set; ++i )
{
        cout << "p_values[" << i << "] = "
             << p_values[ i ] << endl;
}
}
```

Sample Code 36: resize_array.cpp

Let's think about how to grow the array for a moment. What do we need to do? We can't just ask to extend the memory we have—unlike Excel, you can't add an entire new column when you want more space. We have to request more memory and copy over the old values.

Another question is how much memory we should get—it would be inefficient to grow the array by a single integer at a time. It would cause a lot of unnecessary memory allocations—you won't run out of memory, but it will slow things down. A good strategy is to take the current size of the array and double it. This won't waste too much space if we stop reading in new values—it won't use more than twice what's in use—and it means we won't have to constantly reallocate memory. Clearly we need to know the current size of the array, as well as the original array of values to copy them.

```
int *growArray (int* p_values, int *size)
{
        *size *= 2;
        int *p_new_values = new int[ *size ];
        for ( int i = 0; i < *size; ++i )
        {
                p_new_values[ i ] = p_values[ i ];
        }
        delete [] p_values;
        return p_new_values;
}
```
Sample Code 37: resize_array.cpp (continued)

Notice how this code is careful to delete the value in p_values after it finishes copying the data from that array—otherwise, we'd leak memory since we are overwriting the pointer that holds our array upon the return from growArray.

Multidimensional arrays

Resizing a single big array is very useful, a technique that you'll definitely want to remember. Sometimes, though, you want to do more than work with a single big array. Remember how exciting it was when we talked about multidimensional arrays? Wouldn't it be nice to be able to choose the size for our multidimensional arrays? We can do this, and it's a very good exercise for helping you really deeply understand pointers, in addition to being useful. It does, however, require some additional background to really understand. The next couple of sections of this chapter will cover the background and then finally show you how you can allocate multidimensional data structures dynamically.

Pointer arithmetic

This section is going to go a bit deeper into pointers, and it may flex your mind! But these concepts, while challenging, will start to make sense. If you don't understand this section the first time around—reread it. If you can understand everything in this section, including the allocation of two-dimensional arrays, you are going to be in great shape to understand pretty much everything about pointers. So yeah, it's a little tough, and unlike some sections, the payoff isn't immediately obvious, but by taking a bit of time to understand this stuff, you'll spend less time on the rest of the book. Trust me.

Let's talk a little bit about memory addresses and how to think about them. Pointers represent memory addresses, and memory addresses are ultimately just numbers. So just like numbers, you can actually perform some mathematical operations on pointers—for example, adding a number and a pointer, or subtracting two pointers. Why might you want to do this? For one thing, there are times when you want to write a block of memory, and you know the exact offset into which you wish to place a value. If that all sounds like gobbledygook, you've already run across this situation quite frequently—arrays!

As it turns out, when you write:

```
int x[ 10 ];
x[ 3 ] = 120;
```

You are performing **pointer arithmetic** to set the 3rd memory slot to the value 120. The bracket operator is just **syntactic sugar**—a term meaning special, simplified syntax—for doing pointer arithmetic. You can perform the same operation by writing:

```
* ( x + 3 ) = 120;
```

Let's break down what is going on here—amazingly (or confusingly), this is *not* adding 3 to the value of x, it is adding `3 * sizeof ( int )`. `sizeof` is a special keyword that gives you the size, in bytes, of a variable of type. This is something you often need to do when working with memory. Pointer arithmetic always adds "slots" of memory rather than treating the pointer like a number (just like using the brackets of an array gives you access to a particular array slot). Adding in increments of the variable size prevents you from accidentally using pointer arithmetic to write (or read) between two values (for example, the last two bytes of one slot and the first two bytes of another).[29]

In most cases, you should just use array syntax rather than trying to get the pointer arithmetic correct. It's very hard to keep straight the math that is going on when you are doing pointer arithmetic, and it's easy to forget that you aren't adding slots of memory instead of individual bytes. However, understanding pointer arithmetic will make it easier for you to do some pretty sophisticated stuff, and we'll need all of that power in later chapters. It will also help you understand how to dynamically allocate multidimensional arrays.

Understanding two-dimensional arrays

Before we get to allocating multidimensional arrays, you need to know what it really means to be a multidimensional array—again, this is a section that you should really make an effort to understand despite the difficulty. It *will* pay off.

Let's start with an odd curiosity: when you declare that a function takes a two-dimensional array as an argument, you always need to provide the size not of both the parts of the array but just the second.

---

[29] By the way, you can also subtract two pointers, in order to compute their distance. Again the distance will be the number of slots, rather than the number of bytes. (For this reason, you cannot subtract two pointers of different types because they may have different sized slots.) I very very rarely see subtraction between pointers, though. It's never possible to add pointers, since you can only add a pointer and an offset. (Isn't it interesting that subtracting pointers and adding pointers results in different types of value?)

You can either provide both sizes:

```
int sumTwoDArray( int array[ 4 ][ 4 ] );
```

Or one size:

```
int sumTwoDArray( int array[][ 4 ] );
```

But you can never omit both sizes:

```
int sumTwoDArray( int array[][] );
```

Nor can you put only the first size:

```
int sumTwoDArray( int array[ 4 ][] );
```

What's happening is that only certain sizes are needed to do the correct pointer arithmetic! Two-dimensional arrays are actually laid out flat in memory—the compiler lets you, the programmer, treat it as a square block of memory, but it's really just a linear collection of addresses. The way the compiler does this is by transforming an array access, like `array[ 3 ][ 2 ]` into a position in memory. Here's an easy way to think about it. If you visualize a 4x4 array like this, with the row marked in the array:

[0][0][0][0]
[1][1][1][1]
[2][2][2][2]
[3][3][3][3]

The array is actually laid out in memory like this:

[0][0][0][0][1][1][1][1][2][2][2][2][3][3][3][3]

In order to use `array[ 3 ][ 2 ]` (which is located in the blue section), the compiler needs to access memory three rows down (past the magenta, yellow and green rows) and two columns across. To go three rows down with each row being four integers wide, we have to go 4 * 3 integer slots, and then add 2 more integer slots (to get to the 3rd element in the last row).

In other words, `array[ 3 ][ 2 ]` turns into this pointer arithmetic:

```
*(array + 3 * <width of array> + 2)
```

Now you can see that we need the width of the array—without it, the math won't work. And the second dimension of a two-dimensional array is the width. You can't do the same thing with the height of the array because of how the data is physically laid out in memory. (The height would be needed if the array were laid out in the other direction, by row). Because of this, you can actually take as a function argument an array with a variable length for the height of the array, but the second dimension must always be fully specified. In fact, for any multidimensional array, you must specify the sizes for all dimensions except the height. You can think of a single dimensional array as just a special case of an array that only has a height.

Unfortunately, because a hard-coded width is required when declaring a two-dimensional array, dynamically allocating a two-dimensional array with an arbitrary width requires one more feature of C++, pointers to pointers.

Pointers to pointers

In addition to pointing to normal data, pointers can also point to other pointers. A pointer, after all, like any other variable, has an address that you can access.

To declare a pointer-to-a-pointer, you write:

```
int **p_p_x;
```

p_p_x points to a memory address that contains a pointer to integer; I use the prefix p_p to indicate that the pointer itself points to another pointer. This means you need to provide it the memory address of a pointer. E.g.

```
int *p_y;
int **p_p_x;
p_p_x = & p_y;
```

And then you can assign a pointer to p_y by using p_p_x:

```
*p_p_x = new int;
```

We can use pointers-to-pointers to make a two-dimensional array in the same way that we can use a single pointer to make an arbitrary-sized one-dimensional array.

The way to think about it is that you have a one-dimensional array of pointers, and each of those pointers points to a second one-dimensional array. Let's look at that visually, as if we had declared a pointer to a pointer to store a tic-tac-toe board:

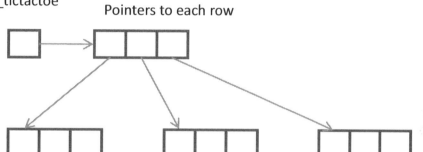

p_p_tictactoe   Pointers to each row

Row of the board   Row of the board   Row of the board

The first pointer points to a collection of pointers, each of which points to one row of the board. Here's the code that we need to allocate this kind of data structure:

```
int **p_p_tictactoe;
// notice that it's a int*, since we are allocating an
// array of pointers
p_p_tictactoe = new int*[ 3 ];

// now make each pointer store the address of an array of
// integers
for ( int i = 0; i < 3; i++ )
{
    p_p_tictactoe[ i ] = new int[ 3 ];
}
```

At this point, we can now use the allocated memory just like a two-dimensional array. For example, we can initialize the entire board with a pair of for loops:

```
for ( int i = 0; i < 3; i++ )
{
```

```
    for ( int j = 0; j < 3; j++ )
    {
         p_p_tictactoe[ i ][ j ] = 0;
    }
}
```

To free the memory, we go in exactly the opposite order that we used to initialize it—first free each row, then free the pointer that holds the rows:

```
for ( int i = 0; i < 3; i++ )
{
     delete [] p_p_tictactoe[ i ];
}

delete [] p_p_tictactoe;
```

You wouldn't typically use this approach when you already know the size of memory that you require (as in the case of creating a tic-tac-toe board) because it is somewhat more complicated than writing simply:

```
int tic_tac_toe_board[ 3][ 3 ];
```

But if you wanted to create an arbitrarily large game board, then this is the approach you need.

Pointers to pointers and two-dimensional arrays

Notice that a pointer to a pointer, when used to hold a two-dimensional array, is not laid out in memory in the same way that a two-dimensional array is laid out. A standard two-dimensional array is all contiguous memory, but the pointer-based approach is not! The diagram shows that each row is a separate chunk of data; in fact, each row is stored in memory that may be quite far away from the other memory.

This has consequences for any function that takes an array as an argument. As you know, you can assign an array to a pointer:

```
int x[ 8 ];
int *y = x;
```

However, you cannot assign a two-dimensional array to a pointer to a pointer:

BAD CODE
```
int x[ 8 ][ 8 ];
```

```
int **y = x; // does not compile!
```

In the first case, the array can be treated as a pointer to a block of memory that contains all the data. In the second case, though, the array is still just a single pointer to a block of memory.

The most important consequence of the difference in layout is that you cannot pass a pointer to a pointer into a function expecting a multidimensional array (even though you can pass a pointer to a function taking an array with only one dimension).

```
int sum_matrix (int values[][ 4 ], int num_rows)
{
        int running_total = 0;
        for ( int i = 0; i < num_vals; i++ )
        {
                for ( int j = 0; j < 4; j++ )
                {
                        running_total += values[ i ][ j ];
                }
        }
        return running_total;
}
```

Here, if you allocate a pointer-to-a-pointer and pass it to this function, the compiler will complain:

BAD CODE
```
int **x;
// allocate x to have 10 rows
sum_matrix( x, 10 ); // does not compile
```

In the one-dimensional case, both operations just go a particular offset from the pointer address. But in the two-dimensional case, the pointer-to-pointer approach needs to take two pointer dereferences—one to find the right row, the other to get the right value out of the row. In the array case, it just uses pointer arithmetic to get the right value. Since a pointer to a pointer doesn't do this pointer math, the compiler can't let you pass in a pointer to a pointer as though it were really a two-dimensional array, even though you write code that otherwise looks the same!

Taking stock of pointers

Pointers may feel like a very confusing topic at first, but you can understand them. If you haven't absorbed everything about them, just take a few deep breaths and re-read the chapter, work through the quiz, and try the practice problems. You don't need to feel like you've fully grasped every nuance of when and why you need to use pointers, but you should know the syntax for working with and initializing pointers and understand how to allocate memory.

Quiz yourself

1. Which of the following is the proper keyword to allocate memory in C++?

A. `new`

B. `malloc`

C. `create`

D. `value`

2. Which of the following is the proper keyword to deallocate memory in C++?[30]

A. `free`

B. `delete`

C. `clear`

D. `remove`

3. Which of the following statements is true?

A. Arrays and pointers are the same

B. Arrays cannot be assigned to pointers

C. Pointers can be treated like an array, but pointers are not arrays

D. You can use pointers like arrays, but you cannot allocate pointers like arrays

4. What are the final values of x, p_int, and p_p_int in the following code? (Note that because integers and pointers are different types, compilers will not accept this code directly, but the exercise is useful for working through on paper what is going on with multiple pointers.)

```
int x = 0;
int *p_int = & x;
int **p_p_int = & p_int;
*p_int = 12;
**p_p_int = 25;
```

---

[30] Okay, if you answered malloc and free to these last two questions, you're also right as these are the functions from C—but you might not have read the chapter!

```
p_int = 12;
*p_p_int = 3;
p_p_int = 27;
```

A. x = 0, p_p_int = 27, p_int = 12
B. x = 25, p_p_int = 27, p_int = 12
C. x = 25, p_p_int = 27, p_int = 3
D. x = 3, p_p_int = 27, p_int = 12

5. How can you indicate that a pointer has no valid value that it points to?
A. Set it to a negative number
B. Set it to NULL
C. Free the memory associated with that pointer
D. Set the pointer to false

(View solution on page 496)

Practice problems

1. Write a function that builds a two-dimensional multiplication table with arbitrary sizes for the two dimensions.

2. Write a function that takes three arguments, a length, width and height, dynamically allocates a three-dimensional array with those values and fills the three-dimensional array with multiplication tables. Make sure to free the array when you are done.

3. Write a program that prints out the memory addresses of each element in a two-dimensional array. Check to see if the values printed out make sense to you based on the way I explained it before.

4. Write a program that lets users keep track of the last time they talked to each of their friends. Users should be able to add new friends (as many as they want!) and store the number of days ago that they last talked to each friend. Let users update this value (but don't let them put in bogus numbers like negative values). Make it possible to display the list sorted by the names of the friends of by how recently it was since they talked to each friend.

5. Write a two-player game of Connect Four[31] where the user can set the width and height of the board and each player gets a turn to drop a token into the slot. Display the board using + for one side, x for the other, and _ to indicate blank spaces.

6. Write a program that takes a width and a height and dynamically generates a maze with the given width and height. The maze must always have a valid path through it (how can you ensure this?). Print the maze to the screen once it's been generated.

For all practice problems, try to write one version with pointers, and one version with references. Make sure to free any memory you allocate.

---

[31] http://en.wikipedia.org/wiki/Connect_Four

Chapter 15
Introduction to Data Structures with Linked Lists

Last chapter you learned how to dynamically allocate arrays, taking advantage of the ability to allocate memory. This chapter you'll learn about even more flexible uses of dynamic memory allocation. The great thing about having lots of memory is that you now have lots of places to put data; you can store quite a few things. But then the next question is: how, exactly, do you store it quickly and make it so that you can easily get access to it later? And that's what we're going to talk about.

First, some terms: a **data structure** is a way of organizing data in memory. For example, an array is a very simple data structure that organizes memory in a linear fashion. Each item in the array is an item in the data structure. A two-dimensional array implemented using pointers to pointers is a somewhat more sophisticated data structure.

The value of advanced data structures
The problem is that, with arrays, if you want to add to an array with no empty slots, you can't. As we saw, you have to start from scratch, allocate a new array, and then copy all the existing items in the array to your new one. This is what

computer programmers call an **expensive** operation—it takes a long time, by your computer processor's standards. Expensive operations are not necessarily a big deal from the perspective of your user; if you don't do them a lot, then it might not be something that anyone can really notice. Computer processors are really fast. But in many cases, expensive operations can become real a problem.

A second problem with arrays is that you can't easily insert data between existing elements of an array. For example, if you want to put a new element between items one and two, and your array has 1000 items, guess what, you have to move items 2 through 1000! This, too, is expensive.

You know how your computer chugs along sometimes, making you painfully wait for it? That's because your computer is doing some kind of expensive operation. Data structures are all about coming up with efficient ways of storing data so that your users don't have to watch the beach ball of death.

A second reason for using different data structures is that they allow you to think about programming at a higher level. Rather than talking about needing a "loop" you'll start to talk about needing a "list". Data structures provide logical ways to organize data and a shorthand way of communicating the basic operations that your program will need. For example, if you say that you need a "list" then you make it clear that you have to store some data in a way that lets you add and remove data efficiently. As you learn about more data structures you will start to think about your programs more and more in terms of the data you need and how you need to organize that data. But enough of all that theoretical stuff—let's talk a bit about linked lists.

Remember the problem of how to easily add new data items? How with an array you had to copy everything? (I sure hope so; that was just a few paragraphs ago!) Wouldn't it be great if you could make a data structure where each item of data told you where to find the next one? Then you could easily add an element at the end of the data structure by making the last element point to the newly added element. You could also insert between two items just by changing where one of those two elements points. Let's go back to the example I've used before, of storing enemies in a game. You'd love to have some kind of list of enemies, where each element of that list is a structure storing information about the enemy. (Why keep a list of enemies at all? You would do that if you needed to be able to take actions each round of the game with all of the enemies—for example, if you needed to go through the list of enemies and have each one of them move. This isn't a "list" like your grocery list or a list of students in a class. Sometimes you need lists just to keep track of every "thing" you have—enemies, in this case.) But you'd also like to be able to quickly add or remove enemies. Well, what if each enemy had information about the next enemy?

Let's look at this visually with each element having x and y screen coordinates, and a weapon of a particular power:

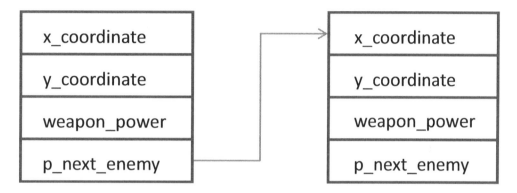

Here, we have one `EnemySpaceShip` structure that has a link of some sort to the next structure. What might that link be? A pointer! Each space ship has a pointer to the next space ship:

```
struct EnemySpaceShip
{
        int x_coordinate;
        int y_coordinate;
        int weapon_power;
        EnemySpaceShip* p_next_enemy;
};
```

Wait a second! We're using `EnemySpaceShip` inside of the structure definition of `EnemySpaceShip`. Is that really ok? Yes, it is! C++ is perfectly capable of handling this kind of self-reference. Now it would be a real problem if you wrote inside the structure:

```
EnemySpaceShip next_enemy;
```

Then we would have a structure that repeated itself infinitely. Declaring a single ship would require all the memory on the system. But notice that we have a pointer to `EnemySpaceShip`, not an actual `EnemySpaceShip`. Because pointers don't have to point to valid memory, you don't have an infinite list of space ships—you only have a space ship that *might* point to another ship. If it does point to another ship, then you will need some more memory, but until you do, the only memory used is the space taken up by a pointer—just a few bytes. A pointer just means that there might be valid memory being pointed to. It only requires enough space to store a memory address. When you declare an `EnemySpaceShip`, you need enough space to hold the fields `x_coordinate`, `y_coordinate`, and `weapon_power`, as well as a final pointer. You don't need to also hold another space ship (which itself would need another space ship). Just a pointer.

Here's one final analogy. Think of it like a train. Each car in a train has a connection that can hook it onto another car. To add a new car, you just hook up a new train car to the car in front of it and the car behind it. The connection can be unused if there is no car to hook on to. That would be the equivalent of having a `NULL` pointer.

Now that we've talked about the concept of creating these kinds of lists, we need to get into some of the details and syntax of how you can use pointers with structures.

Pointers and structures

To access the fields of a structure through a pointer, you use the '`->`' operator in place of the '`.`' operator:

```
p_my_struct->my_field;
```

Each field of a structure has a different memory address, usually a few bytes away from the start of the structure—the arrow syntax computes the exact offset needed to get that particular field of the structure. All other properties of pointers still apply (a pointer points to a piece of memory, don't use an invalid pointer, etc.). The arrow syntax is exactly equivalent to writing

```
(*p_my_struct).my_field;
```

But it is much easier to read (and type!) once you get used to it.

If a function takes a pointer to a structure as an argument, then that function is able to modify the memory at the address associated with the structure, allowing it to modify the structure it is given. This works exactly the same way as when you pass an array to a structure. Let's see how this would work with our EnemySpaceShip structure:

```cpp
// this header is needed for NULL; normally it's included
// by other header files, but we don't need any other
// headers here.
#include <cstddef>

struct EnemySpaceShip
{
        int x_coordinate;
        int y_coordinate;
        int weapon_power;
        EnemySpaceShip* p_next_enemy;
};

EnemySpaceShip* getNewEnemy ()
{
        EnemySpaceShip* p_ship = new EnemySpaceShip;
        p_ship->x_coordinate = 0;
        p_ship->y_coordinate = 0;
        p_ship->weapon_power = 20;
        p_ship->p_next_enemy = NULL;
        return p_ship;
}

void upgradeWeapons (EnemySpaceShip* p_ship)
{
        p_ship->weapon_power += 10;
}

int main ()
{
        EnemySpaceShip* p_enemy = getNewEnemy();
        upgradeWeapons( p_enemy );
}
```
Sample Code 38: upgrade.cpp

In getNewEnemy we use new to allocate the memory for a new ship. In upgradeWeapons we are able to modify p_ship directly because p_ship points to a block of memory containing all of the fields of the structure.

Creating a linked list

Now that we have the syntax for working with pointers to structures, we can create our lists. Any time you create a list by using a structure that contains a pointer to the next element, it is called a **linked list**. To identify the list, you need some way of holding on to the start of the list. Let's go back to our example and add a way of holding on to space ships:

```
struct EnemySpaceShip
{
        int x_coordinate;
        int y_coordinate;
        int weapon_power;
        EnemySpaceShip* p_next_enemy;
};

EnemySpaceShip* p_enemies = NULL;
```

p_enemies is a variable that we will use to store the list of enemies; each time we add a new enemy to our game, we will add it to this list. (This list will be our one-stop point for doing things with enemies in the game.) Another name for this variable could be p_first, or p_head, to indicate that it is the first element of our list.

When we add a new enemy to the game, we will add that enemy to the front of the list.

```
EnemySpaceShip* getNewEnemy ()
{
        EnemySpaceShip* p_ship = new EnemySpaceShip;
        p_ship->x_coordinate = 0;
        p_ship->y_coordinate = 0;
        p_ship->weapon_power = 20;
        p_ship->p_next_enemy = p_enemies;
        p_enemies = p_ship;
        return p_ship;
}
```

We start with p_enemies being empty (NULL). When we get a new enemy, we update the newly created enemy to point to the previous first element in the list (stored in p_enemies), and then we make p_enemies point to the newly created enemy. We're basically adding every new element to the front of the list by sliding the rest of the elements down the list. This sliding does not require any copying; we're just modifying two pointers.

This might be a bit confusing, so let's walk through it with a sequence of steps and a diagram that appears right after the sequence of steps.

First time through

In the initial state, p_enemies starts off as NULL; in other words, there are no enemies (we will always use NULL to indicate that we are at the end of the list).

1. A new ship, p_ship, is allocated—now we have an enemy that I call SHIP 1, which is not yet in the list of links—in the diagram, you can see that that p_next_enemy has not yet been set, and points to unknown memory.

2. The p_next_enemy field of SHIP 1 is set to point to the current list of enemies (which in this case is NULL).

3. Then p_enemies is updated to point to our newly created ship.

4. Our function now returns p_ship to the caller for whatever use is needed, while p_enemies provides access to the entire list (which happens to be only a single element so far).

Initial State

p_enemies ··············→ NULL

Step 1: Create ship

Steps 2 and 3: Update p_next_enemy and p_enemies

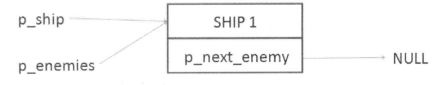

Second time through

> When we start going through the second time, p_enemies is pointing to the ship we just created.

1. A new ship, p_ship, is allocated—now we have a second enemy, which again has a p_next_enemy that points to unknown memory.

2. Next p_next_enemy is set to point to the current list of enemies, in this case the enemy that we created the first time through.

3. Then p_enemies is updated to point to our newly created ship (it now points to the second ship, which points to the first ship).

4. Our function now returns p_ship to the caller for whatever use is needed, while p_enemies provides access to the entire list—both elements, in this case.

Start State

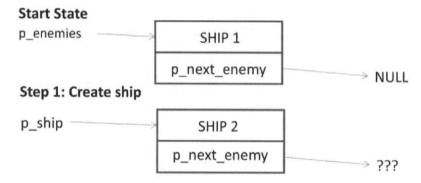

Step 1: Create ship

Steps 2 and 3: Update p_next_enemy and p_enemies

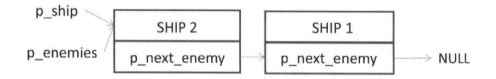

You can think of this operation as sliding all the existing elements of the list down each time you insert a new element. This sliding doesn't involve copying the whole list, as it would with an array. Instead, it means that you update the pointer to the start of the list so that it points to a new starting element. The first element in the list is called the **head** of the list, and you will typically have a pointer that points to the head element of the list, which in this case is p_enemies. At the end of the function, both p_ship and p_enemies point to the same place, but before then, we needed the p_ship pointer to hold on to the new memory so that we could modify p_next_enemy to point to the previous head of the list stored in p_enemies.

Although the function that I wrote uses a global variable, you can make the function simply take the head of the list, so that you can have it work on any list, rather than only a single global list. Here's what that might look like:

```
EnemySpaceShip* addNewEnemyToList (EnemySpaceShip* p_list)
{
        EnemySpaceShip* p_ship = new EnemySpaceShip;
        p_ship->x_coordinate = 0;
        p_ship->y_coordinate = 0;
        p_ship->weapon_power = 20;
        p_ship->p_next_enemy = p_list;
        return p_ship;
}
```

Notice that this function differs from getNewEnemy because it returns a pointer to the list, rather than the new enemy. Since this function cannot modify a global variable associated with the list, and it cannot modify the pointer that is passed to it (only the thing pointed to), it needs a way of giving the caller the new start of the list.[32] The caller can then write:

```
p_list = addNewEnemyToList( p_list );
```

in order to add a new item to the list.

This interface for addNewEnemyToList lets callers choose the base list to use and where to store the newly returned list.

To mimic the behavior we had before with a global p_enemies variable, you would write:

```
p_enemies = addNewEnemyToList( p_enemies );
```

---

[32] If you want to give yourself a real mental workout, try solving the same problem by using a pointer to a pointer instead of returning the original value.

Traversing a linked list

So far, so good—we now know how to store stuff in a list. What about actually using the list to...do stuff? We all know how to access every element of an array by using a for loop to **iterate** (a fancy word for loop) over it. Let's learn how to do the same thing for a linked list, a technique called **traversing** the list.

To get to the next item in the list, all you need is the current item; you can write a loop that has a variable that holds a pointer to the current element of the list and, after performing an operation on that element, updates it to point to the next element in the list.

Let' see an example of code that upgrades all the enemy weapons in the game (perhaps because the player has advanced to the next level):

```
EnemySpaceShip *p_current = p_enemies;

while ( p_current != NULL )
{
    upgradeWeapons( p_current );
    p_current = p_current->p_next_enemy;
}
```

Whoa, that's almost as short as going through an array! The variable p_current keeps track of the current item in the list that we are looking at. p_current starts by pointing to the first enemy in the list (whatever p_enemies points to). While p_current isn't NULL (meaning we aren't at the end of the list), we upgrade the weapons on the current enemy and update p_current to be the next enemy in the list.

Notice that p_current simply changes what it points to, while p_enemies and everything else continue to point to the same place. This is the power of a pointer! It can move you along a data structure simply by changing where it points, without doing copies. There is only a single copy of each ship at any time. This allows our weapon upgrade code to modify the original ship in the list rather than a copy. Here's a visual representation of what the data structure and variables look like as we iterate over the list.

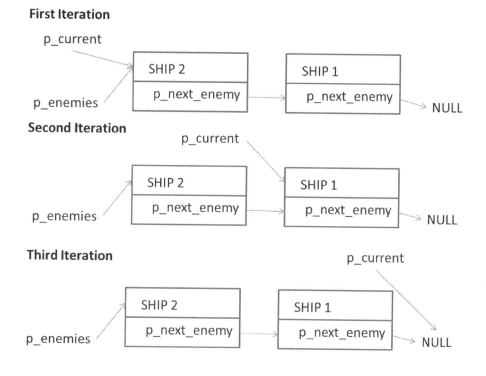

Taking stock of linked lists

Linked lists allow you to easily add new memory to your data structures, without a lot of copying of memory and shuffling of arrays. You can also implement operations such as adding elements into the middle of the list or removing elements. For a complete implementation of a linked list, you'd want to provide all of these operations.

The dirty little secret of linked lists is that you probably won't ever need to implement a linked list yourself! You can use the standard template library instead, which I will discuss soon. The importance of linked lists, however, is that we will often use very similar techniques to create more interesting data structures. I haven't lead you astray—what you've learned here will definitely be valuable even if you never write your own linked list. Moreover, by understanding how a linked list is implemented, you can better understand the tradeoffs of using a linked list or an array.

Arrays vs. linked lists

The primary advantage of a linked list over an array is that linked lists can be easily resized or added to, and that doing so doesn't require moving every element. For example, it's easy to add a new node into a linked list.

What if you want to keep your list sorted, and you need to add a new element to it? If your list is 1, 2, 5, 9, 10 and you want to insert the element 6, it needs to go between 5 and 9. With an array, you need to resize the array to fit the new element in, and then you have to move every single element from 9 to the end of the list. If your list had a thousand elements after the 10, you'd have to move every single one of them over one slot in the list. In other words, the performance of inserting into the middle of an array is proportional to the length of the array. With a linked list, you can just modify element 5 to point to your new element, modify your new element to point to element 9, and you're done! The operation takes the same amount of time no matter how big your list is.

The primary advantage of an array over a linked list is that an array lets you choose any element very quickly, just by providing its index. A linked list, on the other hand, requires that you look through every element in the list until you find the one you want. This means that to get any advantage out of the array, the index needs to be meaningfully related to the value stored in the collection of items—otherwise, you'll have to go through the collection to find what you want anyway.

For example, you could use an array to create a vote tally where voters use numbers from 0-9 to express a preference for candidates who are assigned numbers 0 to 9; then the array index corresponds to a candidate, and the value of the array at that location is the number of votes for the candidate. There's no inherent relationship between candidates and these numbers, but we can make one simply by assigning each candidate a number. Then we can use that number to get information about that candidate.

Here's a simple implementation to show you what this looks like with an array:

```
#include <iostream>

using namespace std;

int main ()
```

```
{
    int votes[ 10 ];

// make sure the election isn't rigged (by clearing out the
// array)
    for ( int i = 0; i < 10; ++i )
    {
        votes[ i ] = 0;
    }

    int candidate;
    cout << "Vote for the candidate of your choice, using
numbers: 0) Joe 1) Bob 2) Mary 3) Suzy 4) Margaret 5)
Eleanor 6) Alex 7) Thomas 8) Andrew 9) Ilene" << '\n';
    cin >> candidate;

// enter votes until the user exits by entering a non-
// candidate number
    while ( 0 <= candidate && candidate <= 9 )
    {
// notice that we can't use a do-while loop because we need
// to check that the candidate is in the right range before
// updating the array. A do-while loop would require
// reading in the candidate value, then checking it, then
// incrementing the vote.

        votes[ candidate ]++;
        cout << "Please enter another vote: ";
        cin >> candidate;
    }
// display the votes
    for ( int i = 0; i < 10; ++i )
    {
        cout << votes[ i ] << '\n';
    }
}
```
Sample Code 39: vote.cpp

Notice how easy it is to update the count for a particular candidate.

We could get fancier and hold an array of structures, with each structure containing the vote count and the names of the candidates. This approach would make it easy to print out the names along with the votes.

Imagine what would happen if you tried to do the same thing with a linked list. The code would have to go element-by-element until it reached the selected candidate. A vote for candidate 5 would require the loop to go from the node for candidate 0 to the node for candidate 1 to the node for candidate 2—there's no way to jump into the middle of a linked list.

The time that it takes to access an element of the array by its index is **constant**, meaning it doesn't change with the size of the array. The time it takes to find an element in a linked list, on the other hand, is proportional to the size of the list, index or no index. As your list grows in size, this will become slower and slower.

If you were going to do this using a linked list, therefore, it would make no sense to assign numbers to candidates; instead, you might as well look for the candidates by name. (Comparing names will be slower than comparing indices, but if you're already choosing to use a linked list, you probably aren't worried about making the code maximally efficient.)

How much space is required for a linked list?
The amount of space used by a data structure is an important consideration if the number of elements will be very large. For small data structures, you won't see a difference; for enormous data structures, taking up twice the amount of space may be a big deal.

Arrays generally take up less space per element. A linked list requires both the item in the list and a pointer to the next element of the list. This means a linked list starts out requiring about twice as much space per item in the list. However, linked lists can sometimes take up less space if you don't know beforehand how many elements will be stored. Instead of allocating a large array and then leaving much of that array empty, you can allocate new linked list nodes only when you need them, so you have never allocated extra memory that you won't use. (To avoid this problem, you could allocate the array dynamically, but this would require you to copy the elements of the array each time you allocated more memory, negating some of the size benefits.[33])

Other considerations
Arrays can also be multidimensional—for example, representing a chess board with an 8 by 8 array is easy whereas doing this with a linked list would require having a list composed of other lists, and accessing a particular element is going to be much slower and more difficult to understand.

---

[33] You might choose to take this approach anyway, particularly if you wanted to have constant-time access using the array index. With data structures, there's usually no universally correct answer when you're comparing not-obviously-bad solutions.

General rules of thumb

Here are a couple of rules of thumb for when you should use a linked list, and when you should use an array:

Use **arrays** when you need constant time access to elements by index, and you know how many items you need to store in advance or when you need to minimize the space used per element.

Use **linked lists** when you need to be able to continually add new elements,[34] or you need to do a lot of insertions into the middle of your list.

In other words, linked lists and arrays serve complementary purposes, and when you would use one or the other will depend on what you are trying to do.

Quiz yourself

1. What is an advantage of a linked list over an array?
A. Linked lists take up less space per element
B. Linked lists can grow dynamically to hold individual new elements without copying existing elements
C. Linked lists are faster at finding a particular element than arrays
D. Linked lists can hold structures as elements

2. Which of the following statements is true?
A. There is no reason to ever use an array
B. Linked lists and arrays have the same performance characteristics
C. Linked lists and arrays both allow constant time access to elements by index
D. It is faster to add an element into the middle of a linked list than into the middle of an array

3. When would you normally use a linked list?
A. When you only need to store one item
B. When the number of items you need to store is known at compile time
C. When you need to dynamically add and remove items

---

[34] The vector class from the standard template library (STL) actually makes it quite easy to add new elements to an array-like data structure, removing this advantage of linked lists. As a result, the vector class is typically a better choice than either a linked list or an array. We will talk about vectors shortly.

D. When you need instant access to any item in a sorted list without having to do any iteration to access it

4. Why is it ok to declare a linked list with a reference to the type of the list item? (`struct Node { Node* p_next; };`)
A. This isn't allowed
B. Because the compiler is able to figure out that you don't actually need the memory for self-referencing items
C. Because the type is a pointer, you only need enough space to hold a single pointer; the memory for the actual next node is allocated later
D. This is allowed so long as you do not actually assign p_next to point to another structure

5. Why is it important to have a `NULL` at the end of the linked list?
A. It indicates where the list ends and prevents the code from accessing uninitialized memory
B. It prevents the list from becoming a series of circular references
C. It is a debugging aid—if you try to go too far down the list, the program will crash
D. If we don't store a `NULL`, then the list will need infinite memory because of the self-reference

6. How are arrays and linked lists similar?
A. Both allow you to quickly add new elements in the middle of your current list
B. Both allow you to store data sequentially and sequentially access that data
C. Both arrays and linked lists can easily grow larger by incrementally adding elements
D. Both provide fast access to every element in the list

(View solution on page 498)

Practice problems
1. Write a program to remove an element from a linked list; the remove function should take just the element to be removed. Is this function easy to write—and will it be fast? Could this be made easier or faster by adding an additional pointer to the list?[35]

---

[35] Hint: what if you have a pointer to the previous node? Does that help?

2. Write a program that adds elements to a linked list in sorted order, rather than at the beginning.

3. Write a program to find an element in a linked list by name.

4. Implement a two-player tic-tac-toe game. First use a linked list to represent the board. Then use an array. Which is easier? Why?

Chapter 16
Recursion

You have seen many algorithms that are based on looping, repeating some activity over and over again. There is another way to repeatedly execute code that does not require looping, but instead uses repeated function calls. This technique is called **recursion**. Recursion is a technique of expressing operations in terms of themselves. In other words, recursion means writing a function that calls itself. Recursion is similar to looping but more powerful. It can make some programs that are nearly impossible to write with loops nearly trivial! Recursion is particularly powerful when applied to data structures such as linked lists and binary trees (which you'll learn about soon). In this chapter and the next, you'll have a chance to understand the basic ideas of recursion as well as see some concrete examples of when you would use it.

How to think about recursion

A useful way to think of recursive functions is to imagine them as a process being performed where one of the instructions is to "repeat the process". This makes it sound very similar to a loop because it repeats the same code, and in some ways it *is* similar to looping. On the other hand, recursion makes it easier to express ideas in which the result of the recursive call is necessary to complete the task. Of course, it must be possible for the "process" to sometimes be completed without the recursive call. One simple example is the idea of building a wall that is ten feet high. If I want to build a 10-foot high wall, then I will first build a 9-foot high wall, and then add an extra foot of bricks. Conceptually, this is like saying the "build wall" function takes a height and if that height is greater than one, the "build wall" function first calls itself to build a lower wall, and then adds one foot of bricks.

Here's a very basic structure of what this might look like (with a couple of notable flaws that we'll discuss soon). The important idea is that we are saying that building a wall of a specific height can be expressed in terms of building a shorter wall.

```
void buildWall (int height)
{
     buildWall( height - 1 );
     addBrickLayer();
}
```

But doesn't this code have a small problem? When will it stop calling buildWall? The answer, unfortunately, is never. The solution is simple—we need to stop the recursive call when we have a wall of height 0; with a height of 0, we should just add a layer of bricks without building any smaller wall.

```
void buildWall (int height)
{
     if ( height > 0 )
     {
          buildWall( height - 1 );
     }
     addBrickLayer();
}
```

The condition where the function will not call itself is termed the **base case** of the function. In the example, the wall building function knows that if we have reached the ground, we can just add a layer of bricks to build the wall (the base of the wall). Otherwise, we still need to build a smaller wall first and then add a layer of bricks on top. If you have trouble following the code (and recursion can be a bit trippy the first time you see it), think about the physical process of building a wall. You start off with a desire to build a wall at a particular height; you then say, "to put bricks here, I need a wall one brick shorter." Eventually you say, "I don't need a smaller wall; I can build on the ground." That's the base case.

Notice that the algorithm reduces the problem to a smaller problem (build a shorter wall) and then solves that smaller problem; at some point, the smaller problem gets small enough (building a one-layer height wall on the ground) that we don't need to reduce the problem any further and can immediately solve that simple case. In real life, this means we can build a wall; in C++, this ensures that the function will eventually stop making recursive calls. This is a lot like the top-down design process that we saw earlier, where we broke down a problem into smaller sub-problems, created functions for those sub-problems, and then used them to build the full program. In that case, we were breaking down a problem into *different* sub-problems than the one we were solving. In recursion, we are breaking down a problem into *smaller versions* of the same sub-problem.

Once a function has called itself, it will be ready to go to the next line after the call site, when the call returns. After the recursive call returns, the function can still perform operations and call other functions. In the wall-building case, after building the smaller wall, the function continues to execute by adding a new layer of bricks.

Let's look at an example that you can actually run that will show real output. How would you write a recursive function that prints out the numbers 123456789987654321? We can do this by writing a function that takes a number and then prints out that number twice, once before the function recurses and once after.

```cpp
#include <iostream>

using namespace std;

void printNum (int num)
{
    // the two calls in this function to cout will
    // sandwich an inner sequence containing the numbers
    // (num+1)...99...(num+1)
    cout << num;
    // While begin is less than 9, we need to recursively
    // print the sequence for (num+1) ... 99 ... (num+1)
    if ( num < 9 )
    {
        printNum( num + 1 );
    }
    cout << num;
}

int main ()
{
```

```
        printNum( 1 );
}
```
Sample Code 40: printnum.cpp

The recursive function call of `printnum( num + 1 )` prints a sequence `(num+1)...99...(num+1)`. By printing num on both sides of the call to `printnum( num + 1 )`, we are effectively creating a sandwich: num is printed on either side of the sequence `(num+1)...99...(num+1)`, making it `(num)(num+1)...99...(num+1)(num)`. If num is 1, then you have `12...99...21`.

Another way to think about this function is that it first prints out the sequence 1 through 9, each time calling `printnum` again. When the base case is reached, `printnum` will return to each recursive call, printing the numbers out again in the order from which the functions are returned—since the last function call made was with the value 9, it will immediately print out when the base case is hit, rather than calling the function again.

When that call returns, it will return to the call where the value of num is 8, and 8 is printed; then it returns, and the value of num is 7, and so on, until all the recursive calls have completed, back to the first call, with the value 1; and then 1 is printed, and we are done.

Recursion and data structures

Some data structures lend themselves to recursive algorithms because the composition of the data structure can be described as containing smaller versions of the same data structure. Since recursive algorithms work by making a problem a smaller version of the original, they work well with data structures that are made up of smaller versions of the same data structure—linked lists are one such data structure.

So far we've talked about linked lists as a list onto which you can add more nodes at the front. But another way to think of a linked list is that a linked list is made up of a first node, which then points to another smaller linked list. In other words, a linked list is composed of individual nodes, but each node points to another node that is the start of "the rest of the list".

This matters because it provides a very useful property for us: we can write programs to work with linked lists by writing code that handles either the current node or "the rest of the list". For example, to find a particular node in a list, you could use this basic algorithm:

If we're at the end of the list, return NULL.
Else if the current node is the target, return it.
Else repeat the search on the rest of the list.

In code, that would look like this:

```
struct node
{
        int value;
        node *next;
};

node* search (node* list, int value_to_find)
{
        if ( list == NULL )
        {
                return NULL;
        }
        if ( list->value == value_to_find )
        {
                return list;
        }
        else
        {
                return search( list->next, value_to_find );
        }
}
```

When thinking about a recursive call, I've talked about the called function doing some work for us. The promise of what a particular function will do, given a particular input, is termed the **contract** of the function. A function's contract summarizes what the function does. The contract of the search function is to find a given node in a list. The search function happens to be implemented by saying, "if the current node is the one we want, return it; otherwise, the contract of the search function is to find a node in the list—let's use that to look through the rest of the list."

It is important to call the search function on the remainder of the list—not the whole list again. Recursion will only work if you can:

1) Come up with a way to solve the problem by working with the solution to a smaller version of the same problem.
2) Solve the base case.

The search function solves two possible base cases—either we are at the end of the list or we have found the node we wanted. If neither of the two current cases matches, then we use the search function to solve a smaller version of the same problem. And that's the key—recursion works when you can recursively solve smaller versions of the same problem and use that result to solve the larger problem.

Sometimes, the value returned from the recursive call is actually used rather than being immediately returned. Let's look at an example—we'll use the factorial function from mathematics. (Everyone uses factorial in their recursion examples!)

```
Factorial( x ) = x * ( x - 1 ) *( x - 2 )...*1
```

Or, said another way:

```
Factorial( x ) =
      If ( x == 1 ) 1
      Else x * Factorial( x - 1 )
```

In other words, factorial is solved by multiplying the current value times the factorial of a smaller value. This is a case where we are using the value returned by the recursive call and doing something else with it—here, multiplying it by another value.

In code:

```
int factorial (int x)
{
      if ( x == 1 )
      {
            return 1;
      }
      return x * factorial( x - 1 );
}
```

Here, we can either solve the base case where x is 1 or we solve the smaller problem of factorial(x - 1) and then use the result to compute the factorial of x. Again, each call to factorial makes x smaller, so eventually we will reach the base case.

Notice that we are solving the sub-problem and then taking the result and doing something with it. When searching a linked list, all we did was return the result of solving the sub-problem. Recursion can be used in both ways—either hand off full responsibility for solving a problem by making a recursive call, or get the result of solving a sub-problem and then use that result to do more computation.

Loops and recursion

In some cases, a recursive algorithm can be easily expressed as a loop that has the same structure. For example, searching the list could be written:

```
node *search (node *list, int value_to_find)
{
        while ( 1 )
        {
                if ( list == NULL )
                {
                        return NULL;
                }
                if ( list->value == value_to_find )
                {
                        return list;
                }
                else
                {
                        list = list->next;
                }
        }
}
```

This code uses exactly the same checks so that you can easily see the comparison with the recursive version. The only difference between the two algorithms is that instead of using recursion, this code uses a loop, and, instead of making a recursive call, it shortens list each time by setting list to point to the "rest of the list". This is a case where both the recursive solution and the **iterative** (loop-based) solution work in a similar way.

In general, it is quite easy to write a recursive algorithm as a loop, and vice versa, when you don't need to do anything with the result that comes from calling the recursive function. This is called **tail recursion**—when the recursive call is the last thing the function does, at the tail of the function. Because the recursive call is the last operation, it's no different from going to the next step in the loop. Nothing from the previous call is needed once the next call completes. The list search example is a situation where we have tail recursion.

On the other hand, consider factorial. There's a small problem with turning it into a loop based on the recursive implementation.

```
int factorial (int x)
{
      while ( 1 )
      {
            if ( x == 1 )
            {
                  return 1;
            }
            // what to put here??
            // return x * factorial( x - 1 );
      }
}
```

We need to do something with the result of `factorial( x - 1 )`, so we can't just loop here. We really need the sub-problem solved (the rest of the loop to complete) before we can figure this out.

However, factorial turns out to be easy to translate into a loop if you re-think the problem! Consider the original definition

```
Factorial( x ) = x * ( x - 1 ) *( x - 2 )...*1
```

If we keep track of the current value, we could compute factorial by storing the running result of multiplying x * (x - 1) * (x - 2) ...

```
int factorial (int x)
{
      int cur = x;
      while ( x > 1 )
      {
            x--;
            cur *= x;
```

```
    }
    return x;
}
```

Notice that rather than solving this by taking the result of a sub-problem (a smaller factorial) we're actually doing the multiplications in the opposite way. For example, if we computed the factorial of five, then the recursive solution would do multiplication in this order:

```
1 * 2 * 3 * 4 * 5
```

On the other hand, the iterative solution would do multiplication in the opposite order:

```
5 * 4 * 3 * 2 * 1
```

In this case, both recursive and iterative solutions are possible—but they're structured differently. By rethinking the structure of the algorithm, we were able to write factorial as a very simple loop. In some cases, it can be much harder to come up with a loop than in this example. Whether or not you choose to use recursion will depend on how easy it is to discover the iterative algorithm. In the case of factorial, it isn't very difficult—but in some cases, it can be very hard. We'll see some examples of that soon.

The stack

It's time to talk a bit more about how function calls work and look at some nice diagrams. Once you understand how function calls work, recursion will be easier to follow and you should have some insight into why some algorithms are easier to write using recursion instead of loops.

All the information a function uses is stored internally on the **stack**. Imagine a stack of plates. You can either put a new plate on top or take off the top plate. The stack, like our stack of plates, works the same way, but instead of plates, we have something called **stack frames**. When a function is called, it gets a new stack frame at the top of the stack, and it uses the stack frame to keep all of the local variables that will be used. When it calls another function, the original stack frame space is kept around, and a new stack frame is added to the top of the stack, giving the newly called function space for its own variables. The currently executing function always uses the stack frame at the top of the stack.

In the simplest case, when just the main function is executing, the stack looks like this:

Variables in main

We have only a single function—main—and the stack has just the variables for main.

Now if main calls some other function, the new function will create a stack frame, on top of the main function. It will look like this:

Variables in 2nd func

Variables in main

The current function now has a place to keep its variables and work with them, without interfering with the variables that the main function was using. If this second function calls a third function, the stack will look like this:

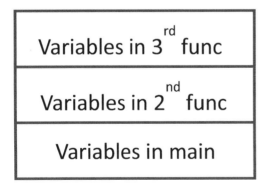

Variables in 3rd func

Variables in 2nd func

Variables in main

The newly called function has its own stack frame. Every function call creates a new stack frame. Upon returning from the function, the stack will go back to looking like it did before:

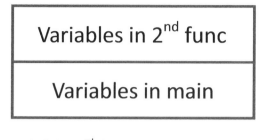

And if the 2nd function returns to main, the stack goes back to having just a single stack frame:

Variables in main

The active frame is always the one associated with the current function being executed, and it is always at the top of the stack.

In addition to containing the variables that are used by the function, the stack frame also contains the arguments to the function and the line of code the function should return to when it completes. In other words, the stack frame stores where a function is and all the data a function is using. Recursively calling a function will create a new stack frame for the new call, even if it is the same function. This is why recursion works—every function call has its own unique stack frame, arguments and variables. This allows each function call to have its own information, and therefore each function can work on a smaller version of the original problem as represented by its own variables.

When a function completes, as we saw in the diagram, the function removes its stack frame from the top of the stack, and it returns to the point of execution in its caller. By removing its stack frame, it restores the stack frame for its caller to use.

It is critical that the stack frame both store the place to return to and that the stack frame be removed from the stack after the function completes. Without the right stack frame, the calling function cannot continue to execute correctly after the called function returns—for example, it won't have the correct values for its local variables.

Think of it this way: when a new function is called, everything the previous function needs to continue executing is kept around. It would be as if you were working on a project, and you decided to get dinner; you'd write down some notes for yourself to help you remember where you were in the project so that after dinner you could come back and finish up. The stack allows the computer to keep extremely detailed notes about what it was doing at any time—far more detailed than you or I could write ourselves.

Here's a stack that demonstrates three recursive calls to `buildWall`, starting at a height of 2. You can see that each stack frame holds the new height value that was passed into `buildWall`. (Notice that the call with a value of 0 is at the stop of the stack, which happens to be the *bottom* of the physical wall.)

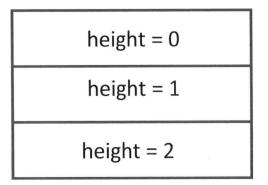

This approach to drawing a stack is often abbreviated like this:

```
buildWall( x = 0 )
buildWall( x = 1 )
buildWall( height = 2 )
main( )
```

Each function is shown on top of the function that called it, and the arguments for that function call are displayed. You can use this technique yourself to help you understand how a particular recursive function works. Sometimes you may find it helpful to write out the local variables next to each frame, in addition to the function name and function arguments.

The power of the stack

The key value that you get from recursion is that you have a stack of function calls, rather than a single stack frame. Recursive algorithms can take advantage of having all of the extra information that is stored in each stack frame, whereas a loop only gets one set of local variables. As a result, a recursive function can wait for a recursive call to return and pick up right where it left off. To write a loop that would work this way, you would have to implement your own version of a stack.

Downsides of recursion

The stack is a fixed size, which means that you cannot have limitless recursion. At some point, there won't be any more room for a new stack frame to be added onto the top of the stack—just like running out of space to stack up another plate in your cabinet.

A simple example of recursion that would theoretically go forever is:

```
void recurse ()
{
        recurse(); // Function calls itself
}

int main ()
{
        recurse(); // Sets off the recursion
}
```

But eventually the stack space will be used up, and the program will crash with a **stack overflow**. A stack overflow is when no more space remains on the stack. At this point, no more function calls can be made, so if your program does try to make one, it will crash. These kinds of crashes, while infrequent, are typically the result of a recursive function with a bad base case. For example, the example factorial I wrote earlier had a small problem: it didn't check for negative numbers in its base case. If the caller passed in -1, it would almost certainly overflow the stack. (Give it a try—overflowing the stack will cause your program to crash, but it won't damage your computer.)

Here is a simple program that shows you how many recursive function calls it would take to run out of stack space with a very small function. (The larger the stack frame of your function, the fewer recursive calls that you can make—though this is rarely a limitation in situations where the base cases are correct.)

```
#include <iostream>

using namespace std;

void recurse (int count) // Each call gets its own count
{
        cout << count << "\n";
        // It is not necessary to increment count since each
        // function's variables are separate (so the count in
        // each stack frame will be initialized one greater
        // than the last count)
        recurse( count + 1 );
}

int main ()
{
        // First function call, so it starts at one
        recurse( 1 );
}
```

Debugging stack overflows

When you try to debug a stack overflow, the most important thing to figure out is what function (or group of functions) is repeatedly adding new stack frames. For example, if you were using a debugger (which we'll talk about in Debugging with Code::Blocks), you'd see from the previous example that the stack looked like this when the program eventually crashed:

```
recurse( 10000 );
recurse( 9999 );
recurse( 9998 );
...
recurse( 1 )
main()
```

This is an easy case to analyze because only one function is involved—clearly, this function has a missing base case of some kind, probably related to not stopping when the recursive argument reaches a certain size.

Sometimes you can have **mutual recursion** where two functions call each other.

Here's a very contrived example using factorial again, where there are two functions used to compute factorial—one to compute factorial for odd numbers and one for even numbers:

```
int factorial_odd (int x)
{
      if ( x == 0 )
      {
            return 1;
      }
      return factorial_even( x - 1 );
}

int factorial_even (int x)
{
      if ( x == 0 )
      {
            return 1;
      }
      return factorial_odd( x - 1 );
}

int factorial (int x)
{
      if ( x % 2 == 0 )
      {
            return factorial_even( x );
      }
      else
      {
            return factorial_odd( x );
      }
}
```

Notice that the base cases here do not guard against negative inputs. Calling factorial(-1) will result in a call stack like this:

```
factorial_even( -10000 )
factorial_odd( -9999 )
factorial_even( -9998 )
factorial_odd( -9997 )
```

Just from looking at the stack we can get an idea that there is a problem with the base case, and that the two functions keep calling each other. The next step is to look at the code and try to figure out which one is supposed to have a check for negative numbers in its base case. For computing factorial, it would make sense for both functions to have separate base cases containing the same check; in other cases, only one of the functions may be responsible for having the final base case.

Whenever you debug complex recursive calls, it helps to find the series of functions that repeat—in this case, just `factorial_even` and `factorial_odd` calling each other. In some cases, you may have a much longer period between repetitions; you must discover the whole set of function calls that repeat, and then figure out why that set of functions is repeating.

Performance
Recursion requires making many function calls—each function call needs to set up a stack frame and pass arguments, which adds overhead that isn't there when you're looping. In almost all cases, this will not be significant on modern computers, but if you have code that is very frequently executed (millions or billions of times in a short period of time) then you might start to notice the overhead from making the function call.

Taking stock of recursion
Recursion makes it possible to create algorithms that solve problems by breaking those problems into smaller versions of the same problem. Recursion also provides more power than loops because recursive functions maintain a stack holding the current state of each recursive call, allowing the function to continue processing after getting the result of the sub-problem.

A recursive implementation of an algorithm will often feel more natural than the equivalent loop-based implementation. We'll see some examples in the next chapter, which covers binary trees. As you develop more code, you'll find recursion makes it easy to think about a much wider range of problems than can be solved by looping alone.

Here are some rules of thumb for when you should use recursion or looping.

Use recursion when...

1) The solution to a problem requires breaking down the problem into smaller versions of the same problem, and there isn't an obvious way of writing it as a loop.

2) The data structure you are working with is recursive (such as a linked list).

Use a loop when...

1) It's obvious how to solve the problem with a simple loop—for example, if you're adding a list of numbers together, you could write a recursive function, but it's not worth it.

2) When you're using a data structure that is indexed by number, such as an array.

Quiz yourself

1. What is tail recursion?

A. When you call your dog

B. When a function calls itself

C. When a recursive function calls itself as the last thing it does before returning

D. When you can write a recursive algorithm as a loop

2. When would you use recursion?

A. When you can't write the algorithm as a loop

B. When it is more natural to express an algorithm in terms of a sub-problem than in terms of a loop

C. Never, really, it's too hard ☹

D. When working with arrays and linked lists

3. What are the required elements for a recursive algorithm?

A. A base case and a recursive call

B. A base case and a way of breaking down the problem into a smaller version of itself

C. A way of recombining the smaller versions of a problem

D. All of the above

4. What can happen if your base case is incomplete?

A. The algorithm might finish early

B. The compiler will detect it and complain

C. This isn't a problem

D. You may have a stack overflow

(View solution on page 500)

Practice problems

1. Write a recursive algorithm to compute the power function pow(x, y) = x^y

2. Write a recursive function that takes an array and displays the elements in reverse order without starting the index of the array at the end. (In other words, don't write the equivalent of a loop that starts printing at the end of the array.)

3. Write a recursive algorithm to remove elements from a linked list. Write a recursive algorithm to add elements into a linked list. Try writing the same algorithms using iteration. Do the recursive implementations or the iterative implementations feel more natural?

4. Write a recursive function that takes a sorted array and a target element and finds that element in the array (returning the index, or -1 if the element isn't in the array). How fast can you make this search? Can you do better than having to look at every element?

5. Write a recursive algorithm to solve the Tower of Hanoi problem. Here's a website that describes the problem and lets you try your hand at solving it yourself: http://www.mazeworks.com/hanoi/index.htm

Chapter 17
Binary Trees

Note: This chapter covers one of the most interesting and useful basic data structures, the binary tree. Binary trees are a perfect example of how to use recursion and pointers to do amazingly useful things. But they are going to require that you really understand recursion and the concepts underlying linked lists. How do I know? I have seen more than one student struggle with binary trees after glossing over pointers and recursion. There's nothing inherently hard about binary trees—nothing that should prevent you from understanding them. But you really do need to have a strong foundation. If you struggle with the concepts in this chapter, you probably need to get a deeper grasp of pointers or recursion—try rereading those chapters and implementing their exercises.

Why do we need binary trees?

Linked lists are a great technique for making lists of things, but it can take a lot of time to find a particular element in your list. Moreover, even arrays don't help if the data is just one big long list without any structure. You might try sorting your array, which would allow you to do very quick searches. But your array is still going to be difficult to insert into; if you want to keep an array sorted, you're going to do a lot of shuffling every time you add a new element. Moreover, looking up things quickly is pretty important. Just to name a few examples:

1) If you are creating an MMORPG like World of Warcraft and you need to allow players to quickly sign in to the game—you have to be able to look up the player quickly

2) If you're working on credit card processing software and you need to handle millions of transactions every hour—you need to be able to find the account balance for a credit card number quickly

3) If you are working on a low-powered device like a smartphone and you're displaying an address book to the user, you don't want the user to wait because you're using a slow data structure

This chapter is all about the tools we need to solve problems like these—and many more.

The basic idea of this solution is to store your elements in a linked-list-like structure—meaning, that you use pointers to structure memory, just as we did with linked lists—but in a way that makes it easier to search for values. To do this, we need to give more structure to the memory than just a simple list.

What is a binary tree?

Let's look at what this idea of structuring data really means. When you started out, all you had was arrays; these arrays didn't provide the ability to have any data structure other than a sequential list. A linked list uses pointers to incrementally grow a sequential list, but it doesn't take advantage of the flexibility pointers provide to build more sophisticated structures.

What do I mean by a sophisticated structure in memory? Well, for one thing, you can build a structure that holds more than one next node at a time. Why would you do this? If you have two "next" nodes, one of them can represent elements less than your current element, and the other can represent elements greater than your current element. This kind of structure is called a **binary tree**. A binary tree is so named because there are at most two branches from each node. The "next" nodes are called **children** and the node linking to a child is called the **parent** node for that child.

You can visualize a binary tree like this:

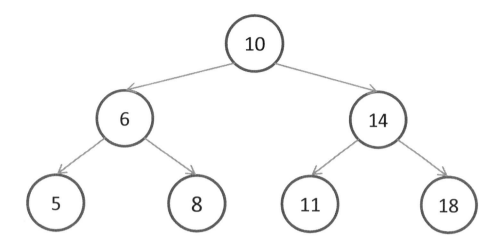

Notice that in this tree, the left child of each element is a smaller value than the element, and the right child of each element is larger than the element. Node 10 is the parent of the entire tree. Its child nodes, 6 and 14, are the parents of their own, smaller, trees. These smaller trees are called **subtrees**.

One important property of a binary tree is that each child of a node is itself an entire binary tree. This property, combined with the rule that left children are smaller than the current node, and right children are larger, makes it easy to design an algorithm to find a node in a tree. First, you look at the value of the current node; if it is equal to the search target, you're done. If the search target is less than the current node, you go to the left; otherwise, you got to the right. This algorithm works because every node on the left of the tree is less than the current node, and every node on the right is greater than the current node.

It would be ideal to have a **balanced** tree, meaning that there are the same number of nodes in the left tree as in the right tree. When this happens, each child binary tree is about half the size of the whole tree, and if you are searching for a value in the tree, your search can remove half of the elements every time it goes to a child node. So when you have a 1000 element tree, you can immediately chop off about 500 elements. Now your search is reduced to looking in a 500 element tree. Searching in the 500 element tree again allows us to lop off about half the elements, or 250 elements. It won't take you very long to find what you are looking for if you keep removing half of the elements. How many times must you subdivide a tree before reaching only a single element? The answer is $\log_2 n$—where n is the number of elements in the tree. This value is small, even for very large trees (for a tree with about 4 billion elements, it will be 32, which is nearly one hundred million times faster than the same search in a linked list of 4 billion elements where you have to look at every element). However, if the tree is not balanced, you might not be able to cut the tree exactly in half. In the worst case, every node has only a single child node, meaning that your tree is just a glorified linked list (with some extra pointers), taking you back to having to search through n elements.

As you can see, when the tree is approximately balanced (it doesn't have to be perfect) searching for nodes is much much faster than the search you would do with a linked list. And all of this happens because you can structure memory to your liking rather than being stuck with simple lists.[36]

Talking about trees

In order to walk through sample code with binary trees, we'll need a convenient way to refer to different parts of the tree, so let's establish some basic conventions for diagramming and referring to trees.

The most basic tree is an **empty tree**, which is represented by NULL. When I diagram trees, I will not show links to empty trees.

Whenever I want to talk about a particular subtree, I will say "<tree headed by [value of parent node]>". For example, in the tree

---

[36] The basic binary tree we will discuss here can, in rare cases, end up with the same structure as a linked list, depending on the order that nodes are inserted. There are more sophisticated kinds of binary trees that always force proper balance, but that's outside the scope of this book. One such data structure is the red-black tree: http://en.wikipedia.org/wiki/Red%E2%80%93black_tree

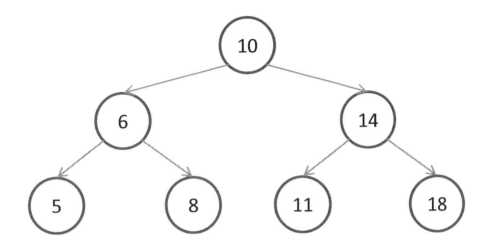

<tree headed by 6> would refer to this subtree:

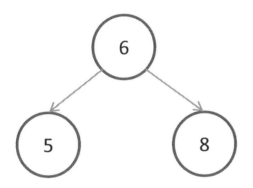

Implementing binary trees

Let's look at the necessary code for a simple implementation of a binary tree. We'll start off by declaring a node structure:

```
struct node
{
        int key_value;
        node *p_left;
        node *p_right;
};
```

Our node has the ability to store the value as a simple integer, key_value, and contains two child trees called p_left and p_right.

There are a couple of common functions you'll want to perform on binary trees—the main ones are inserting into the tree, searching for a value in the tree, removing a node from the tree, and destroying the tree to free the memory.

```
node* insert (node* p_tree, int key);
node *search (node* p_tree, int key);
void destroyTree (node* p_tree);
node *remove (node* p_tree, int key);
```

Inserting into the tree

Let's start with insertion using a recursive algorithm. Recursion really shines on trees because each tree contains two smaller trees, so the whole data structure is itself recursive in nature. (Which it wouldn't be if each tree contained, say, an array or a pointer to a linked list rather than to more trees.)

Our function will take a key and an existing tree (possibly empty) and return a new tree containing the inserted value.

```
node* insert (node *p_tree, int key)
{
    // base case--we have reached an empty tree and need
    // to insert our new node here
    if ( p_tree == NULL )
    {
        node* p_new_tree = new node;
        p_new_tree->p_left = NULL;
        p_new_tree->p_right = NULL;
        p_new_tree->key_value = key;
        return p_new_tree;
    }
    // decide whether to insert into the left subtree or
    // the right subtree depending on the value of the
    // node
    if( key < p_tree->key_value )
    {
        // build a new tree based on p_tree->left by
        // adding the key. Then replace the existing
        // p_tree->left pointer with a pointer to the
        // new tree. We need to set the p_tree->p_left
        // pointer in case p_tree->left is NULL. (If it
        // isn't NULL, p_tree->p_left won't actually
        // change, but it doesn't hurt to set it.)
        p_tree->p_left = insert( p_tree->p_left, key );
    }
    else
```

```
        {
                // Insertion into the right is exactly
                // symmetric to insertion into the left
                p_tree->p_right =
                        insert ( p_tree->p_right, key );
        }
        return p_tree;
}
```

The basic logic of this algorithm is: if we have an empty tree, create a new one. Otherwise, if the value being inserted is greater than the current node, insert it into the left subtree and replace the left subtree with the new subtree created. Otherwise, insert it into the right subtree and do the same replacement.

Let's see this code in action, building an empty tree into a tree with a couple of nodes. If we insert the value 10 into an empty tree (NULL), we immediately hit the base case. The result is a very simple tree:

10

With both child trees pointing to NULL.

If we then insert the value 5 into the tree, we will make the call

```
insert ( <tree with parent 10>, 5 )
```

Since 5 is less than 10, we'll get a recursive call onto the left subtree:

```
insert ( NULL, 5 )
insert ( <tree with parent 10>, 5 )
```

The call insert (NULL, 5)

will create a new tree and return it:

5

Upon receiving the returned tree, `insert ( <tree with parent 10>, 5 )`, will link the two trees together. In this case, the left child of 10 was `NULL` before, so this sets the left child of 10 to be a completely new tree:

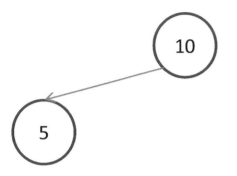

If we now add 7 to the tree, we'll get

```
insert ( NULL, 7 )
insert ( <tree with parent 5>, 7 )
insert ( <tree with parent 10>, 7 )
```

First,

```
insert ( NULL, 7 )
```

returns a new tree:

Then

```
insert ( <tree with parent 5>, 7 )
```

links up the subtree 7, like this:

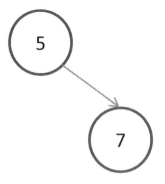

And finally this tree is returned to

```
insert ( <tree with parent 10>, 7 )
```

which links it back:

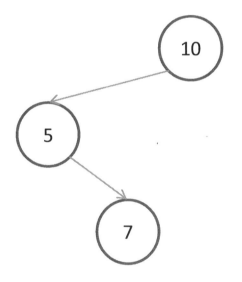

Since 10 already had a pointer to the node containing 5, re-linking the left child of 10 to the tree with parent 5 isn't strictly necessary, but it removes an extra conditional check from the code to check whether the subtree is empty.

Searching the tree

Now let's look at how you'd implement a search of the tree. The basic logic is going to be almost exactly the same as for inserting into a tree—first check the two base cases (have we found the node or are we looking at an empty tree) and then, if we're not on the base case, figure out which subtree to search.

```
node *search (node *p_tree, int key)
{
      // if we reach the empty tree, clearly it's not here!
      if ( p_tree == NULL )
      {
            return NULL;
      }
      // if we find the key, we're done!
      else if ( key == p_tree->key_value )
      {
            return p_tree;
      }
      // otherwise, try looking in either the left or the
      // right subtree
      else if ( key < p_tree->key_value )
      {
            return search( p_tree->p_left, key );
      }
      else
      {
            return search( p_tree->p_right, key );
      }
}
```

The search function shown above first checks two base cases: either we're at the end of this branch of the tree, or we've found our key. In either case, we know what to return—NULL for the end of the tree or the tree itself if we've found the key.

If we aren't at a base case, we reduce the problem to that of finding the key in one of the child trees, either the left or the right tree, depending on the value of the key. Notice that each time we make a recursive call when searching for a node we cut the size of the tree roughly in half—just as I said at the beginning of the chapter, where we saw that searching a balanced tree would take time proportional to $\log_2 n$ which will be far more efficient for a large amount of data when compared with looking through a large linked list or array.

Destroying the tree
The destroy_tree function should also be recursive. The algorithm will destroy the two subtrees at the current node and then delete the current node.

```
void destroy_tree (node *p_tree)
{
      if ( p_tree != NULL )
```

```
    {
            destroy_tree( p_tree->p_left );
            destroy_tree( p_tree->p_right );
            delete p_tree;
    }
}
```

To help you understand how this works, imagine if you printed out the value of the node right before deleting it:

```
void destroy_tree (node *p_tree)
{
    if ( p_tree != NULL )
    {
            destroy_tree( p_tree->p_left );
            destroy_tree( p_tree->p_right );
            cout << "Deleting node: " << p_tree->key_value;
            delete p_tree;
    }
}
```

You'll see that the tree is deleted "bottom up". First the nodes 5 and 8 are deleted; then the node 6. Then the other side of the tree is deleted, 11 and 18; then 14. And finally, once all its children are deleted, 10. The values in the tree don't matter; what is important is where the node is located. Here's a binary tree where instead of putting in the value for each node, I've put in the order in which it will be deleted:

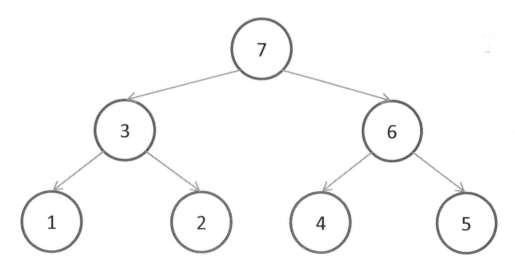

It can be quite helpful to manually walk through what the code does on a couple of trees. This will make it much clearer.

Deleting from a tree is an example of a recursive algorithm that would not be easy to implement iteratively! You would have to write a loop that could somehow handle dealing with both the left and the right branch of the tree simultaneously! The problem is that you need to be able to delete one subtree, while keeping track of the second subtree to be deleted—and you need to do that for every single level in the tree. The stack helps you keep your place. The way to visualize it is that each stack frame effectively stores which branch of the tree has already been destroyed:

```
destroy_tree( <subtree> )
destroy_tree( <tree> ) - knows whether the subtree was the
subtree to the left, or the subtree to the right
```

Each stack frame knows which parts of the tree need to be destroyed by knowing where in the function to continue execution. When making the first call to destroy_tree, the stack frame tells the program to continue execution on the second call to destroy_tree. When making that second call, the stack frame tells the program to continue with delete tree. Since each function call has its own stack frame, it keeps track of the entire current state of the tree's destruction, one level of the tree at a time.

The only way to implement this non-recursively would be to have a data structure that kept the equivalent amount of information for us. For example, you could simulate the stack by writing a function that kept a linked list (emulating the stack) of subtrees that were in the process of being destroyed. This linked list could store which sides of the tree remained to be deleted. Then you could write a loop-based algorithm to add subtrees into this list and remove them when they were fully destroyed. In other words, recursion allows you to take advantage of the built-in stack data structure rather than having to write your own. As an exercise, I suggest that you try to implement the equivalent non-recursive implementation of destroy_tree; you'll see how much easier it is to express this algorithm without having to build your own stack and gain a much deeper understanding of recursion as a result.

Removing from a tree

The algorithm for removing from a binary tree is more complex. The basic structure is similar to the pattern we've seen before: if we have an empty tree, we're done; if the value being removed is in the left subtree, remove the value from the left subtree; if the value being removed is in the right subtree, remove the value from the right subtree. If we find the value, remove it.

```
node* remove (node* p_tree, int key)
{
      if ( p_tree == NULL )
      {
            return NULL;
      }
      if ( p_tree->key_value == key )
      {
            // what to do?
      }
      else if ( key < p_tree->key_value )
      {
            p_tree->left = remove( p_tree->left, key );
      }
      else
      {
            p_tree->right = remove( p_tree->right, key );
      }
      return p_tree;
}
```

But there's trouble in paradise in one of the base cases—what exactly do you need to do when you actually find the value being removed? Remember that a binary tree needs to maintain the following condition:

Every value in the tree to the left of the current node must be less than its key value; every value in the tree to the right of the current node must be greater than its key value.

There are three basic cases to consider:

1) The node being removed has no children
2) The node being removed has one child
3) The node being removed has two children

Case 1 is the easiest—if we're removing a node with no children, all we need to do is return NULL. Case 2 is also easy—if there's only one child, we just return that child. But case 3 is harder.

You can't just take one of the two children and promote it. For example, what if we used the node to the left of the element you're going to remove. If you do, what happens to the elements to the right of that node? Consider the example tree from earlier:

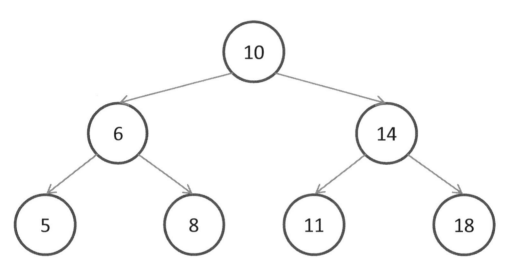

What if you remove element 10? You can't just replace it with element 6 because you'd end up with this tree:

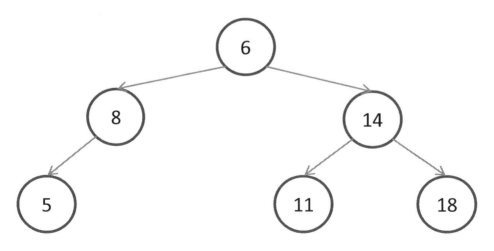

8 is now to the left of 6, even though 8 is greater than 6. This clearly breaks our tree—a search for the value 8 will go to the right of 6, never finding 8.

Similarly, you can't just take the element to the right for the same reason:

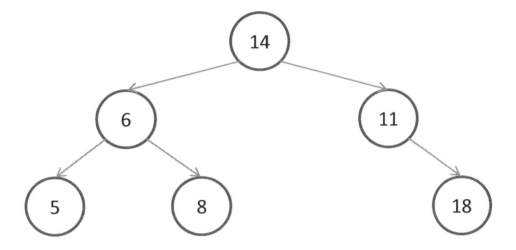

Here, 11 is smaller than 14, but it's still to the right of the tree—a no-no. In a binary tree, you can't promote a node up the tree willy-nilly.

So what do you do? Everything on the left of a node must have a value less than that node's value. So why not find the greatest value to the left of the node we're removing, and promote it to the top of the tree. Since it's the greatest value to the left of the tree, it's perfectly safe to use it to replace the current node—it's guaranteed to be greater than every other node to its left, and since it ended up in the left side of the tree to begin with, it's guaranteed to be less than every node to its right.[37]

In our example, we'd want to reach this final tree since 8 is the greatest value to the left of 10:

---

[37] Using the same reasoning, you can also pick the node on the right side of the tree with the lowest value. In practice, a good algorithm should not consistently pick one direction or another to avoid unbalancing the tree, but we will implement a simpler version ignoring this randomization.

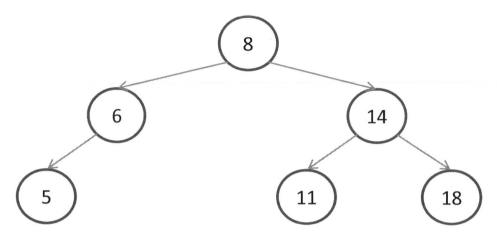

In order to do this, we need an algorithm that can find the greatest value stored in the left side of the tree—basically, a find_max function. We can implement find_max by taking advantage of the property that greater values are always in the right subtree, so we can just follow the right branch of a tree until we hit NULL. In other words, for a basic find_max function, taking a tree and returning the maximum value in that tree, we treat the tree as though it were a linked list of right tree pointers:

```
node* find_max (node* p_tree)
{
     if ( p_tree == NULL )
     {
          return NULL;
     }
     if ( p_tree->p_right == NULL )
     {
          return p_tree;
     }
     return find_max( p_tree->p_right );
}
```

Notice that we need two base cases—one for having no tree at all, and another for hitting the end of our list of child trees to the right.[38] In order to return a pointer to the last node, we need to "look ahead" one node while we still have a valid pointer.

---

[38] The way we will implement remove will actually make the first base case (checking for an empty tree) unnecessary, but it is good style to code defensively against bad inputs.

Let's see if we can use this to write our remove function. In our base case, if `find_max` returns NULL, we know that we can just use the left tree to replace the removed node as there is no value greater than it. Otherwise, we'll need to replace the removed node with the result from `find_max`.

```
node* remove (node* p_tree, int key)
{
      if ( p_tree == NULL )
      {
            return NULL;
      }
      if ( p_tree->key_value == key )
      {
            // the first two cases handle having zero or
            // one child node
            if ( p_tree->p_left == NULL )
            {
                  node* p_right_subtree = p_tree->p_right;
                  delete p_tree;
            // this might return NULL if there are zero
            // child nodes, but that is what we want anyway
                  return p_right_subtree;
            }
            if ( p_tree->p_right == NULL )
            {
                  node* p_left_subtree = p_tree->p_left;
                  delete p_tree;
            // this will always return a valid node, since
            // we know p_tree->p_left is not NULL from the
            // previous if statement
                  return p_left_subtree;
            }
            node* p_max_node = find_max( p_tree->p_left );
            p_max_node->p_left = p_tree->p_left;
            p_max_node->p_right = p_tree->p_right;
            delete p_tree;
            return p_max_node;
      }
      else if ( key < p_tree->key_value )
      {
            p_tree->p_left = remove( p_tree->p_left, key );
      }
      else
      {
            p_tree->p_right =
                  remove( p_tree->p_right, key );
      }
      return p_tree;
```

```
}
```

But does this work? There's a subtle bug here—we never actually removed max_node from its original place in the tree! This means that somewhere in the tree, there's a pointer to max_node that points back up the tree. Moreover, the original child trees of max_node are no longer available.

We need to remove max_node from the tree. Fortunately, we know that max_node has no right subtree, only a left subtree, meaning it has at most one child,[39] so it falls into one of the easy cases to handle. We only need to modify the parent of max_node to point to max_node's left subtree.

We can write a simple function that, given a pointer to max_node and the head of the tree containing max_node, returns a new tree that properly removes max_node. Note that it relies on the fact that max_node has no right subtree!

```
node* remove_max_node (node* p_tree, node* p_max_node)
{
        // defensive coding--shouldn't actually hit this
        if ( p_tree == NULL )
        {
                return NULL;
        }
        // we found the node, now we can replace it
        if ( p_tree == p_max_node )
        {
                // the only reason we can do this is because we
                // know p_max_node->p_right is NULL so we
                // aren't losing any information. If p_max_node
                // has no left subtree, then we will just
                // return NULL from this branch, which
                // will result in p_max_node being replaced
                // with an empty tree, which is what we want.
                return p_max_node->p_left;
        }
        // each recursive call replaces the right subtree
        // tree with a new subtree that does not contain
        // p_max_node.
        p_tree->p_right =
                remove_max_node( p_tree->p_right, p_max_node );
```

---

[39] We know this because it is the maximum value of a subtree, so it cannot have a node to its right.

```
      return p_tree;
}
```

With this helper function, we can now easily modify the `remove` function so that we remove the max node from the left subtree before replacing the node to remove with the max node.

```
node* remove (node* p_tree, int key)
{
      if ( p_tree == NULL )
      {
            return NULL;
      }
      if ( p_tree->key_value == key )
      {
            // the first two cases handle having zero or
            // one child node
            if ( p_tree->p_left == NULL )
            {
                  node* p_right_subtree = p_tree->p_right;
                  delete p_tree;
                  // this might return NULL if there are
                  // zero child nodes, but that is what we
                  // want anyway
                  return p_right_subtree;
            }
            if ( p_tree->p_right == NULL )
            {
                  node* p_left_subtree = p_tree->p_left;
                  delete p_tree;
                  // this will always return a valid node,
                  // since we know p_tree->p_left is not
                  // NULL from the previous if statement
                  return p_left_subtree;
            }
            node* p_max_node = find_max( p_tree->p_left );
            // since p_max_node came from the left subtree,
            // we need to remove it from that subtree
            // before re-linking that subtree back into the
            // rest of the tree
            p_max_node->p_left =
                  remove_max_node(
                        p_tree->p_left,
                        p_max_node
                  );
            p_max_node->p_right = p_tree->p_right;
            delete p_tree;
            return p_max_node;
```

```
        }
        else if ( key < p_tree->key_value )
        {
                p_tree->p_left = remove( p_tree->p_left, key );
        }
        else
        {
                p_tree->p_right =
                        remove( p_tree->p_right, key );
        }
        return p_tree;
}
```

Let's look what this code would do with our example tree from earlier:

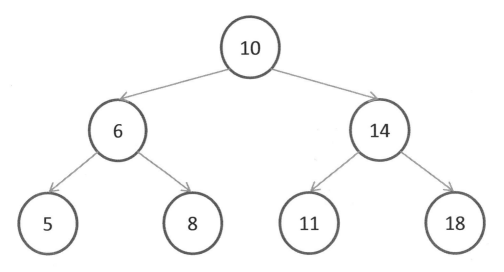

If we remove 10 from the tree, the `remove` function will immediately hit the "found" case. It will find that there are both left and right subtrees, so it will find the node with the maximum value in the subtree headed by 6. That node is 8. It will then link 8's left subtree to point to the new subtree headed by 6, but that does not contain 8.

Removing 8 from the subtree is easy. We start off with this subtree:

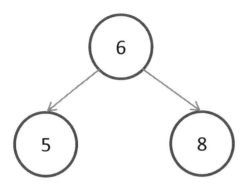

The first call to `remove_max_node` sees that 6 is not the correct node to remove, so `remove_max_node` is recursively called on the subtree headed by 8. Since 8 is the node we're looking for, 8's left subtree (NULL) is returned, and 6's right pointer changes to point to NULL. We now have the tree:

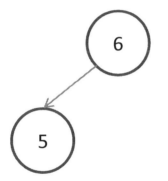

In the call to `remove`, we now have the tree that was returned from `remove_max_node` (shown above) set into the left pointer of the 8 node, so our new tree is:

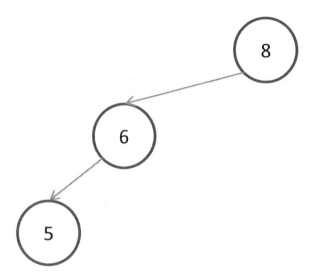

Finally, the right pointer of 8 is set to the right subtree headed by 14, and our tree is now fully rebuilt:

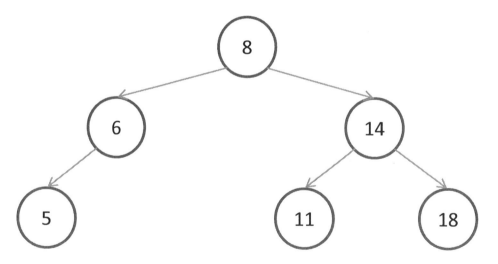

And then we free the original 10 node.

You can find the entire source code from this chapter, along with a simple program that lets you manipulate the tree, in the file binary_tree.cpp.

Real world use of binary trees

Although I've talked a lot about being able to quickly search for stuff, you might be wondering: does it really matter how fast you can find a particular value in a data structure? Aren't computers really fast? And when do I need to do all of these lookups anyway?

In general, there are two cases where searching is important. The first is checking for whether you already have a particular value. For example, if you have a game that allows users to register a username, you would want to be able to check whether a particular username is already taken when the user registers. If you're working on a game like World of Warcraft, you want to be able to do this check really fast even with millions of users. Since usernames are actually strings, rather than integers, they will also take longer to compare since you must do a comparison on each individual letter. This will not take so long that it will be slow if you do it a few times, but it is slow enough to add up over millions of comparisons. So using a binary tree to store usernames would certainly make the sign-up experience much better—and if you are trying to get users to play your online game, you definitely want it to be easy to sign up.

Another common situation where you want fast look-ups is when you have some additional data associated with the value being stored. This data structure is called a **map**. A map stores a key and a value associated with that key (the value doesn't have to be a single piece of data—it can be a structure or even a list or another map, if you need to store a lot of information).

For example, take a game like World of Warcraft. Any massively multiplayer online game will need to have a map from your username to your password,[40] to handle logins and probably also your character's stats. Each time you log in with your username and password, World of Warcraft would look up your username in the map and find the associated password, compare the password

---

[40] In practice, the password itself won't be stored in the map. Instead, a **hashed** version of the password would be stored. A **hash** is an algorithm that turns a string of text into another string of text (or into a number) in a way that makes the original value unrecoverable. In this case, the hashed version of the password would make it impossible to get the original password. Storing passwords in hashed form prevents passwords from being stolen by looking in the file or database that stores the passwords. Passwords are hashed using algorithms that make it highly unlikely that two passwords will hash to the same string.

against what the user typed in, and if the password is valid, retrieve the rest of the character information and let the user play the game.

You could implement such a map by using a binary tree. To implement a map as a binary tree, the binary tree would use the key for inserting nodes (in this case, the username) and store the value (in this case, the password) in the same node, next to the key.

The concept of a map shows up all the time. For example, on an even larger scale, credit card companies would want to use a map of some sort as well—every time you make a purchase with your credit card, some data about your account needs to be changed. Hundreds of millions of people have credit cards; doing a scan through that many credit card numbers on every credit card transaction would grind commerce to a halt around the world. The basic idea is that you need to be able to look up account balances very quickly, given a credit card number. To do this, you could again use a binary tree to build a map from each credit card number to the account balance associated with that number. Now every credit card transaction can be a simple search of a binary tree for a node, and then an update to the balance stored in that node.

If you have a million credit card numbers, with a balanced tree, this lookup will average looking at $\log_2 1000000$ nodes, which works out to about 20 nodes. That's 50,000 times better than doing a linear scan through the list of nodes. There's no doubt that credit card companies have even more sophisticated data structures than binary trees at work here. For one thing, all the account information needs to be stored permanently in a database rather than just temporarily in memory. There may also be more sophisticated, complex structures beyond simple maps. The important point is that the idea of the binary tree and the map are building blocks that can be used to build those more sophisticated structures.

Finally, quick lookups matter even on a smaller scale. For example, your cell phone probably has a feature where it will show you the name of any caller in your phone's address book. That's another example where you want to be able to quickly look up a name by a number (in this case, a telephone number). I don't know how cell phones are actually implemented—address books may not be large enough to get a significant advantage out of a binary tree—but it's another case where you want to use the concept of a map for its organizational power, and maps are often built as a binary tree structure in order to allow fast lookups.[41]

Cost of building trees and maps

Building a map using a binary tree will take some time. You have to add every node into the tree, and each node will take on average $\log_2 n$ operations to be added (the same as searching for a node since adding and searching both cut the tree in half each time). That means that it will actually take $n \log_2 n$ operations to build your entire tree. Since each linear search in a linked list would look at an average of about $\frac{n}{2}$ nodes, if you do $2\log_2 n$ searches on a linked list, then you're spending about as much time doing these searches as it would take to build a binary tree. (Why is that? The total time is the average time of each search times the number of searches: $\frac{n}{2} \times 2\log_2 n = n\log_2 n$.) In other words, you don't want to construct a binary tree if you're only going to use it once, but if you know it'll be used many times, go for it (even a map of a million nodes needs only about 40 lookups to occur to increase average performance). For a credit card company processing millions of transactions, it's a clear win. For a cell phone, it will depend on how many phone calls you get and the size of the address book. (Try doing some of the math to see if you think it would be useful for your cell phone.)

Quiz yourself

1. What is the primary virtue of a binary tree?
A. It uses pointers
B. It can store arbitrary amounts of data
C. It allows fast lookups of data
D. It is easy to remove from the binary tree

2. When would you consider using a linked list instead of a binary tree?
A. When you need to maintain data in a way that allows fast lookups
B. When you want to be able to access the elements in sorted order
C. When you need to be able to quickly add to the front or end, but never access items in the middle
D. When you don't need to free the memory you are using

3. Which of the following is a true statement?

---

[41] There are other data structures, including the hash table, that are also used for implementing maps.

A. The order in which you add items to a binary tree can change the tree structure

B. A binary tree should have items inserted in sorted order to provide the best structure

C. A linked list will be faster than a binary tree for finding elements if the elements are inserted in random order to the binary tree

D. A binary tree can never be reduced to having the same structure as a linked list

4. Which of the following describes why binary trees are fast at finding nodes?

A. They aren't—having two pointers means you have to do more work to traverse the tree

B. Each level you go down the tree, you cut the number of remaining nodes you have to search through approximately in half

C. They aren't really any better than linked lists

D. Recursive calls on binary trees are faster than looping over a linked list

(View solution on page 501)

Practice problems

1. Write a program to display the contents of a binary tree. Can you write a program that prints the nodes in a binary tree in sorted order? What about in reverse sorted order?

2. Write a program that counts the number of nodes in a binary tree.

3. Write a program that checks whether a binary tree is properly balanced.

4. Write a program that checks if the binary tree is properly sorted so that all nodes to the left of a given node are less than the value of that node, and all nodes to the right are greater than the value of that node.

5. Write a program that deletes all of the nodes in a binary tree without using recursion.

6. Implement a simple map, in the form of a binary tree, that holds an address book; the key for the map should be a person's name and the value should be the person's email address. You should provide the ability to add email addresses to the map, remove email addresses, update email addresses, and of

course find email addresses. You'll also want to clean up your address book when your program shuts down. As a reminder, you can use any of the standard C++ comparison operators (such as ==, < or >) to compare two strings.

Chapter 18
The Standard Template Library

It's a great thing to be able to write your own data structures, but it's not as common as you might have gathered from the last chapter. Don't worry; I didn't make you read through that for nothing! You learned a lot about how to build your own data structures when you *do* need them, you learned the properties of several common data structures, and there are times when it does make sense to write your own implementations of data structures.

That said, one of the great features of C++ (that isn't available in C) is the large library of reusable code that comes with your compiler; this library is called the **standard template library**, or **STL**. The standard template library is a collection of commonly used data structures, including linked lists and several data structures built on top of binary trees. Each of these data structures allows you to specify the type(s) of data that they store when you create them, so you can use them for holding anything you'd like—integers, strings, or structured data.

Because of that flexibility, in many cases the standard template library replaces the need for you to build your own data structures for your basic programming needs. In fact, the STL allows you to raise the level of your code in a couple of significant ways:

1) You can start to think about your programs in terms of the data structures you need, without having to worry about whether you can implement those data structures yourself

2) You have ready access to world-class implementations of these data structures, with performance and space usage that's very good for most problems

3) You don't need to worry about the memory allocation and deallocation for the data structures you are using

There are some tradeoffs to using the standard template library, though:

1) You will need to learn the interfaces to the standard template library, and how to use them

2) The compiler errors that are generated when you misuse the STL are hideously difficult to read

3) Not every data structure you might want is available in the STL

The STL is a large topic—there are books written just on using the STL, so there's no chance I can cover it all.[42] The purpose of this chapter is to give you an overview of the absolutely most useful and common STL data structures. From here on out, I'll use these data structures when appropriate.

Vectors, a resizable array

The STL has a replacement for the array, called the **vector**. The STL's vector is very similar to an array, but it can be automatically resized without you, the programmer, having to worry about the details of the memory allocation and moving around the existing elements of the vector.

The syntax for using a vector is, however, different from using an array. Here's a comparison of declaring an array vs. a vector:

```
int an_array[ 10 ];
```

---

[42] Effective STL, by Scott Meyers is a good choice.

vs.

```
#include <vector>

using namespace std;
vector<int> a_vector( 10 );
```

First of all, you'll notice that you need to include the `vector` header file to get anywhere at all, and you need to use the namespace `std`. That's because the vector is part of the standard library, similar to `cin` and `cout`.

Second, when you declare a vector, you have to provide the type of data you will store in the vector using angle brackets:

```
vector<int>
```

This syntax uses a feature of C++ called templates (hence the name standard *template* library). The vector type is coded in such a way that it can store any kind of data, as long as you tell the compiler which type of data a particular vector will store. In other words, there are really two types involved here: the type of the data structure, which governs how the data is organized, and the type of data held in that data structure. Templates allow combining different types of data structures with different types of data held in that data structure.

Finally, when you provide the size of the vector, you put it in parentheses instead of brackets:

```
vector<int> a_vector( 10 );
```

This syntax is used when initializing certain kinds of variables—in this case, we are passing the value ten into an initialization routine, called a constructor, that will set up the vector with a size of ten. In upcoming chapters, we'll learn more about constructors and objects that have them.

Once you've created your vector, you can access individual elements the same way you do with an array:

```
for ( int i = 0; i < 10; i++ )
{
    a_vector[ i ] = 0;
    an_array[ i ] = 0;
```

```
}
```

Calling methods on vectors

Vectors provide more than just the basic functionality associated with an array, though. You can do things like add an element past the end of the vector. These operations are provided by functions that are part of the vector. The syntax for using these functions is different from what you've seen before. Vectors take advantage of a C++ feature called the **method**. A method is a function that is declared along with the data type itself (in this case, the vector), and calling a method uses new syntax. Here's an example:

```
a_vector.size();
```

This code calls the method `size` on `a_vector`, returning the size of the vector. It's a bit like accessing a field of a structure, except instead of accessing a field of the structure, you're calling a method that belongs to that structure. Even though the `size` method is clearly doing something to `a_vector`, you do not need to provide `a_vector` as a separate argument to the method! The method syntax knows to pass `a_vector` into the size method as an implicit argument.

You can think of this syntax:

```
<variable>.<function call>( <args> );
```

as calling a function that belongs to the variable's type. In other words, it's sort of like writing

```
<function call>( <variable>, <args> );
```

In our example,

```
a_vector.size();
```

would be like writing

```
size( a_vector );
```

In the coming chapters, we'll talk a lot more about methods and how to declare and use them. For now, just know there many methods that are callable on vectors, and you need to use this special syntax to use them. This method

syntax is the *only* way to make this kind of function call—you can't write `size(
a_vector)`.

Other features of vectors

So what are these great features we get from vectors? Vectors make it easy to increase the number of values they hold without having to do any tedious memory allocation. For example, if you wanted to add more items to your vector, you would write:

```
a_vector.push_back( 10 );
```

This adds one more new item to the vector. Specifically, what it says is, "add the item 10 at the end of the current vector". The vector itself will handle all of the resizing for you! To do this with an array, you'd have to allocate new memory, copy all the values over, and then finally add your new item. Sure, vectors do allocate memory and copy elements internally, but vectors choose smart allocation sizes so that if you are constantly adding new elements, they don't allocate memory on every resize.

A word of warning: even though you can add to the end of a vector using `push_back`, you can't simply use the brackets to get the same effect. This is a quirk of how the language defined the feature—the brackets only let you work with already-allocated data. The reason is likely to avoid doing memory allocation without the user of the code being aware of it.

So writing code like this:

```
vector<int> a_vector( 10 );
a_vector[ 10 ] = 10; // the last valid element is 9
```

will not actually work—it might crash your program, and it's certainly dangerous. Whereas if you write

```
vector<int> a_vector( 10 );
// add a new element to the vector
a_vector.push_back( 10 );
```

The vector will be resized so that it will have a new size, 11.

Maps

We've already talked a little bit about the idea of a map—taking one value and using it to look up another. This comes up all the time in programming—implementing an email address book where you look up an address by a name, looking up account information by account number, or allowing a user to log in to a game.

The STL provides a very convenient map type, which allows you to specify the types of the key and the value. For example, a data structure to hold a simple email address book, similar to the one you may have created as part of the exercises in the last chapter, could be implemented like this:

```
#include <map>
#include <string>

using namespace std;

map<string, string> name_to_email;
```

Here, we need to tell the map data structure about two different types—the first type, string, is for the key, and the second type, also a string, is for the value, which in this case is an email address.

One great feature of the STL map is that when you actually use the map, you can use the same syntax as an array!

To add a value to a map, you'd treat it like an array, except instead of using an integer you use the key type:

```
name_to_email[ "Alex Allain" ] =
     "webmaster@cprogramming.com";
```

To get a value out of a map is almost exactly the same:

```
cout << name_to_email[ "Alex Allain" ];
```

How's that for convenient! All the simplicity of using an array but the ability to store any type. Even better, unlike with vectors, you don't even need to set the size of the map before you use the [] operator to add elements.

You can also easily remove items from a map.

Let's say you don't want to email me anymore—you can just remove me from your address book with the `erase` method:

```
name_to_email.erase( "Alex Allain" );
```

Bye!

You can also check the size of the map using the `size` method:

```
name_to_address.size();
```

And you can check if a map is empty by using the `empty` method:

```
if ( name_to_address.empty() )
{
        cout << "You have an empty address book. Don't you
wish you hadn't deleted Alex?";
}
```

This is not to be confused with the way you actually make the map empty, which is the clear method:

```
name_to_address.clear();
```

By the way, the STL containers use a consistent naming convention, so you can use `clear`, `empty` and `size` on vectors as well as maps.

Iterators

In addition to storing data and accessing individual elements, sometimes you just want to be able to go through every item in a particular data structure. If you were using an array, or a vector, you could use the length of the array and read each individual element. What do you do about maps, though? Since maps often have non-numeric keys, it's not always possible to iterate through the keys in a map using a counter variable.

To solve this problem, the STL has a concept called an **iterator**; an iterator is a variable that allows you to sequentially access each element of any given data structure, even if the data structure doesn't normally provide a simple way of doing this. Let's start off by looking at how to use an iterator with a vector and then move on to using an iterator to access elements in a map. The basic idea will be that the iterator stores your position in a data structure, letting you access the element at that position. You can then move to the next element in the data structure by calling a method on the iterator.

Declaring an iterator requires some unusual syntax. Here's what it would look like to declare an iterator for a vector of integers:

```
vector<int>::iterator
```

This syntax basically says that you have a `vector<int>`, and you want to have an iterator that works for this type, hence the `::iterator`. So how do you use an iterator? Since an iterator marks the position in a data structure, you request an iterator from that data structure:

```
vector<int> vec;
vec.push_back( 1 );
vec.push_back( 2 );

vector<int>::iterator itr = vec.begin();
```

The call to the `begin` method returns an iterator that lets you access the first element of the vector. You can think of an iterator as being quite similar to a pointer—it lets you talk about the location of an element in the data structure, or you can use it to get that element. In this case, you can read the first element of the vector with the syntax:

```
cout << *itr; // print out the first element of the vector
```

The star operator is used, just as if you were using a pointer. This should make some sense—an iterator is a way of storing a location, just like a pointer.

To get the next element of the vector, you increment your iterator:

```
itr++;
```

This tells the iterator to go to the next element of the vector.

You can also use the prefix operator:

```
++itr;
```

This approach is slightly more efficient with some iterators.[43]

You can check to see if you're at the end of the iteration by comparing the iterator to the end iterator, which you can get by calling

```
vec.end();
```

So to write code that loops over an entire vector, you would write:

```
for ( vector<int>::iterator itr = vec.begin();
      itr != vec.end();
      ++itr )
{
    cout << *itr << endl;
}
```

This code says: create an iterator, and get the first element of the vector of integers; while the iterator isn't equal to the end iterator, keep iterating through the vector. Print out each element.

There a few minor improvements we can make to this loop. We should avoid making a call to vec.end() every time through the loop:

```
vector<int>::iterator end = vec.end();
for ( vector<int>::iterator itr = vec.begin();
      itr != end;
      ++itr )
{
    cout << *itr << endl;
}
```

And you can actually put multiple variables into the first part of the for loop, so we can make this code a little bit nicer:

```
for ( vector<int>::iterator itr = vec.begin(),
      end = vec.end();
      itr != end; ++itr )
{
```

---

[43] The reason is that the prefix operator (++itr) returns the value of the expression after doing the increment, whereas if you use the postfix operator (itr++) it has to return the previous value of itr, which means that it needs to keep the old value around. The prefix operator already has the value it needs to return, since it has the result of the operation.

```
            cout << *itr << endl;
}
```

We can use a very similar approach to looping over a map. But a map has not just a single value that it stores: it has both a key and a value. How do you get this from the iterator? The iterator, when you dereference it, has two fields, first and second. The first field is the key, and the second field is the value.

```
int key = itr->first; // get key from iterator
int value = itr->second; // get value from iterator
```

Let's take a look at some code that displays the contents of a map in a nice readable format:

```
void displayMap (map<string, string> map_to_print)
{
        for ( map<string, string>::iterator itr =
                    map_to_print.begin(),
                    end = map_to_print.end();
                itr != end;
                ++itr )
        {
                cout << itr->first << " --> "
                        << itr->second << endl;
        }
}
```

This map display code is quite similar to the code that iterates over vectors; the only real difference is the use of the map data structure and the use of first and second on the iterator.

Checking whether a value is in a map

Sometimes with maps, you want to be able to check whether a given key is already stored in the map. For example, if you're looking up someone in an address book, you might want to know if that person isn't actually in the address book. The find method on the map is exactly what you want if you need to see if a value exists in a map and retrieve it, if it does. The find method returns an iterator: either an iterator holding the location of the object with the given key, or the end iterator, if no object was found.

```
map<string, string>::iterator itr =
        name_to_email.find( "Alex Allain" );
if ( itr != name_to_email.end() )
{
```

```
        cout << "How nice to see Alex again. His email is: "
            << itr->second;
}
```

On the other hand, if you just access a map element that isn't in the list using the normal bracket operation:

```
name_to_email[ "John Doe" ];
```

Then the map will insert an empty element for you if the value doesn't already exist. So if you really need to know if a value is in the map or not—use `find`, otherwise you can safely use the bracket operation.

Taking stock of the STL

There is a lot more to the STL than what I've just covered, but you've now learned enough to take advantage of many of the foundational STL types. The `vector` is a complete replacement for arrays, and it can be used in place of linked lists when you don't need to worry about the time it takes to insert or modify the list. There are very few reasons why you'd need to use an array once you have the vector type, and most of those are advanced uses of arrays such as when working with file I/O.

The `map` is probably the single best data type out there—I use map-like structures all the time, and it makes writing sophisticated programs much more natural because you no longer need to worry about how you create many of the data structures. Instead, you can focus on how you solve the problems that you want to solve. In many ways, maps provide a replacement for a basic binary tree—you probably wouldn't implement your own binary tree most of the time, unless you had specific performance requirements or really needed to be able to use the tree structure. That is the true power of the STL—about 80% of the time, it will provide you with the core data structures, so you can write code that solves your specific problem. The other 20% of the time is why you need to know how to build your own data structures.[44]

Some programmers suffer from not-invented-here syndrome—a tendency to use their own code, rather than code someone else wrote. In most cases, you *shouldn't* implement your own data structures—the built-in structures are

---

[44] These aren't scientifically measured statistics; in fact, I just made them up. Your ratio may vary, but I doubt it will ever be 100% in either direction.

typically better, faster and more complete than what you could build yourself. But knowing how to build them will give you greater insight into how to use them, and how to make your own data structures when you do need to.

So when might you need your own data structure? Let's say that you wanted to build a small calculator that lets users input arithmetic expressions and evaluate those inputs using the right order of operations, for example reading in an expression like 5 * 8 + 9 / 3 and then evaluating it so the multiplication and division come before the addition.

It turns out that a very natural way to think about this kind of structure is as a tree. Here's a way to express the expression 5 + 8 + 9 / 3 in a tree form:

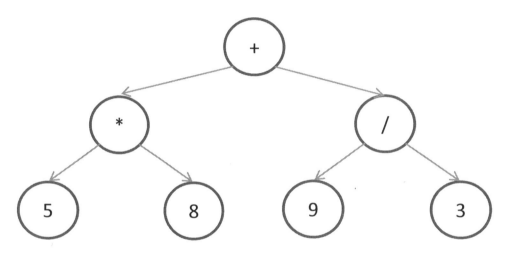

You evaluate each node in one of two ways:

1) If it's a number, return its value
2) If it's an operator, compute the values of the two subtrees and perform the operation

Building such a tree requires that you work with the raw data structure—you're not going to be able to do it with just a map. If your only tool is the STL, it will be hard to solve this problem; if you understand binary trees and recursion, it becomes much simpler.

Learning more about the STL

If you want to learn more about what is available in the STL, there are a few good resources:

The SGI has a website with a great deal of STL documentation: http://www.sgi.com/tech/stl/. Another good resource is Scott Meyer's book *Effective STL*, which will introduce you to many STL concepts and idioms. The site http://en.cppreference.com/w/cpp also has excellent documentation for many STL elements and while not meant as an introduction to the STL, it provides good reference material for the C++ standard library.

Quiz yourself

1. When is using a vector appropriate?
A. When you need to store an association between a key and a value
B. When you need to be able to maximize performance when changing the collection of items
C. When you don't want to worry about the details of updating your data structure
D. Like a suit at a job interview, a vector is always appropriate

2. How do you remove all items at once from a map?
A. Set the item to an empty string
B. Call `erase`
C. Call `empty`
D. Call `clear`

3. When should you implement your own data structures?
A. When you need something really fast
B. When you need something more robust
C. When you need to take advantage of the raw structure of the data, such as building an expression tree
D. You really won't implement your own data structures, unless you like it

4. Which of the following properly declares an iterator you can use with `vector<int>`?
A. `iterator<int> itr;`
B. `vector::iterator itr;`
C. `vector<int>::iterator itr;`
D. `vector<int>::iterator<int> itr;`

5. Which of the following accesses the key of the element an iterator over a map is currently on?

A. `itr.first`

B. `itr->first`

C. `itr->key`

D. `itr.key`

6. How do you tell if an iterator can be used?

A. Compare it with `NULL`

B. Compare it to the result of calling `end()` on the container you are iterating over

C. Check it against 0

D. Compare it with result of calling `begin()` on the container you are iterating over

(View solution on page 502)

Practice problems

1. Implement a small address book program that allows users to enter names and email addresses, remove or change entries, and list the entries in their address book. Don't worry about saving the address book to disk; it's ok to lose the data when the program exits.[45]

2. Use vectors to implement a high score list for a video game. Make it so that scores are updated automatically, and new scores are added into the right place in the list. You may find the SGI website listed above useful for finding more operations you can do on vectors.

3. Write a program with two options: register user and log in. Register user allows a new user to create a login name and password. Log in allows a user to log in and access a second area, with options for "change password" and "log out". Change password allows the user to change the password, and log out will return the user to the original screen.

---

[45] This is only true because you are both the programmer and the user ☺

Chapter 19
More about Strings

Wow, we've just gone through a ton of difficult material! Congratulations on getting through that! Let's take a short break from learning new data structures and go back to working with a data structure you've already seen: the humble string. Despite their simplicity, strings are used all over the place; many programs are written almost entirely in order to read in and modify strings. You often want to read in strings to display back to the user, but you'll also often want to get some meaning out of a string. For example, you might want to look for a specific value in a string to implement a search function. You might read a bunch of tabular data separated by commas, implement a high score list, or create an interface for a text-based adventure game. One of the most common apps you use every day, the web browser, is largely a giant string processor—processing HTML web pages. All of these problems require you to be able to do more than just read in and print back a string as a whole.

Strings can also be quite large, holding lots of characters in memory, and so we can take advantage of some of the features we just learned about—specifically references—to create maximally efficient programs even when passing strings between functions. This chapter will introduce you to a variety of operations you can use to work with strings as well as explain how to keep your program fast when using them. In the practice problems, you'll get a chance to write some interesting string processing code that gives you a chance to learn the power of string manipulation.

Reading in strings

Sometimes when you read in a string to your program, you want to read an entire line rather than using the normal space separator that allows you to read a word at a time.

There is a special function, `getline`, which reads an entire line at a time. Getline takes an "input stream", and reads a line of text from that stream. An example of an input stream is `cin`, which you normally use to read a word at a time. (Let me let you in on a little secret that I haven't mentioned yet: the `cin` method is really an object, like a string or vector, that is a type called input stream, and `cin>>` is the method that reads in data. Explaining all of that in the first chapter didn't seem like a good idea!)

Here's a basic example that demonstrates reading a single line from the user:

```
#include <iostream>
#include <string>

using namespace std;

int main ()
{
    string input;
    cout << "Please enter a line of text: ";
    getline( cin, input, '\n' );
    cout << "You typed in the line " << '\n' << input;
}
```
Sample Code 41: getline.cpp

This program reads a sequence of characters into the string `input`, until the newline character is hit—in other words, until the user presses enter.

The newline itself will be discarded—your input will contain everything up to the newline, but if you want a newline in the string, you will have to add it yourself if you want it. You can use any character you want, not just newline, as the marker to stop reading. (This character is called a **delimiter**, because it indicates the limit of what should be read.) The user will still need to press enter before `getline` returns, but only the text up to the delimiter will be read in.

Let's look at an example that shows you how to read in text formatted using the comma separated value (CSV) format. CSV formatted data looks like this:

Sam, Jones, 40 Asparagus Ave, New York, New York, USA

Each comma separates one section of data; it's like having a spreadsheet but instead of having columns in a spreadsheet, you have columns separated by commas. Let's write a program that can read in CSV data entered by a user that stores a roster of players in a video game with the format:

```
<player first name>,<player last name>,<player class>
```

When you read the section on file I/O later in this book, you'll be able to make a few modifications to this program and read in CSV files from disk, but for now we'll just read in values from the user. This program will end when the first name is empty.

```cpp
#include <iostream>
#include <string>

using namespace std;

int main ()
{
    while ( 1 )
    {
        string first_name;
        getline( cin, first_name, ',' );

        if ( first_name.size () == 0 )
        {
            break;
        }
        string last_name;
        getline( cin, last_name, ',' );

        string player_class;
        getline( cin, player_class, '\n' );
        cout << first_name << " " << last_name
            << " is a " << player_class << endl;
    }
}
```
Sample Code 42: csv.cpp

Notice the use of the `size` method on string, allowing us to detect if we have an empty string. This is just one of the many methods available on strings.

String length and accessing individual elements

To find the length of a string, you can use either the `length` or `size` function that you just saw. These functions are part of the string class, and each returns the number of characters in a string:

```
string my_string1 = "ten chars.";
int len = my_string1.length(); // or .size();
```

There is no difference between the `size` and `length` methods—use whichever feels more natural.[46]

Strings can be indexed numerically, like an array. For instance, you could iterate over all of the characters in a string, accessing each character by index, as though the string were an array. This is useful if you wanted to work with individual characters of string—for example, looking for a specific character like a comma.

Note that the use of the `length` or `size` function is important here so that you don't try to go past the end of a string—just like going past the end of an array, going past the end of a string would be dangerous.

Here's a small example that demonstrates looping over a string in order to display it:

```
for( int i = 0; i < my_string.length(); i++ )
{
    cout << my_string[ i ];
}
```

Searching and substrings

The string class supports simple searching and substring retrieval using the methods `find`, `rfind`, and `substr`. The `find` method takes a substring and a position in the original string and finds the first occurrence of the substring starting from the given position. The result is either the index of the first occurrence of the substring, or a special integer value, `string::npos`, which indicates no substring was found.

---

[46] The reason that both methods exist is that `size` is used across all STL container objects, so size is included for consistency. To most programmers working with strings, using the term `length` sounds more natural.

This sample code searches for every instance of the string "cat" in a given string and counts the total number of instances:

```cpp
#include <iostream>
#include <string>

using namespace std;

int main ()
{
      string input;
      int i = 0;
      int cat_appearances = 0;

      cout << "Please enter a line of text: ";
      getline( cin, input, '\n' );

      for ( i = input.find( "cat", 0 );
            i != string::npos;
            i = input.find( "cat", i ) )
{

            cat_appearances++;
            // Move past the last discovered instance to
            // avoid finding same string again
            i++;
      }
      cout << "The word cat appears " << cat_appearances
            << " in the string " << '"' << input << '"';

}
```
Sample Code 43: search.cpp

If you want to find a substring starting from the end of the string, you can use the `rfind` function in almost the exact same way, except that the search goes backward from the starting point, rather than forward. (String matches are still left-to-right—that is, calling `rfind` to search for "cat" would not match on the string "tac".)

The `substr` function creates a new string containing a slice of the string of a given length, beginning at a given position:

```cpp
// sample prototype
string substr (int position, int length);
```

For instance, to extract the first ten characters of a string, you might write

```cpp
#include <iostream>
```

```
#include <string>

using namespace std;

int main ()
{
    string my_string = "abcdefghijklmnop";
    string first_ten_of_alphabet =
    my_string.substr( 0, 10 );
    cout << "The first ten letters of the alphabet are "
        << first_ten_of_alphabet;
}
```

Passing by reference

Strings can be quite large, holding a lot of data. Of course, not every string is going to be large, but in general it is a good practice to take a string parameters by reference:

```
void printString (string& str);
```

As a refresher: a reference parameter is a bit like a pointer—rather than copying the string variable, a reference is passed to the original string variable:

```
string str_to_show = "there is one x in this string";
printString( str_to_show );
```

Here, rather than copying the variable `str_to_show`, the `printString` takes the address of the variable; the `str` parameter can be used just like the original string.

But there is a possible downside to passing by reference—remember that a reference takes the address of the original variable, so your function can modify the variable. While you probably won't do this by accident when you first write your function, when you go back and maintain it—adding new functionality— you might forget that the variable passed in is not supposed to change and, gasp, modify it. Someone calling the function will be shocked to discover that their data has been changed!

C++ provides a mechanism to prevent accidental modification of reference parameters. The function can specify that the reference is constant. C++ has a special keyword to designate that a reference is constant, `const`. A `const` reference cannot be modified, but it can be read.

```
void print_string (const string& str)
{
     cout << str; // legal, doesn't modify str
     str = "abc"; // not legal!
}
```

Whenever you add a reference parameter to a function, consider whether the function should modify the reference or not. If you do not want to modify the parameter, mark it as const to ensure that the function does not—and cannot—modify the parameter. Using const makes it totally clear that the parameter will not be modified.

Const isn't limited to references. You can also do the same thing with memory pointed to by a pointer. In this case, you could write something like:

```
void print_ptr (const int* p_val)
{
     if ( p_val == NULL ) // ok, memory p_val points to
                          // not modified
     {
          return;
     }
     cout << *p_val; // ok, memory access is ok
     *p_val = 20; // NOT ok, memory p_val points to is
                  // modified
     p_val = NULL; // ok, not modifying memory, just the
                   // pointer itself
}
```

Notice that your compiler is awfully clever and can tell if your code is assigning a value to the memory pointed to or not. It looks beyond just whether the pointer is being dereferenced to see what is being done with the reference. It is perfectly legitimate to modify the pointer itself because the pointer's value is copied; changing p_val has no effect on the variable passed into the function.

You can also use const more broadly, to document and enforce that any given variable will never change. If you ever do try to modify it, the compiler will tell you that you're doing something that you did not intend to do. When you declare a const variable, you must assign to it immediately (since you can never change it again).

```
const int x = 4; // ok to assign when the variable is
```

```
                    // created
x = 4; // not ok, x can't be modified
```

It is good programming style to use `const` whenever possible. Making a variable `const` makes it much easier to read the rest of the code because you know that no one will modify it, so once you see an assignment to that variable, you can be sure it won't change later. You don't have to keep track of whether it takes on some other value. You are free to focus on what happens to the non-`const` variables, and whether they are modified. It also ensures that you don't later modify the variable by accident, changing the behavior of code that assumed the variable had the same value that it started with.

For example, if you have some code that prompts a user for a first and last name, and then creates a new string that contains the user's full name, you would make that full name variable `const` since it shouldn't change.

Const propagation

Const is viral. Once you have declared a variable as `const`, it cannot be passed by reference into a method that takes a non-const reference, and it can't be passed by pointer to a method that takes a non-const pointer since that method might try to modify the value via the pointer. A `const X*` is a different type than an `X*` and a `const X&` (declaring a reference to an X) is a different type than an `X&`. You can convert an `X*` to a `const X*` or an `X&` to a `const X&`, but you can't go the other way. For example, if you write a method like this, it will not compile:

```
void print_nonconst_val (int& p_val)
{
        cout << p_val;
}

const int x = 10;

// will not compile, cannot pass a const int to a function
// taking a non-const reference
print_nonconst_val( x );
```

This restriction only applies to reference and pointers, where the original value is being shared. If the variable is copied, such as when passing by value, you don't need to make the function parameter `const`:

```
void print_nonconst_val (int val)
```

```
{
    cout << val;
}

const int x = 10;

// fine, x is copied, so it doesn't matter that val isn't
// const since it's local to the print_nonconst_val
// function
print_nonconst_val( x );
```

As a result, as soon as you make one variable const, you may find that you need to make other variables const—especially pointer and reference function parameters.

Using const can be tricky if you are working with a library or a set of helper methods that do not use const-ness anywhere. On the other hand, if you are building a library or your own helper methods, you should use const, so that the code that uses your methods can also take advantage of const-ness.

The C++ standard library is built with const-ness in mind, so that you can safely use const variables in your own code and use those variables with the standard library.

Throughout the rest of the book, I will use const variables when appropriate.

One thing to be aware of is that you can declare a variable to be const inside of a loop, even if you reset the variable each time through the loop:

```
for ( int i = 0; i < 10; i++ )
{
    const i_squared = i * i;
    cout << i_squared;
}
```

The variable i_squared can be declared const even though it is being set each time through the loop. The reason is that the variable i_squared has a scope that is entirely within the loop body. Each time through the loop, the i_squared variable is, from the compiler's perspective, recreated.

Const and the STL

In the last chapter on the STL, we looked at a function that could display a map. You might have noticed that the map is being passed by value, which means the whole map needs to be copied to get passed into the `displayMap` function. Here's that function again:

```
// map is copied!
void displayMap (map<string, string> map_to_print)
{
    for ( map<string, string>::iterator itr =
            map_to_print.begin(),
            end = map_to_print.end();
        itr != end;
        ++itr )
    {
        cout << itr->first << " --> " << itr->second
            << endl;
    }
}
```

It would be great to use references here to avoid copying the map by making it a reference, and it would be even better to make it a const reference, to make it clear that this is purely a display function, not something that edits the map in any way.

```
void displayMap (const map<string, string>& map_to_print)
{
    for ( map<string, string>::iterator itr =
            map_to_print.begin(),
            end = map_to_print.end();
        itr != end;
        ++itr )
    {
        cout << itr->first << " --> " << itr->second
            << endl;
    }
}
```

If you do this, you'll run into a wall of compiler errors! The problem is that by making the map `const`, you're saying that no one should be able to modify elements in the map, but iterators allow modifications to the map. For example, you could write:

```
if ( itr->first == "Alex Allain" )
{
```

```
        itr->second = "webmaster2@cprogramming.com"
}
```

In order to change my address in your address book. Fortunately, the STL is const-friendly and all of the STL containers have a second, special, kind of iterator, called a `const_iterator`. You can use `const_iterator` just like a normal iterator, except that you cannot modify the container you're iterating over by writing to the `const_iterator`:

```
void displayMap (const map<string, string>& map_to_print)
{
    for ( map<string, string>::const_iterator itr =
            map_to_print.begin(),
            end = map_to_print.end();
          itr != end;
          ++itr )
    {
        cout << itr->first << " --> " << itr->second
            << endl;
    }
}
```

You must always use a `const_iterator` when the container you want to iterate over is `const`, and it's a good idea to use one whenever you want to use an iterator for accessing data but not for modifying the container.

Quiz yourself

1. Which of the following is valid code?
A. `const int& x;`
B. `const int x = 3; int *p_int = & x;`
C. `const int x = 12; const int *p_int = & x;`
D. `int x = 3; const int y = x; int& z = y;`

2. Which of these function signatures allows the following code to compile: const int x = 3; fun(x);
A. `void fun (int x);`
B. `void fun (int& x);`
C. `void fun (const int& x);`
D. `A and C`

3. What's the best way to tell if a string search failed?
A. Compare the result position to 0

B. Compare the result position to -1

C. Compare the result position to `string::npos`

D. Check if the result position is greater than the length of the string

4. How do you create an iterator for a const STL container?

A. Declare the iterator `const`

B. Use indices to loop over it rather than using an iterator

C. Use a `const_iterator`

D. Declare the template types to be `const`

(View solution on page 504)

Practice problems

Note: for all practice problems, use const and const references whenever appropriate! This means that almost any time you write a function that takes a string, you will probably want to pass it by const reference.

1. Write a program that reads in two strings, a "needle" and a "haystack" and counts the number of times the "needle" appears in the "haystack".

2. Write a program that allows a user to type in tabular data similar to a CSV file, but instead of using commas a separator, you should try to detect valid separators. First let the user type in the lines of tabular data. Then detect possible separator characters by looking through the input for non-number, non-letter, non-space characters. Find all of these characters that appear on every single line, and display the user these characters to ask which one to use. For example, if you see input like this:

Alex Allain, webmaster@cprogramming.com
John Smith, john@nowhere.com

You should prompt the user to choose between comma, at sign, and period for the separator.

3. Write a program that reads in HTML text that the user types in (don't worry, we'll cover how to read from a file later). It should support the following HTML tags: <html>, <head>, <body>, <b>, <i>, and <a>. Each HTML tag has an open tag, e.g. <html>, and a closing tag that has a forward-slash at the start: </html>. Inside the tag is text that is controlled by that tag: <b>text to be bolded</b> or

<i>text to be italicized</i>. The <head> </head> tags control text that is metadata, and the <body></body> tags surround text that is to be displayed. <a> tags are used for hyperlinks, and have an URL in the following format: <a href=URL>text</a>.

Once your program has read in some HTML, it should simply ignore <html>. It should remove any text from the <head> section so that it doesn't show up when you output it. It should then display all text in the body, modifying it so that any text between a <b> and a </b> will show up with asterisks (*) around it, any text inside <i> and </i> will show up with underscores (_) around it, and any text with a <a href=linkurl>link text</a> tag shows up as link text (linkurl).

Chapter 20
Debugging with Code::Blocks

You've now learned many powerful programming techniques, but it can be difficult to track down bugs in more complicated programs. Fortunately, there is a tool that can help you with this, called a **debugger**. A debugger is a tool that allows you to check the state of your program while it's running to make it easier to understand what it's really doing. New programmers often put off learning to use a debugger because it seems onerous or unnecessary. It is true that you have to learn the tool in order to use it. But not learning to use a debugger is penny-wise, pound-foolish. Debuggers save scads of time—using a debugger is like learning to walk instead of crawl. You'll need some practice, and you'll stumble along at first—but when you get it working, you'll really be cranking.

This chapter will cover the Code::Blocks debugger, since you should have it already installed if you're running Windows and went through the Code::Blocks setup from earlier. However, the concepts are generic, and there are many different debuggers. I've provided plenty of screenshots so that you can follow along even if you aren't using Windows, so you can see what a debugger looks like. Your development environment will almost certainly have its own debugger.[47]

Throughout this chapter, I'll use buggy programs to demonstrate real-live debugging. For each example, you can create a new Code::Blocks project with this program (or create a project in your development environment of choice) if you want to follow along.

The first program below is supposed to compute interest rates, compounded annually, on a particular amount of money. Unfortunately, it has a bug and prints out the wrong value.

```cpp
#include <iostream>
using namespace std;

double computeInterest (double base_val, double rate, int
years)
{
        double final_multiplier;
        for ( int i = 0; i < years; i++ )
        {
                final_multiplier *= (1 + rate);
        }
        return base_val * final_multiplier;
}

int main ()
{
        double base_val;
        double rate;
        int years;
        cout << "Enter a base value: ";
        cin >> base_val;
        cout << "Enter an interest rate: ";
        cin >> rate;
        cout << "Enter the number of years to compound: ";
        cin >> years;
```

---

[47] If you run Linux, you can use GDB. If you are using Visual Studio or Visual Studio Express, it comes with its own very good debugger. There are also other standalone debuggers you can use that are beyond the scope of this book, including WinDbg, which comes as part of Microsoft's Debugging Tools for Windows: http://www.microsoft.com/whdc/devtools/debugging/default.mspx. Apple Xcode also provides a debugger.

```
        cout << "After " << years << " you will have "
             << computeInterest( base_val, rate, years )
             << " money" << endl;
}
```

Sample Code 44: bug1.cpp

Here's the result of running this program:

```
Enter a base value: 100
Enter an interest rate: .1
Enter the number of years to compound: 1
After 1 you will have 1.40619e-306 money
```

Not so good! $1.40618e-306$ is definitely the wrong amount of money! Clearly we have a bug. Let's try running this in a debugger to see where our problem comes from.

Starting out

We need to make sure that Code::Blocks is properly configured to make debugging easy.

To do this, we need to produce what are called **debugging symbols**. Debugging symbols let the debugger figure out which line of code is currently being executed so that you can know where you are in the program. To make sure you have your symbols set up correctly, in Code::Blocks go to Project|Build Options. You should see a dialog like this:

You want to make sure that you have the "Produce debugging symbols" option checked for the "Debug" target. You will also want to make sure that you have selected "Debug" as the target for the project, under Build|Select Target|Debug.

This will make sure that you build your program using the debugging symbols that you set up for the "Debug" target.

If you don't have both a "Debug" and a "Release" target, then you can just set the "Produce debugging symbols [-g]" checkbox for your current build target.[48] Also make sure that "Strip all symbols from binary (minimizes size) [-s]" is NOT checked. (You normally create these build target types when creating your project. The easiest way to make sure that you've got the right settings is to just go with the Code::Blocks defaults during project setup.)

Once everything is set up, you're ready to go. If you built your program earlier but had to change your configuration, you will need to rebuild it now. Once that's done, you are able to debug!

Breaking in

The value of the debugger is that it lets us see what the program is doing—what code is executing and the values of our variables. To look at this information, we need to have it **break** into the program, but not in the burglary sense; we need to make our debugger pause the program execution. We do this by setting a breakpoint somewhere in the program and then running the program under the debugger. The debugger will execute the program until it hits the line of code with the breakpoint. At that point, the debugger will let you look around your program or advance the program line-by-line and check how the each line of code affects your variables.

Let's set a breakpoint early in the program, at the start of the main function, so we can watch the execution of the entire program. To do that, put your cursor on the line

```
double base_val;
```

and go to "Debug|Toggle Breakpoint" (or press F5). This will set a little red dot on the sidebar next to this line of code—this dot tells you that this line is a breakpoint:

---

[48] If you are using g++ then you need to provide the −g command line argument to the compiler in order to produce symbols. If you're using Xcode, it will automatically take care of including symbols.

```
15        int main()
16     □ {
17 ●          double base_val;
18             double rate;
19             int years;
20             cout << "Enter a base value: ";
21             cin >> base_val;
22             cout << "Enter an interest rate: ";
23             cin >> rate;
24             cout << "Enter the number of years to compound: ";
25             cin >> years;
```

You can set or unset the breakpoint using the toggle breakpoint command, or you can click on the dot.

Now that we have a breakpoint, we can execute our program! Go to Debug|Start (or press F8).

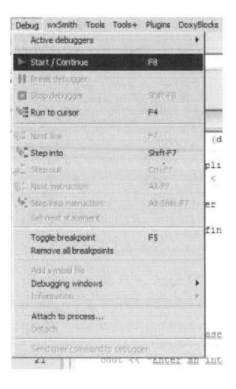

Once you do this, your program will execute as it normally would, until the breakpoint is hit. In this case, it will hit the breakpoint pretty much immediately since it's the first line of the program.

Now you should see the debugger open, and it should look something like this:

(There may also be some other windows open—we'll talk about those in a minute.) The first thing to notice is the yellow triangle below the red dot. This triangle shows you the line of code that will execute next. It's a couple of lines below our dot. It's not right on the dot because there isn't really any machine code—the code the processor executes that resulted from compiling your C++ code—associated with the variable declarations, so our breakpoint, despite looking like it is on line 17, is actually on line 20! (The numbers to the left of the dot and triangle are line numbers.)

Now we want to take a look at some of the other windows, starting with the "Watches" window. Depending on what version of Code::Blocks you have, this window may have popped open on its own, or you may have to open it. If you don't see the "Watches" window, go to Debug|Debugging Windows|Watches to open it. Depending on what version of Code::Blocks you have, it may have numbers in it, or it might be blank. Here's one example of what it might look like in Code::Blocks 12:

Well, that window looks really useful, doesn't it? But actually, there's a lot you can do here. First, click on the narrow rectangle space on the left; you should get a blinking cursor. From there, you can enter the name of any variable that is in scope. For example, here's what it looks like after manually entering the three variables available to the main function:

This will show you the variable names, along with the value stored in the variable in the middle column, and the variable type on the right. Notice that the values here look like gibberish! The reason is that we haven't initialized them yet—that's what the next couple of lines in the program are for.[49]

In order to execute the next couple of lines, we need to ask the debugger to go to the next line of code. Going to the next line will execute the current line of

---

[49] Remember that variables are not initialized when they are declared.

code (the one with the yellow arrow). The Code::Blocks debugger calls this the "Next line" instruction:

You can use F7 as a keyboard shortcut for "Next line".[50]

Once we've gone to the next line, the program will run the `cout` statement and output a message to the screen asking you to enter a value. If you try to type a value though, it won't work—the program is back in the debugger. Let's press F7 again, to execute the next line of code. After we press F7, the program will wait

---

[50] You might wonder why there's both "Next line" and "Next instruction". We will always use "Next line". "Next instruction" is for debugging without debugging symbols, which is beyond the scope of this book.

for user input because the `cin` function hasn't returned yet—it needs to get user input before it will return. Go ahead and put in the value 100, to match the bug report, and then repeat the process to provide inputs for the next two variables, using the values we put in earlier: .1 for the interest and 1 for the number of years to compound.

Now we're at this line of code:

```
cout << "After " << years << " you will have "
     << computeInterest( base_val, rate, years )
     << " money" << endl;
```

Let's double-check that we handled the inputs correctly. We can do this by using the watch window to check the values of the local variables.

So far, so good—base is 100, the rate is .1, and years is 1. What's that you say? Rate isn't .1? That's true, it is actually .10000000000000001. But that little 1 at the end is just a quirk of how floating-point numbers are represented— remember, they aren't perfectly precise. But it's so small that it won't make a real difference in most programs.[51]

Now that we know everything is ok so far, let's investigate what happens inside the `computeInterest` function. The way to do that is to use another debugger command, "Step Into":

---

[51] It's true, however, that floating-point errors can compound, and in some applications this can cause serious problems. This just isn't one of them.

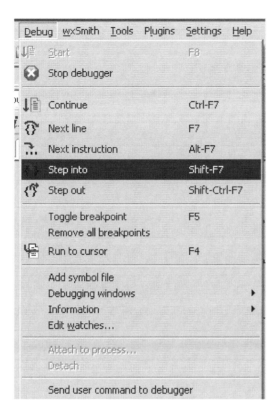

The Step Into command goes *into* the function that is about to be called on the current line, unlike Next, which will merely execute the whole function and show you the result, as we saw with the `cin` function. You use Step Into when you need to debug inside of a function, as we do here.

So let's step into `computeInterest`. But first, you might be wondering, doesn't this line have a bunch of function calls?

```
cout << "After " << years << " you will have "
    << computeInterest( base_val, rate, years )
    << " money" << endl;
```

What about all those `cout` calls? The Code::Blocks debugger is smart—it won't step into functions that are in the standard library. We can just do a step into and it will go directly into `computeInterest`, bypassing the functions that aren't interesting to us. Let's do that now.

Now that we're inside `computeInterest` the first thing to do is verify that the function arguments are correct—maybe we mixed up the order of arguments. The Watches window is now showing us the variables within the scope of the current `computeInterest` function, so let's make sure they're correct:

Watches			☒
base_val	100	double	
rate	0.1000000000000001	double	
years	1	int	
		...	

That all looks right!

Now let's take a look at the other local variables—we'll have to add them to the watches first:

Watches			☒
base_val	100	double	
rate	0.1000000000000001	double	
years	1	int	
i	No symbol "i" in current conte:		
final_multiplier	0	double	
		...	

See anything odd? Well, the window says that there's no symbol `i`. That's because we haven't yet executed the line where `i` is declared, so the window doesn't know about it yet. `final_multiplier` doesn't look right at all, either. But remember that last time we looked at the watch window and saw crazy values it was because the variables weren't initialized yet. Let's use next line (F7) to execute the initialization associated with our loop and see what happens.

It only takes one line to initialize the loop, so we can now check our local variables again—they should look something like this:

So i is just fine, but what about `final_multiplier`? It doesn't look like it's initialized properly. Moreover, the line of code we're on is about to use `final_multiplier`:

```
final_multiplier *= (1 + rate);
```

This line says, multiply `final_multiplier * (1 + rate)`, and reassign that value to `final_multiplier`, but `final_multiplier` is totally off, so this multiplication is going to give a bogus value.

Do you see how to fix this?

We need to initialize `final_multiplier` on the line that declares it. In this case, it should be initialized to 1.

That's it; we've found the problem and we have a solution. Thanks, debugger!

Debugging crashes

Let's take look at another kind of bug—a crash. Crashes are often the scariest bugs for new programmers because they seem so extreme. Over time, though, crashes will be your favorite bugs to track down. The reason is that you will know exactly where the problem happened. The program crashed because it had bad data, and you can stop the program at exactly the point where it crashed to figure out what that bad data was and where it came from.

The following simple (but buggy) program creates a couple of nodes in a linked list, then prints out each value in the list.

```cpp
#include <iostream>

using namespace std;

struct LinkedList
{
      int val;
      LinkedList *next;
};

void printList (const LinkedList *lst)
{
      if ( lst != NULL )
      {
            cout << lst->val;
            cout << "\n";
            printList( lst->next );
      }
}

int main ()
{
      LinkedList *lst;
      lst = new LinkedList;
      lst->val = 10;
      lst->next = new LinkedList;
      lst->next->val = 11;
      printList( lst );

      return 0;
}
```
Sample Code 45: bug2.cpp

When you run this program, however, it won't work. It may crash, or it may go into an infinite loop. Something is not right!

Let's run this under the debugger to see if it can help. Go to Debug|Start, or hit F8.

Almost immediately, the debugger will pop up with a message:

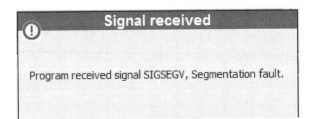

A Segmentation Fault (aka segfault) is caused by using pointers that aren't valid—generally, it means that a program tried to dereference either a NULL pointer or an invalid pointer (either a pointer that was previously freed or a pointer that was never initialized). Think of it as the program trying to access a segment of memory that it didn't have access to.[52]

How can we figure out where the bad pointer came from? Well, the debugger has broken right on the line where the crash happened. Go ahead and hit OK in the dialog, and then look for the yellow arrow to see the line of code that has crashed:

```
cout << lst->val;
```

There's only one pointer on this line—lst. Let's see what the value of lst is— we'll use the watch window. You can see from the watch window that the value of lst is 0xbaadf00d![53] Pretty weird, huh? That's a special value used by the compiler to initialize memory when it is allocated. This feature is only used when running under a debugger, which is why you may see different behavior under the debugger than when running the program outside the debugger. The debugger helps you by using a consistent value that is known to cause a segfault if accessed—that way, if you use an uninitialized pointer, it will show up immediately.[54]

---

[52]Some environments use the term **Access Violation**, which evokes the same meaning.

[53] If you're not familiar with this syntax, it is used for hexadecimal numbers—numbers that are in base 16. These numbers usually are prefixed with 0x and use the letters A-F to mean the digits 10-15. So 0xA in hexadecimal is the same as the number 10 in decimal.

[54] The alternative is to use the value that was stored in the variable previously located where the pointer is stored. Since that memory is unpredictable, and might even appear

Now we know that `lst` was uninitialized. But why wasn't it initialized? Let's use another debugger feature, the **call stack**. To view it, go to Debug|Debug Windows|Call Stack. The call stack shows all of the functions that are currently in the process of executing. Here's what the call stack looks like in the call stack window:

Nr	Address	Function	File	Line
0	00401343	printList(lst=0xbaadf00d)	C:\debugger demos\main.cpp	16
1	00401377	printList(lst=0x5f1090)	C:\debugger demos\main.cpp	18
2	00401377	printList(lst=0x5f1070)	C:\debugger demos\main.cpp	18
3	004013CF	main()	C:\debugger demos\main.cpp	29

There are several columns—Nr is just a number that you can use to refer to each stack frame. Address is the address of the function.[55] Function is the name of the function and the arguments (in fact, you can see that `lst=0xbadf00d` just by looking at the call stack), and you also have the file and line number, so you can find the line of code that was executing.

The top function on the call stack is currently executing, the function beneath it called the current function, etc. The bottom function is `main`, because it is the function that starts the program.

We can see that there were three calls to `printList`, the first two calls have valid pointer values, and the third has `0xbaadf00d`. Remember that our main function created two list nodes. The first two calls to `printList` must be

---

valid, it can make the program behave quite strangely and be more difficult to track down. For example, rather than crashing immediately, it might read bogus memory and crash later when using that memory. The debugger tries to make life easier for you by making the behavior consistent and making sure that the program crashes as early as possible, so you are as close to the original problem as possible.

[55] The function address can be useful if you're debugging at the assembly level, but most of the time you won't be.

using those nodes, and the third call is using an uninitialized pointer. We now know to look at the code that initializes the list again, and we can see that we never set the next value to NULL for the node at the end of the list.

Although we've solved this issue, there are times when you want to find more information about different stack frames. You can switch the debugger's context to go to any stack frame to inspect local variables. To do so, right click on the stack frame you are interested in and select "Switch to this frame":

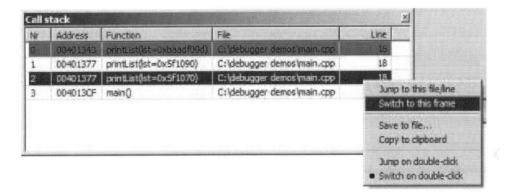

The debugger will move the yellow arrow to show you the function call being made in that stack frame. You will also be able to use the watches window to inspect local variables that are part of that stack frame.

Breaking into a hung program

Sometimes you don't get a simple crash but instead you have a program that is "stuck"—perhaps in an infinite loop or waiting for some slow system call to finish. If you have a situation like this, you can run under the debugger, wait until you hit the problem, and then ask the debugger to break into the program.

Let's use another piece of example code to see how this works:

```
#include <iostream>

using namespace std;

int main ()
{
        int factorial = 1;
        for ( int i = 0; i < 10; i++ )
        {
```

```
            factorial *= i;
    }
    int sum = 0;
    for ( int i = 0; i < 10; i++ )
    {
            sum += i;
    }
    // factorial w/o two
    int factorial_without_two = 1;
    for ( int i = 0; i < 10; i++ )
    {
            if ( i == 2 )
            {
                    continue;
            }
            factorial_without_two *= i;
    }
    // sum w/o two
    int sum_without_two = 0;
    for ( int i = 0; i < 10; i++ )
    {
            if ( i = 2 )
            {
                    continue;
            }
            sum_without_two += i;
    }
}
```

Sample Code 46: bug3.cpp

This program, when you run it, will never exit. It gets stuck somewhere. In order to find out where, we will run it under the debugger, wait for it to get stuck, and then take a look around.

First, build this program and run it under the debugger (Debug|Start or the shortcut F8). Once the program has run, you'll see that it doesn't exit; it's gotten stuck somewhere, presumably some kind of infinite loop. Let's ask the debugger to break into the running program, so we can see what's going on. To do this, go to Debug|Break Debugger. (If you don't see a Break Debugger option, you might be using an older version of Code::Blocks. In that case, you should use Stop Debugger instead. But if you see both Break Debugger and Stop Debugger, make sure to use Break Debugger.) Break Debugger will cause the debugger to break into the program and let you look around at the point of execution. (You can also use it to end the debugging session, if the program is already in the debugger.)

Once you've stopped the program, you should see the call stack (or pull it up again via Debug|Debugging Windows|Call stack if you don't see it)—but in this case, the call stack will look pretty weird—like this:

Call stack				
Nr	Address	Function	File	
0	770C000D	ntdll!LdrFindResource_U()	C:\Windows\system32\ntdll.dll	
1	7714F896	ntdll!RtlQueryTimeZoneInformation()	C:\Windows\system32\ntdll.dll	
2	78BC3672	?? ()		
3		?? ()		

None of that is our code! What's going on here!? What you're seeing is the result of breaking into a running program—notice that the top of the call stack starts with `ntdll`, a core Windows DLL. But where is the program code that was being executed? It turns out that to break into the process, the debugger created another thread—a thread is a way of executing code simultaneously. In order to break into the process the debugger needs to be able to execute some code while our original code was executing. It does this by creating a new thread that executes the break in code. We didn't have this second thread in previous examples because the process was started with an already-set breakpoint, so the debugger had enough control to break in without creating a second thread. In this case, we wanted to be able to break into the program at a point in time, to find out what code was being executed, rather than breaking at a particular line of code. Now, to find our own code, we need to switch to the right thread.

To switch threads, we need to bring up the threads window—Debug|Debugging windows|Running threads:

In the threads window, you will see two threads:

The Active column uses a * to show the current thread—in this case, the thread that was used to break into the process. We want to switch to the other thread, so we can see the information about it. To do that, right click on the other thread, and select "Switch to this thread":

Now we can go back to the call stack, and we see much more understandable information (you may have to press F7 first before anything will populate here):

This is our code. You'll see that the debugger has put the yellow arrow at line 29, indicating that's the next line to be executed. That's this code here:

```
for ( int i = 0; i < 10; i++ )
{
        if ( i = 2 )
        {
                continue;
        }
        sum_without_two += i;
}
```

Since this program was stuck, and we're in the middle of a loop, a good theory is that this loop is not terminating. How can we prove this? Let's step through the program.

We need to be a little careful here, though. If we just do "Next Line" in the debugger, it will execute code from the other thread that was used to break into the process because that is the currently executing thread. Instead of doing "Next line" we need to put in a breakpoint in our own code, and let the program run until it hits our breakpoint.[56] Let's put a breakpoint on the if statement line, and then hit Continue (Ctrl-F7). Once the breakpoint is hit, we'll be on the right thread, and you can go back to using "Next line" to step and see what is happening in the program.

What you'll see is that we are always hitting the `if ( i = 2 )` statement and then going to the start of the loop.

What's going on here? Let's take a look at the value of `i` in the locals window. When we're on the loop line, `i` is two. After executing the for loop code, `i` is 3. Then when we execute the if statement line, you can see that `i` drops back to two!

It looks like someone is setting the value of `i` to two—in this case, it must be the if statement. And indeed, there's the common typo of a single equals sign instead of a double equals sign.

By the way, you might be wondering—why doesn't the program ever actually reach the continue line, why does it just jump back to the for loop directly from the if statement? This is a quirk of the debugger—it can sometimes be hard to match the machine code directly up with a particular line of code. In this case, the debugger is having trouble telling `if ( x = 2 )` apart from the continue statement. You'll see this from time to time in a debugger where the code that is executed doesn't seem to quite match what you expect. You'll start to pick up on specific cases, like this one, as you debug.

---

[56] Some debuggers allow you to control which thread is running by "freezing" threads, but Code::Blocks does not have this option.

Modifying variables

Sometimes when you're debugging, you may want to modify the value of a variable—for example, to make sure that if the variable is set to a particular value, the rest of the code really will work. You can do this by using the Watch Window—if you click on a variable's value, you can start typing and set the value of the variable to whatever value you'd like.

 Be careful not to do this right before the code initializes the value or it will just be overwritten.

Summary

Code::Blocks is a debugger that you can use to quickly get started debugging. If you're on a non-Windows system, many if not all of the same concepts will apply, possibly in modified form. The basic idea of debugging is to understand more about the state of your program, using tools like breakpoints, stepping through code to get you to the right place, and then looking at what is going on by understanding the call stack and the values of different variables.

Practice problems

Unlike other chapters, rather than quizzing you on debugging or asking you to write code, I have some buggy programs for you to debug. Each of these programs behaves badly; you should create a project for each one in Code::Blocks and debug it. In some cases, there may be more than one bug!

Problem 1: Issues with exponents

```
#include <iostream>

using namespace std;
int exponent (int base, int exp)
```

```
{
      int running_value;
      for ( int i = 0; i < exp; i++ )
      {
            running_value *= base;
      }
      return base;
}

int main()
{
      int base;
      int exp;

      cout << "Enter a base value: ";
      cin >> base;
      cout << "Enter an exponent: ";
      cin >> exp;
      exponent( exp, base );
}
```
Sample Code 47: practice1.cpp

Problem 2: Trouble adding numbers

```
#include <iostream>

using namespace std;

int sumValues (int *values, int n)
{
      int sum;
      for ( int i = 0; i <= n; i++ )
      {
            sum += values[ i ];
      }
      return sum;
}

int main()
{
      int size;
      cout << "Enter a size: ";
      cin >> size;
      int *values = new int[ size ];
      int i;
      while ( i < size )
      {
            cout << "Enter value to add: ";
            cin >> values[ ++i ];
      }
```

```
        cout << "Total sum is: "
             << sumValues( values, size );
}
```
Sample Code 48: practice2.cpp

Problem 3: Bugs with Fibonacci[57]

```cpp
#include <iostream>

using namespace std;

int fibonacci (int n)
{
        if ( n == 0 )
        {
                return 1;
        }
        return fibonacci( n - 1 ) + fibonacci( n - 2 );
}

int main()
{
        int n;
        cout << "Enter the number to compute fibonacci for: "
             << endl;
        cin >> n;
        cout << fibonacci( n );
}
```
Sample Code 49: practice3.cpp

Problem 4: Misreading and misprinting a list

```cpp
#include <iostream>

using namespace std;

struct Node
{
        int val;
        Node *p_next;
};

int main()
{
        int val;
        Node *p_head;
        while ( 1 )
```

---

[57] If you aren't familiar with the Fibonacci sequence, you may find this webpage useful: http://en.wikipedia.org/wiki/Fibonacci_number

```
        {
                cout << "Enter a value, 0 to replay: " <<endl;
                cin >> val;
                if ( val = 0 )
                {
                        break;
                }
                Node *p_temp = new Node;
                p_temp = p_head;
                p_temp->val = val;
                p_head = p_temp;
        }
        Node *p_itr = p_head;
        while ( p_itr != NULL )
        {
                cout << p_itr->val << endl;
                p_itr = p_itr->p_next;
                delete p_itr;
        }
}
```

Sample Code 50: practice4.cpp

Part 3: Writing Larger Programs

NOTE: *If you have been reading this book straight-through, and you haven't yet worked any of the practice problems—***STOP***. You cannot appreciate or use the information in this part of the book if you have not done some programming. You are reaching some of the most important information in this book, but it is meaningless without some practical experience.*

Many concepts that we have talked about so far have enabled you to do new things. But now it is time to talk not just about doing new things, but about doing bigger things. So far, you've written very small programs, I'd guess generally not more than a few hundred lines. When your programs are not very big, they are, fortunately, not very hard to keep in your head, but you might have already started to notice that longer programs are harder to work on. Even if you haven't, you will reach a point where a program gets too big. For some people it will be a few hundred lines, for some people a few thousand lines, or maybe even more, but it doesn't really matter; good memory is a nice skill, but no one has enough to do anything truly interesting with memory alone. All programs become too large to understand completely. Want to write a computer game? Scientific software? An operating system? You'll need techniques that make it easier to structure and understand large programs.

Fortunately, many programmers have run into this problem and have developed techniques that make it easier to build larger programs. The principles outlined in the next few chapters will make it possible to write larger, more sophisticated programs. They will also make it easier to design smaller programs too.

Let's dive into a couple of concepts that we'll keep coming back to as we talk about how to design large programs. We'll start off with the physical code—how you lay out your program on disk so that it's not just a single enormous cpp file. Then we'll talk about the logical design of your program--how you make it possible to write programs without needing to keep every single detail of how it works in your head at the same time.

Chapter 21
Breaking Programs Up Into Smaller Pieces

As your programs get bigger and bigger, you won't want to have your whole program in a single source file. Making changes will be cumbersome, and you'll start to get lost in the file when you need to find things. Once your programs reach a couple of thousand lines, you'll definitely want to start splitting your program across multiple source files. [58]

Using more than one source file makes it easier to know where to find something because each file is smaller and can contain code relevant to one particular aspect of the program. It also makes it easier for you to design your program because each header file will contain the specific interface for the associated source code, and it will not be possible for other files to use functions or data structures that aren't defined in the header file. This might sound like a limitation, but in reality it makes it easier for you to separate the implementation of each subsystem from the functionality it provides to other subsystems.

---

[58] I once had to work with a file that was nearly 20,000 lines and a half-megabyte in size. No one wanted to touch it!

Understanding the C++ build process

Before you can split up your code into multiple files, you need to understand more about the basics of how C++ compilation works.

In fact, compiling isn't quite the right word—compiling doesn't even mean creating an executable file. Creating an executable is a multistage process; the most important stages are **preprocessing**, **compilation** and **linking**. The total process of going from source code files to an executable is best referred to as a **build**. Compiling is a single part of the build process, not the entire build process. Nonetheless, you will often see people use the word compile to refer to the whole process. Usually you do not need to run separate commands for each stage—the compiler itself invokes the preprocessor, for example.

Preprocessing

The first step in the build process is when the compiler runs the C **preprocessor**. The purpose of the C preprocessor is to make textual changes to the file before the compile step. The preprocessor understands **preprocessor directives**, commands that are written directly into the source file, but that are intended for the preprocessor rather than the compiler.

All preprocessor directives begin with the pound sign (#). The compiler itself will never actually see the preprocessor directives!

For example, a statement such as

```
#include <iostream>
```

tells the preprocessor to grab the text of the file `iostream` directly into the current file. Every time you include a header file it will literally be pasted into the file before the compiler sees it, and the `#include` directive will be removed.

The preprocessor also expands out **macros**. A macro is a string of text that is replaced by another, generally more complicated, string of text. Macros allow you to put constants in a single, central point, so that you can easily change them.

For example, you can write

```
#define MY_NAME "Alex"
```

You can then use MY_NAME instead of "Alex" throughout your source file.

```
cout << "Hello " << MY_NAME << '\n';
```

The compiler will see:

```
cout << "Hello " << "Alex" << '\n';
```

If you want to change the name being used, you need only change the line that contains the #define, rather than having to do a global search/replace across your code. Macros centralize pieces of information so that you can change them more easily. If you want to give your program a version number that can be referred to throughout the code, you could do so with a macro:

```
#define VERSION 4
// ...
cout <<  "The version is " << VERSION
```

Because the preprocessor runs before the compiler processes the code, it can also be used to remove code—sometimes you want to have the ability to compile certain code only in a debugging build. You can do this by telling the preprocessor to include source code only if a macro has been defined. Then, when you want the code, you can define the macro, and if you don't want the code, you can remove the macro.

For example, you might have debugging code that prints out the values of some variables, but you don't want these printouts to happen all the time. You can make it so that the debugging code is conditionally included into the build.

```
#include <iostream>

#define DEBUG

using namespace std;

int main ()
{
     int x;
     int y;
     cout << "Enter value for x: ";
     cin >> x;
```

```
      cout << "Enter value for y: ";
      cin >> y;
      x *= y;

#ifdef DEBUG
      cout << "Variable x: " << x << '\n' << "Variable y: "
          << y;
#endif
      // further use of x and y
}
```
Sample Code 51: define.cpp

If you want to turn off the display of the variables, you can simply comment out the #define DEBUG:

```
// #define DEBUG
```

The C preprocessor also supports checking that a macro is NOT defined—for example, you can execute code only if DEBUG is NOT set, using **#ifndef (if n**ot **def**ined). We will use this technique when we talk about working with multiple header files.

Compilation
Compilation means turning a source code file (a .cpp file) into an **object** file (a .o or .obj file). An object file contains your program in a form suitable for the computer processor to understand—**machine language instructions**—for each function that you wrote in your source file. Each source file is **separately compiled**, meaning that the object file contains machine language only for the source code file that was compiled. For instance, if you compile (but don't link) three separate files, you will have three object files created as output, each with the name <filename>.o or <filename>.obj (the extension will depend on your compiler). Each of these files contains a translation of one source code file into machine language. But you can't run them yet. You need to turn them into executable files that your operating system can use. That's where the linker comes in.

Linking
Linking means creating a single executable file (e.g. an EXE or DLL) out of a bunch of object files and libraries.[59] The linker creates a file in the proper format

---

[59] Or possibly just one object file, if you have only one source file. Linking always happens, even for the simplest single file programs.

for an executable and transfers the contents of each individual object file into the resulting executable. The linker also deals with object files that have references to functions defined outside the object file's original source file—for example, for functions that are part of the C++ standard library. When you make a call into the C++ standard library (e.g. cout << "Hi"), you are using a function that is not defined in your code. It is defined in the equivalent of an object file, but not one of yours—the compiler vendor provides the object file. At the time of compilation, the compiler knew the function call was valid because you included the iostream header file, but since that function was not part of the cpp file, the compiler just leaves a stub at the call site. The linker goes through the object file, and for each stub, it finds the correct function address and replaces the stub with the correct address from one of the other object files being linked.

This operation is sometimes called a **fixup**. When you split your program into multiple source files, you take advantage of the linker's ability to do this fixup for all functions that make calls into other source files. If the linker cannot find a definition for a function anywhere, then it will generate an undefined function error—even though the compiler let the code through, it doesn't mean the code is correct. The linker is the first place that looks at the whole program at once in a way that can detect this kind of problem.

Why separate compiling and linking?

Because not every function needs to be defined in the same object file, it is possible to compile individual source files one at a time, and then link them together later. If you change one file, FrequentlyUpdated.cpp, but don't change another file, InfrequentlyChanged.cpp, then the object file for InfrequentlyChanged.cpp doesn't need to be recompiled. Skipping unnecessary compilation can save tons of time during builds. The larger your codebase, the more time you will save.[60]

To get the full benefits of conditional compilation, you need a tool that will remember whether a particular object file is **out of date**, meaning that you've changed the corresponding source file (or one of the headers included by that source file) since the last compile. If you are on Windows and using Code::Blocks, then this is already taken care of for you. If you're on a Mac, then

---

[60] I've seen codebases that take hours to build from scratch, and I've heard of codebases that take days.

Xcode will handle this for you automatically when you add new files via File|New|New file.... If you're using Linux, you can use a utility called make that comes with most *nix distributions.[61]

How to split your program across multiple files

So how do you structure your code to take advantage of separate compilation? Let's walk through a simple example of having some shared code in one program, Orig.cpp, which you now wish to reuse in a new program. I will describe this process in a very structured way, so that you can see each step, but in practice multiple steps can be done at once.

Step 1: Splitting our declarations and definitions

If you haven't been trying to split out the code into multiple files, you probably don't have a clean separation of function declarations from the function definitions, so the first step is to make sure that all of your functions have function declarations, and move them to the top of your file. Visually, it looks like this:

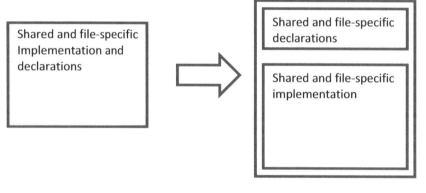

Orig.cpp

Step 2: Figure out which functions need to be shared

Now that your function declarations and function definitions have been separated, you can go through and figure out which ones are specific to this file, and which should be in the common file.

---

[61] You can read more about makefiles here:
http://www.cprogramming.com/tutorial/makefiles.html

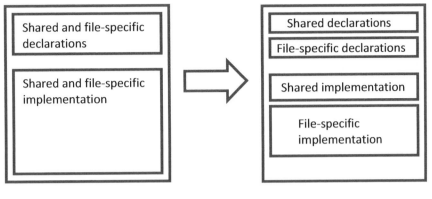

Step 3: Move shared functions into their new files

Now you can move your shared declarations into a new file, `Shared.h`, and your shared implementation into `Shared.cpp`. At the same time, you will need to include `"Shared.h"` from `Orig.cpp`. You can continue to call the shared functions, since all of the declarations are in `Shared.h`. You will need to set it up so that when you build `Orig.cpp`, it will also link with the object file `Shared.obj`. We'll cover that detail below.

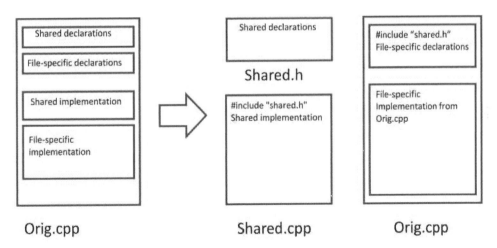

Going through an example

Here's a small program with generic linked list code that happens to be written inside of the file `Orig.cpp`. We're going to take this code and split it into a header file and source file that can be reused.

orig.cpp
```cpp
#include <iostream>

using namespace std;

struct Node
{
     Node *p_next;
     int value;
};

Node* addNode (Node* p_list, int value)
{
     Node *p_new_node = new Node;
     p_new_node->value = value;
     p_new_node->p_next = p_list;

     return p_new_node;
}

void printList (const Node* p_list)
{
     const Node* p_cur_node = p_list;
     while ( p_cur_node != NULL )
     {
          cout << p_cur_node->value << endl;
          p_cur_node = p_cur_node->p_next;
     }
}

int main ()
{
     Node *p_list = NULL;
     for ( int i = 0; i < 10; ++i )
     {
          int value;
          cout << "Enter value for list node: ";
          cin >> value;
          p_list = addNode( p_list, value );
     }
     printList( p_list );
}
```
Sample Code 52: orig.cpp

First, let's split out the declarations from the definitions. For brevity, I show only the actual declarations; the rest of the file is unchanged.

orig.cpp

```
struct Node
{
        Node *p_next;
        int value;
};

Node* addNode (Node* p_list, int value);
void printList (const Node* p_list);
```

Since there are no file-specific declarations, we don't need to do any work to separate them out; we can immediately go and put all of these declarations into a new header file, Shared.h (or, in this case, we'll call it linkedlist.h). I will show the entirety of each file.

linkedlist.h

```
struct Node
{
    Node *p_next;
    int value;
};

Node* addNode (Node* p_list, int value);
void printList (const Node* p_list);
```
Sample Code 53: linkedlist.h

linkedlist.cpp

```cpp
#include <iostream>
#include "linkedlist.h"

using namespace std;

Node* addNode (Node* p_list, int value)
{
        Node *p_new_node = new Node;
        p_new_node->value = value;
        p_new_node->p_next = p_list;

        return p_new_node;
}

void printList (const Node* p_list)
{
        const Node* p_cur_node = p_list;
```

```
        while ( p_cur_node != NULL )
        {
                cout << p_cur_node->value << endl;
                p_cur_node = p_cur_node->p_next;
        }
}
```
Sample Code 54: linkedlist.cpp

orig.cpp
```
#include <iostream>
#include "linkedlist.h"

using namespace std;

int main ()
{
        Node *p_list = NULL;
        for ( int i = 0; i < 10; ++i )
        {
                int value;
                cout << "Enter value for list node: ";
                cin >> value;
                p_list = addNode( p_list, value );
        }
        printList( p_list );
}
```
Sample Code 55: orig_new.cpp

Notice that the header file should not contain any function definitions. If we had added a function definition to the header file and then included that header file into more than one source file, the function definition would have shown up twice at link time. That will confuse and anger the linker.

We also need to make sure that the function declarations themselves don't show up twice in a single source file. It's possible that Orig.cpp will come to include more header files, and that one of those header files might include linkedlist.h:

newheader.h
```
#include "linkedlist.h"
// other code
```

orig.cpp
```
#include "linkedlist.h"
#include "newheader.h"
```

```
/* rest of code from orig.cpp */
```

Orig.cpp includes `linkedlist.h` twice—once directly, and once indirectly, through the inclusion of `newheader.h`.

Fixing this problem requires an **include guard**. An include guard uses the C preprocessor to control whether or not a file is included. The basic idea is to say:

```
if <we haven't yet included this file>
     <mark that we've included the file>
     <include it>
```

We can safely use this pattern because you should never need to include a header file more than once.

To implement an include guard, we need to use the preprocessor command `#ifndef` that we saw earlier in this chapter. The `#ifndef` statement says, "**if** **not def**ined", include the block of code up to the next `#endif`.

```
#ifndef ORIG_H
// contents of the header
#endif
```

This code says, "if no one has defined `ORIG_H` then go ahead and include the rest of the code up to the `#endif`." The trick is that we can now define `ORIG_H`:

```
#ifndef ORIG_H
#define ORIG_H
// contents of the header

#endif
```

Imagine what happens if someone includes this header file twice—the first time around, `ORIG_H` is undefined, so the `#ifndef` includes the remainder of the file, including the part that defines `ORIG_H`. (Sure, it defines it to be empty—but it's still defined.) The next time the file is included, the `#ifndef` is false, and no code is included.

You do need to come up with unique names for your header file include guards—a good technique is to use the name of the header file, followed by _H.

Doing this should ensure that your include guards are unique, and unlikely to conflict with someone else's real #define values or include guards.[62]

Other dos and don'ts of header files

Never ever include a .cpp file directly. Including a .cpp file will just lead to problems because the compiler will compile a copy of each function definition in the .cpp file into each object file, and the linker will see multiple definitions of the same function—a no-no. Even if you were incredibly careful about how you did this, you would also lose the time-saving benefits of separate compilation.

There is one particularly noteworthy case of the rule that you should have only a single copy of each function: for any given build you're doing, you should have only a single source file containing the main function. Main is the entry point to your program, so there needs to be only one version of it.

Handling multiple source files in your development environment

Setting up the proper linking of multiple source files will depend on your environment. I'll walk through how to do this for each development environment, starting with Code::Blocks.

Code::Blocks

In Code::Blocks, to add a new source file to your current project, you go to "File|New|Empty Source File...".

You will be asked if you want to add the file to the current project:

Select "Yes".

---

[62] You may also want to add your name, or the name of your company, in some way to the #define if you intend to share the code or use a lot of shared code. Someone else might have created a linked list too.

You'll then need to choose a file name. Once you've done that, Code::Blocks will prompt you for which build configurations require this file. For source files, this is the actual step that includes this file in the linking.

Choose all of the available options (typically "Debug" and "Release"). Although you would never link a header file, it is ok to choose these two options for header files as well because Code::Blocks is smart enough not to add them to the linking options.

To use the new files, you'll typically need to add both a header file and a source file, and then make the source code changes that we went through earlier.

g++

If you're using g++, you don't need to do anything special other than create the files and name the files on the command line. For example, if you have source files `orig.cpp`, `shared.cpp`, and a `shared.h` header file, you can compile the two source files with the command:

```
g++ orig.cpp shared.cpp
```

You do not mention the header file on the command line—it should be included by the .cpp files that need it. This will recompile all files given on the command line. If you want to get the full benefits of separate compilation, you can instead compile each file separately with the −c flag:

```
g++ -c orig.cpp
g++ -c shared.cpp
```

And then link them with

```
g++ orig.o shared.o
```

or just

```
g++ *.o
```

If you know there aren't any spurious object files in the current directory.

Manually controlling separate compilation is a tedious process. It is much easier to do this with a **makefile**. A makefile is the definition of your program's build process, and it can encode the dependencies between different source files so that if you change one source file, the makefile will know to recompile any other source files that depend on that file.

Makefiles are beyond the scope of this book, but you can learn more about makefiles at http://www.cprogramming.com/tutorial/makefiles.html. If you prefer not to learn about makefiles, however, for the time being you can continue to just compile all of your C++ files at once with:

```
g++ orig.cpp shared.cpp
```

Xcode

To add a new source file to your Xcode project, use the File|New File menu item. If you want to make sure that your new files show up under the "Sources" folder on the left tree view, select the "Sources" directory where main.cpp is located before you go to File|New File... This isn't necessary, but it will help you keep things organized.

Once you've selected File|New, you will have several options for the type of file:

Choose "C and C++" from the left pane and then "C++ file" on the right (or, if you want to add just a header file, "Header file"). If you want to add both a header and a cpp implementation file, choose "C++ file. You will have the option to create the header file on the next screen. Press Next.

Select the name of the file and, if you don't want to use the default location, fill in a new location. You can just accept the defaults if you like—in this example, I'm adding it directly into the directory add_file that is associated with a project called add_file.

If you select C++ file, you will have the option to create the header file too; I've outlined the checkbox in a box in screen capture above. If you choose this option, the header file will be opened for you when you press Finish.

Xcode will automatically set up the build process to compile the new cpp file you create and link it with the other files.

Quiz yourself
1. Which of the following is not a part of the C++ build process?
A. Linking
B. Compiling

C. Preprocessing
D. Postprocessing

2. When would you get an error related to an undefined function?
A. During the link phase
B. During the compilation phase
C. At program startup
D. When you call the function

3. What can happen if you include a header file multiple times?
A. Errors about multiple declarations
B. Nothing, header files are always loaded only once
C. It depends on how the header file is implemented
D. Header files can only be included by one source file at a time, so this isn't a problem

4. What advantage is there to having separate compile and link steps?
A. None, it's confusing and it probably makes things slower since you have multiple programs running
B. It makes it easier to diagnose errors because you know whether the problem is from the linker or compiler
C. It allows only changed files to be recompiled, saving compilation and linking time
D. It allows only changed files to be recompiled, saving compilation time

(View solution on page 505)

Practice problems

1. Write a program that contains the functions `add`, `subtract`, `multiply` and `divide`. Each of these functions should take two integers and return the result of the operation. Create a small calculator that uses these functions. Put the function declarations into a header file, but include the source code for these functions in your source file.

2. Take the program you wrote above and put the function definitions into a separate source file from the rest of your calculator code.

3. Take the implementation of binary trees that you used in for the exercises in the binary trees chapter and move all function declarations and structure declarations into a header file. Put the structure declarations in one file and the function declarations into another file. Move all the implementation into one source file. Create a small program that exercises the basic functionality of the binary tree.

Chapter 22
Introduction to Program Design

Now that we've solved the problem of how you can physically store code on disk in a way that makes it easy to edit as programs get larger, we can focus on the next level of the problem—how to logically organize your code to make it easy to edit and work with. Let's start out by going through some of the most common issues that come up as your programs get larger.

Redundant code

Although we briefly touched on the issue of repeating code when introducing functions, let's take another, deeper look at that issue. When your programs become bigger, ideas will be repeated over and over again. For example, if you have a video game, it will need code that draws different graphical elements to the screen (a spaceship or a bullet, for example).

Before you can draw a spaceship, you'll need the most basic ability to draw a **pixel**—a pixel is a single point of color on the screen located using two-dimensional coordinates. Most of the time, you can get a graphics library to do this for you.[63]

---

[63] We won't actually do graphics in this book, but you can learn more about it here http://www.cprogramming.com/graphics-programming.html

You'll also want code that uses pixels (or other basic graphical elements that a graphics library would provide, like lines and circles) to draw the actual elements of the game—spaceships, bullets, etc.

You're probably going to want to do this drawing quite frequently in your code—certainly any time one of the spaceships or bullets moves, it needs to be redrawn. If you were to just put in all of the code that draws the bullet each time you needed to draw a bullet, you'd have a lot of redundant code.

This redundancy adds unnecessary complexity to your program, and complexity makes understanding your program much harder. You want to have standard ways of doing things like drawing space ships or bullets, rather than allowing each part of your code to repeat the process. Why is that? Let's say that you want to change something—maybe the color of the bullet. If you have code to display the bullet in 10 different places, you will end up having to change each of those places just to change the color. That's a pain!

Every time you want to display a bullet, you have to figure out the code all over again or go find an example of the code and copy and paste it, maybe tweaking some variable names to avoid conflicts. In either case, you have to think about "how to display the bullet" rather than being able to say, "draw me a bullet". Moreover, when you go back and read your code, you're going to have to figure out what the code does—it's a lot harder to figure out that

```
circle( 10, 10, 5 );
fillCircle( 10, 10, RED );
```

means draw a bullet than it is to figure out that

```
displayBullet( 10, 10 );
```

means draw a bullet.

Functions give code useful names so that when you read the code, you can remember what it's really doing. Although you probably haven't experienced it yet, as you build larger programs, you will start to spend more time reading your code than writing it, so good names and good functions alone can make a big difference.

Assumptions about how data is stored

The disease of redundancy can infect more than your algorithms. Let's take another example of code that has hidden redundancy. What if you wanted to have a chess program that represented the current position on the chess board as an array? Each time you access the board, you could simply access the array.

To initialize the second rank to contain all white pawns, you might write:

```
enum ChessPiece {
      WHITE_PAWN,
      WHITE_ROOK
      /* and others */
};

// ... lots of code

for ( int i = 0; i < 8; i++ )
{
      board[ i ][ 1 ] = WHITE_PAWN;
}
```

Later, if you want to check what piece is located on a particular square, you could just read from the array:

```
// ... lots of code
if ( board[ 0 ][ 0 ] == WHITE_ROOK )
{
      /* do something */
}
```

As your program grows, more and more code that uses the board will end up scattered all over the place. What harm is there in doing that? You are not really repeating yourself each time you read from the array; it's just a single line of code, right? Yet you are repeating yourself—you are repeatedly using the same data structure. By repeatedly using the same data structure, the code makes a very specific assumption about how the chess board is represented. You aren't repeating an algorithm, but you are repeating the assumption of how the data is represented. Think about it this way—just because it happens to only take one line of code to access the board, that doesn't mean that it will always take one line of code to access the board. If you had implemented your board differently, you might have needed a more complex technique for accessing the board.

Sophisticated chess programs use a different board representation than an array (they use multiple bitboards[64] rather than a single array; these bitboards will take more than one line of code each time you need to use them). If I were writing a chess program, I'd probably start by using an array, so I could focus on the basic algorithms I need before worrying about making the code optimally fast. But to make it easy to change my representation of the board, I would hide the array. How can you hide an array, though?

The last time we needed to hide something, we wanted to hide the details of painting bullets. We did this by using a function that we could call, rather than writing code that directly painted to the screen. Here too we can use a function to hide the details of the board representation. Rather than use the array directly, our code will call a function that accesses the array. For example, you might write a function such as getPiece like this:

```
int getPiece (int x, int y)
{
      return board[ x ][ y ];
}
```

Notice that the function takes two arguments, and it returns a value, just like accessing the array. It doesn't really save you any typing because you need all of the same input data that you needed before—an x coordinate and a y coordinate. What's different is that the means of accessing the board is now hidden within this one function. The rest of your program can (and should) use this function to access the array. Then, if you later decide you want to change the representation of the board, you can change just this one function—**and everything else just works**.[65]

The idea of using a function to hide details is sometimes called **functional abstraction**. Applying functional abstraction means that you should put any kind of repeated operation into a function—let the function specify the inputs and the outputs to the caller, but avoid telling the caller anything about HOW the function is implemented. The HOW can be either the algorithm that is being used, or the data structures that are being used. The function allows its callers

---

[64] See http://en.wikipedia.org/wiki/Bitboard

[65] That is, assuming that you were consistent in always using this function to access the board. It's also true that you might need a few more functions to set pieces on the board, but changing two functions is better than changing dozens or hundreds.

to take advantage of the promise the function makes about its interface without knowing how the function is implemented.

There are several advantages to using functions to hide data and algorithms.

1) You make life easier on yourself in the future. Rather than having to remember how to implement an algorithm, you can just use a function you previously wrote. As long as you trust that the function works correctly for all valid inputs, you can trust the output without having to remember how it works.

2) Once you can trust a function to "just work" you can start to solve problems by writing code that uses those functions again and again. You don't have to worry about all the details (like how you access the board), so you can focus on the new problems to solve (like how to make your AI).

3) If you DO find a mistake in your logic, rather than having to update multiple places in the code, you only need to change one function.

4) If you write functions to hide your data structures, you also give yourself flexibility in how your data is stored and represented. You can start with inefficient representations that are easy to write and later replace them with faster implementations, if needed, without having to change anything but a small number of functions.

Design and comments

When you create well-designed functions, you should also document those functions. Documenting a function properly is not quite as simple as it sounds, though.

Good comments answer the questions that a reader of the code will have. The kind of comments that you've seen me put into the examples I've used in this book—like this:

```
// declare variable i and initialize to 3
int i = 3;
```

aren't really the kind of comments you should be writing! A comment like this is intended to answer the questions of readers who are just beginning to learn to program; but in the real world, the people who are reading your program will already know C++.

What's worse, over time the comments fall out of date, so if someone reads the comment, it might not only waste their time, but they might completely misunderstand what is happening.

It's much better to write comments that address questions like, "whoa, that seems like a weird approach. Why'd they do it this way?" Or, "what are the acceptable values for this function to take, and what do they mean?" Here's an example of the kind of documentation you should strive to write for each function you create:

```
/*
 * compute the value of Fibonacci for the given positive
integer, n. If * the value of n is less than 1, the
function  returns 1
*/
int fibonacci (int n);
```

Notice that this function description describes exactly what the function does, what arguments are valid, and what happens if an invalid input is provided. This kind of documentation means that the user of the function doesn't need to go look at how it is implemented—a very good thing!

Good commenting is not necessarily verbose commenting—you shouldn't comment every single line of code. I always include documentation on my functions that are intended to be used outside of a single file, and I add explanatory comments whenever the code is particularly tricky or unusual looking.

There is one bad habit that takes the idea of minimal commenting too far— when you leave the comments until the very end of the development cycle. Once the code is written, it's too late to go back and meaningfully comment it; all you're doing is adding the same information that you could have figured out by reading the code. Comments are most useful when you put them in while you're writing the code.

Quiz yourself

1. What is the advantage of using a function instead of directly accessing data?
A. The function can be optimized by the compiler to provide faster access
B. The function can hide the implementation of the function from callers, making it easier to change the caller of the function
C. Using functions is the only way to share the same data structure across multiple source code files
D. There is no advantage

2. When should you put code into a common function?
A. Whenever you need to call it
B. When you have started calling the same code from more than a couple of places
C. When the compiler starts to complain about the functions being too big to compile
D. B and C

3. Why would you want to hide the representation of a data structure?
A. To make the data structure easier to replace
B. To make the code that uses the data structure easier to understand
C. To make it easier to use the data structure in new parts of the code
D. All of the above

(View solution on page 506)

Chapter 23
Hiding the Representation of Structured Data

So far you've seen how to hide data stored in global variables or in an array. Hiding data is not limited to these few examples. One of the most common places where you want to hide data is when creating a structure. This might strike you as strange: a structure, after all, has a very specific layout and set of values that it can store. When you look at them that way, as a group of fields, structures provide no way of hiding their implementation details (like which fields they store, and in what format). In fact, you might be wondering, "isn't the whole point of a structure is to provide some particular pieces of data? Why would you want to hide the representation?" It turns out that there is another way to think about structures, a world in which you do want these things.

Most of the time when you have a bunch of related data, what really matters is not so much exactly how you store the data, but what you can do with that data. This is a very important point, and it can be a mind shift. So I'm going to repeat it, and put it in bold: **What matters isn't how you store the data, but how you use the data**.

Since bolding text doesn't always lead to immediate clarity, let's take a simple example—the string. Unless you are actually implementing the string class, it really doesn't matter to you how the string is stored. For any code that works with strings, what matters is how to get the length of the string, access individual characters of the string, or display the string. It could be that the implementation of string uses an array of characters and another variable to store the length, or it could use a linked list, or it could use a feature of C++ that you've never heard of.

The important thing is that it doesn't matter, as a user of the string, how the string is implemented—what matters is what you can do with the string. There may be a lot of things you can do, but even the C++ string has only about 35 different things you can do with it—and you don't even need most of them, most of the time.

What you will often want is the ability to create new data types without having to expose the raw data that is used to implement the data type. For example, when creating a string, you don't need to worry about the buffer that holds the characters. STL vectors and maps work just like this; you don't need to know how they are implemented in order to use them—for all you care, when using an STL vector, the implementation could be to feed carrots to hyperactive rabbits with a knack for organization.

Using functions to hide the layout of a structure

You can use functions to hide the exact fields of a structure by creating functions associated with a structure. For example, imagine a small chess board that represents the board and whose move it is (white or black). We'll use enums to store both the pieces and the player to move:

```
enum ChessPiece {
      EMPTY_SQUARE,
      WHITE_PAWN
      /* and others */
};
enum PlayerColor { PC_WHITE, PC_BLACK };

struct ChessBoard
{
      ChessPiece board[ 8 ][ 8 ];
      PlayerColor whose_move;
};
```

You can create functions that operate on the board, taking the board as a parameter to the function:

```
ChessPiece getPiece (
```

```
        const ChessBoard *p_board,
        int x,
        int y
)

{
        return p_board->board[ x ][ y ];
}

PlayerColor getMove (const ChessBoard *p_board)
{
        return p_board->whose_move;
}

void makeMove (
            ChessBoard* p_board,
            int from_x,
            int from_y,
            int to_x,
            int to_y
        )
{
        // normally, we'd want some code that validates the
        // move first
        p_board->board[ to_x ][ to_y ] =
            p_board->board[ from_x ][ from_y ];
        p_board->board[ from_x ][ from_y ] = EMPTY_SQUARE;
}
```

Which you use just like any other function:

```
ChessBoard b;
// first we'd need some code to initialize the board
// then we can use it, like so...
getMove( & b );
// move a piece from 0, 0 to 1, 0
makeMove( & b, 0, 0, 1, 0 );
```

This is a fine approach, and in fact C programmers used this approach for years. On the other hand, all of these functions are only associated with the ChessBoard structure because they happen to take it as an argument. Nothing explicitly says, "This function should be considered a core part of this structure". Wouldn't it be nice to be able to say that a structure contains not just data, but also the ways that it can manipulate data?

C++ takes this idea to heart and builds it directly into the language. To support this style, C++ introduces the concept of a method—a **method** is a function declared to be part of a structure (you have seen methods before, in the section on the STL). Unlike free-floating functions that are not associated with a structure, methods can very easily operate on the data stored in the structure. The method writer declares the method as part of the structure, which directly ties the methods to the structure. By declaring the method part of the structure, the method's caller need not pass the structure as a separate argument! That does require special syntax, though.

Method declaration and call syntax

Let's see what it would look like if we turned our functions into methods:

```
enum ChessPiece {
      EMPTY_SQUARE,
      WHITE_PAWN
      /* and others */
};

enum PlayerColor { PC_WHITE, PC_BLACK };

struct ChessBoard
{
      ChessPiece board[ 8 ][ 8 ];
      PlayerColor whose_move;
      ChessPiece getPiece (int x, int y)
      {
            return board[ x ][ y ];
      }

      PlayerColor getMove ()
      {
            return whose_move;
      }

      void  makeMove (
                  int from_x,
                  int from_y,
                  int to_x,
                  int to_y
            )
      {
            // normally, we'd want some code that validates
            // the move first
            board[ to_x ][ to_y ] =
                  board[ from_x ][ from_y ];
```

```
                board[ from_x ][ from_y ] = EMPTY_SQUARE;
        }
};
```
Sample Code 56: method.cpp

First, you can see that the methods are declared inside the structure. This makes it clear that the methods are supposed to be treated as a fundamental part of the structure.

Moreover, the method declarations don't take a separate argument for the ChessBoard—inside the method, all of the fields of the structure are directly available. Writing board[x][y] directly accesses the board of the structure on which the method was called. But how does the code know which instance of the structure to work on? (What if you have more than one ChessBoard?)

A call to a method looks like this:

```
ChessBoard b;
// code to initialize board
b.getMove();
```

Calling a function associated with the structure looks almost exactly like accessing a field of the structure.

Internally, the compiler is handling the details of letting the method access the data in the structure the method was called on. Conceptually, the <variable>.<method> syntax is a shorthand for passing <variable> to <method>. Now you know why we needed this syntax in the chapter on the STL; the functions worked like these methods.

Moving function definitions out of the structure
Having to include every function body in your structure can get really messy and make it hard to understand. Fortunately, you can split up methods into a declaration that appears inside the structure and a definition that's outside the structure. Here's an example:

```
enum ChessPiece {
        EMPTY_SQUARE,
        WHITE_PAWN
        /* and others */
};
```

```
enum PlayerColor { PC_WHITE, PC_BLACK };

struct ChessBoard
{
     ChessPiece board[ 8 ][ 8 ];
     PlayerColor whose_move;

     // method declarations inside the structure
     ChessPiece getPiece (int x, int y);
     PlayerColor getMove ();
     void makeMove (
               int from_x,
               int from_y,
               int to_x,
               int to_y
          );
};
```

The method declarations are inside the structure, but otherwise look like a normal function prototype.

The method definitions themselves need some way to tie them back to the structure—we can do this by using a special "scoping" syntax that indicates that the method belongs inside a structure. The syntax is to write the name of the method as <structure name>::<method name>, but otherwise the code is the same:

```
ChessPiece ChessBoard::getPiece (int x, int y)
{
     return board[ x ][ y ];
}

PlayerColor ChessBoard::getMove ()
{
     return whose_move;
}

void  ChessBoard::makeMove (
          int from_x,
          int from_y,
          int to_x,
          int to_y
     )
{
     // normally, we'd want some code that validates the
     // move first
```

```
board[ to_x ][ to_y ] = board[ from_x ][ from_y ];
board[ from_x ][ from_y ] = EMPTY_SQUARE;
}
```

For the rest of the book, I will split up the declaration and definition of any method longer than a few lines. Some practitioners recommend *never* defining any method inside a structure because it exposes more than you need about how the methods are implemented. The more you expose about your method implementation, the more likely someone is to write code that depends on the exact details of the implementation rather than on just the interface to the method. In this book, I will sometimes put method declarations with the class anyway to save some space.

Quiz yourself

1. Why would you want to use a method rather than using the field of a structure directly?
A. Because the method is easier to read
B. Because the method is faster
C. You wouldn't, you should use the field directly
D. So that you can change the representation of the data

2. Which of the following defines the method associated with the structure
`struct MyStruct { int func(); };`
A. `int func() { return 1; }`
B. `MyStruct::int func() { return 1; }`
C. `int MyStruct::func() { return 1; }`
D. `int MyStruct func () { return 1;   }`

3. Why would you want to include a method definition inline with the class?
A. So that users of the class can see how it works
B. Because it always makes the code faster
C. You don't! It leaks details about the implementation
D. You don't, it makes the program run more slowly

(View solution on page 507)

Practice problems

1. Write a structure that provides the interface to a tic-tac-toe board. Implement a two-player tic-tac-toe game with the methods on the structure.

You should make it so that basic operations like making a move and checking whether one player has won are part of the interface of the structure.

Chapter 24
The Class

When Bjarne Stroustrup created C++, he wanted to really reinforce the idea of creating structures that were defined by the functions they provided, rather than the data they happened to use for their implementations. He could have done everything he wanted by extending the existing structure concept, but instead he created an entirely new concept: the **class**.

A class is like a structure, but it adds the ability to define what methods and data are internal to the implementation of the class, and what methods are intended for users of the class. You should think of the word class as similar in meaning to category; when you define a class, you are creating an entirely new class, or category, of thing. It no longer carries the connotation of being structured data; instead, classes are defined by the methods that they provide as their interface. Classes can even keep you from accidentally using implementation details.

That's right—in C++, it is possible to prevent methods that don't belong to the class from using the internal data of the class. In fact, when you declare a class, the default is that nothing is available to anyone except the methods that are part of the class! You have to explicitly decide what should be made publicly accessible. The ability to make data inaccessible outside the class allows the compiler to check that programmers are not using data they shouldn't be using. This is a godsend for maintainability. You can change basic things about your class—for example, how a chess board is stored—without having to worry about breaking code outside of the class.

Even if you're the only programmer on your project, having the assurance that no one is "cheating" and looking underneath the method is a very nice thing indeed. In fact, this is another reason why methods are useful—as you'll soon see, only methods can access "internal" data.

From here on out, I will use classes whenever I want to hide the way data is stored, and structures whenever there is absolutely no reason to hide it. You may be surprised how rarely used structures are—data hiding really is that valuable. Just about the only time where I use plain old structures is when I'm implementing a class, and I need some helper structure to hold onto part of the data. Since the helper structure is specific to just this one class, and not exposed publicly, there usually isn't any need to make it a full-fledged class. Like I said, there's no hard and fast need to do so, but it's a common convention.

Hiding how data is stored

Let's dive into the syntax of data hiding with classes—how *would* you use a class to hide some data while making some methods available to everyone? Classes let you classify each method and field (often called **members** of the class) as either public or private—public members are available to anyone, and private members are available only to other members of the class.[66]

Here's an example of declaring methods to be public and all of the data to be private:

```
enum ChessPiece {
      EMPTY_SQUARE,
      WHITE_PAWN
      /* and others */
};

enum PlayerColor { PC_WHITE, PC_BLACK };

class ChessBoard
{
public:

      ChessPiece getPiece (int x, int y);
      PlayerColor getMove ();
      void makeMove (
            int from_x,
```

---

[66] There's also a third type, called protected, that we will talk about later.

```
                int from_y,
                int to_x,
                int to_y
        );

private:
        ChessPiece _board[ 8 ][ 8 ];
        PlayerColor _whose_move;
};

// Method definitions are exactly the same!
ChessPiece ChessBoard::getPiece (int x, int y)
{
        return _board[ x ][ y ];
}

PlayerColor ChessBoard::getMove ()
{
        return _whose_move;
}

void  ChessBoard::makeMove (
                int from_x,
                int from_y,
                int to_x,
                int to_y
        )
{
        // normally, we'd want some code that validates the
        // move first
        _board[ to_x ][ to_y ] = _board[ from_x ][ from_y ];
        _board[ from_x ][ from_y ] = EMPTY_SQUARE;
}
```

Sample Code 57: class.cpp

Notice that this class declaration looks a lot like our structure declaration from before, but with one major difference. I have used two new keywords: **public** and **private**. Anything declared after the keyword public is available for anyone to use on the object (in this case, the methods getPiece, getMove, and makeMove). Anything in the section that begins with private is accessible only by methods implemented as part of the ChessBoard class (_board and _whose_move)[67].

---

[67] I have also put underscores before each private element of the class to make it easier to tell what is private, but it is not a requirement of C++. It looks a bit ugly at first, but I find it makes a big difference when you're reading the code! If you follow this convention, just make sure that you do not use a capital letter after the underscore; this

By the way, you can switch between public and private all you like. This class declaration makes exactly the same things public:

```
class ChessBoard
{
public:
      ChessPiece getPiece (int x, int y);

private:
      ChessPiece _board[ 8 ][ 8 ];
      PlayerColor _whose_move;

public:
      int getMove ();
      void makeMove (int from_x, int from_y, to_x, to_y);
};
```

In my own code, I always start with a public section, followed by a private section. This emphasizes that the public section is meant for users of the class (other programmers) because it is the first thing that a user of the class will see.[68]

Declaring an instance of a class

Declaring an instance of a class is just like declaring an instance of a structure:

```
ChessBoard b;
```

Making a method call on a class is also exactly the same:

```
b.getMove ();
```

There is one small terminology difference though. When you declare a new variable of a particular class, that variable is generally called an **object**. The word object should evoke images of real world things like the steering wheel—something that exposes a pretty narrow interface hiding lots of complexity. When you go to turn your car left, you rotate the steering wheel—you don't worry about how the gears work. All you need to do is turn the wheel and press

---

prefix may cause conflicts with some compilers. As long as you stick with a lowercase letter after the underscore when declaring private fields or methods, you'll be fine.

[68] These users are, of course, other programmers, not the end users of the software. In many cases, you will be the user of your own class in the future.

the gas. All the details are hidden behind a basic user interface. In C++, all the details of an object's implementation are hidden behind the set of public function calls—these functions are what make up its "user interface". Once you've defined an interface, your class can implement it however it wants to—how the data is represented, and how the methods are implemented, is up to you.

The responsibilities of a class

Whenever you create a class in C++, think of it as creating a new kind of variable—a new data type. Your new type is just like an `int` or a `char`, but more powerful. You've already seen this idea—in C++, a string is a class, and the string class is, in fact, a new type of data you can use. The idea of public and private makes perfect sense when you think about creating a new type of data: you want to provide some specific functionality and a specific interface. For example, a string provides the ability to display itself, work with substrings or individual characters, and get basic attributes like the length of the string. It really doesn't matter is how the string is implemented.

If you think of creating a class as defining a new type, then it makes sense that the first thing you should do is figure out what you want to be public: what you want your class to do. Anything that is public can be used by any programmer who uses the class—you should treat it as an interface, just like a function has an interface consisting of its arguments and return value. It's something you want to think about carefully, because once you start to use the interface, changing the interface will require changing all the users of that interface. Since the method is public, there could be many many callers—you have no easy way to limit how much change will be required. No one is going to come up with a totally new way to drive a car because everyone would have to learn how to drive all over again! But it's ok to come up with a new engine type, like going from purely gas powered to a hybrid, because it doesn't change the interface, just the implementation.

Once you've come up with a basic public interface, you should start thinking about how you will implement the public methods that make up the interface. Any methods or fields that you want to use to implement your public methods, but that don't need to be public, should be made private.

In contrast to the public interface, private methods and data are easy to change. These private members of the class are only available to methods of the class (both public methods and private methods). By making the implementation details private, you have the chance to change them later if you decide you want to re-implement the functionality of the class. (It's very hard to get it exactly right the first time!) Just remember the hybrid car!

My advice is simply this: Never make data fields public, ever, and make methods private by default, moving them to the public interface only if you are convinced that the method belongs there. Going from private to public is easy—going from public to private is hard—you can't put the genie back in the bottle. If you need to provide access to a specific field, write methods to get and set the values (these methods are often called **getters,** for reading a variable, and **setters**, for writing it).

It may seem somewhat heavy-handed to never make data fields public. Won't you have to write a lot of getters and setters, writing lots of functions like `getMove` that do nothing but return a private data field such as `_whose_move`?

Yes, sometimes it does mean that. But the small cost of writing these methods is totally outweighed by the trouble you will find yourself in when you realize that you need to change the trivial getter to add some kind of functionality. For example, you might decide to go from storing a value in a variable to computing that value from some other variables. If you have no getter, but instead let everyone access the data as a public field, you're stuck.

You can come up with some examples of fields that can safely be made public. But my advice is not to try—you save yourself a little bit of typing upfront, while adding a potentially very big headache later, and the consequence of guessing wrong is a bad design that you can't easily change.

What does private really mean?
Just because something is declared private doesn't mean that there is any kind of security guarantee. Private fields of a class are stored in memory, just like public fields, usually right next to them; any code can use fancy pointer tricks to read that data. The operating system and the language make no guarantees about protecting private data from a malicious third party. Marking data private allows the compiler to prevent accidental use of private data—not to enforce security guarantees. Even though it doesn't provide a security guarantee, it's still useful.

By the way, that there's a commonly-used programming term for using public methods to hide private data: encapsulation. **Encapsulation** means hiding your implementation (encapsulating it) so that users of the class only work with a specific set of methods that form the interface for a class. Phrases like "data hiding" or "implementation detail" are more evocative, but encapsulation is a term that you'll run across. Now you know what it means.

Summary

The class is one of the fundamental building blocks for most real world C++ programs. Classes allow programmers to create large scale designs that are easy to understand and work with. You've now learned about one of the powerful features of classes—the ability to hide data—and the next several chapters will introduce many more features of classes.

Quiz yourself

1. Why would you use private data?
A. To make data safe from hackers
B. To prevent other programmers from ever touching that data
C. To make it clear what data is supposed to be used only for the implementation of a class
D. You shouldn't, it makes it harder to program

2. How is a class different from a structure?
A. Not at all
B. A class defaults to everything being public
C. A class defaults to everything being private
D. A class lets you say whether fields are public or private, a structure doesn't

3. What should you do with data fields of your class?
A. Make them public by default
B. Make them private by default, but move to public if needed
C. Never make them public
D. Classes don't usually have data, but if they do, rock on Wayne

4. How do you decide if a method should be public?
A. Never make methods public
B. Always make methods public

C. Make methods public if they are needed to use the main features of a class, otherwise make them private

D. Make methods public if there's any chance that someone might want to use that method

(View solution on page 508)

Practice problems

1. Take the structure from the practice problem at the end of the last chapter (representing a tic-tac-toe board) and reimplement it using a class, marking the publicly useful methods as public and marking the data and any helper methods as private. How much of your code did you have to change?

Chapter 25
The Lifecycle of a Class

When you create a class, you want to make it as easy to use as possible. There are three basic operations that any class is likely to need to support:

1) Initializing itself
2) Cleaning up memory or other resources
3) Copying itself

All three of these items are important for creating a good data type. Let's use the string as an example: a string needs to be able to initialize itself, even if just to an empty string. It shouldn't rely on some external code to do that—once you declare a string, it is available for you to use immediately. Moreover, when you're done with the string, it needs to clean up after itself since strings allocate memory. When you use the string class, you don't have to call a method to do that cleanup—it is handled automatically. Finally, it also needs to allow copying from one variable to another, just like an integer can be copied from one variable to another. Taken together, these three pieces of functionality should be part of every class so that the class is easy to use properly and hard to use improperly.

Let's take each of these three features, starting with initializing the object, and see how C++ makes this easy.

Object construction

You may have noticed earlier that there was no code in the `ChessBoard` interface (the public part of the class) to initialize the board. Let's fix that.

When you declare a class variable, there needs to be some means of initializing the variable:

```
ChessBoard board;
```

In C++, the code that runs when an object is declared is called the **constructor**. A constructor should set up the object so that it can be used without further initialization. A constructor can also take arguments—you've seen this already when declaring a vector that is a particular size:

```
vector<int> v( 10 );
```

This calls the vector constructor with the value ten; the vector constructor initializes the new vector so that it can immediately hold ten integers.

To create a constructor, you simply declare a function that has the same name as the class, taking no arguments and returning no return value. (Not even void—you literally don't write in a type for the return value.)

```
enum ChessPiece {
      EMPTY_SQUARE,
      WHITE_PAWN
      /* and others */
};
enum PlayerColor { PC_WHITE, PC_BLACK };

class ChessBoard
{
public:

      ChessBoard (); // <-- no return value at all!

      PlayerColor getMove ();
      ChessPiece getPiece (int x, int y);
      void makeMove (
            int from_x,
            int from_y,
            int to_x,
            int to_y
```

```
        );

private:
        ChessPiece _board[ 8 ][ 8 ];
        PlayerColor _whose_move;
};

ChessBoard::ChessBoard () // <-- still no return value
{
        _whose_move = PC_WHITE;
        // start off by emptying the whole board, then fill
        // it in with pieces
        for ( int i = 0; i < 8; i++ )
        {
                for (int j = 0; j < 8; j++ )
                {
                        _board[ i ][ j ] = EMPTY_SQUARE;
                }
        }
        // other code to initialize the board...
}
```
Sample Code 58: constructor.cpp

(I won't keep showing all of the method definitions if they haven't changed, but I will keep showing you the full class declaration so you can see how it fits together.)

Notice that this constructor is part of the public section of the class. If the ChessBoard constructor were not public, then no instances of the object could be created. Why is that? The constructor must be called any time an object is created, but if it's private, that means that nobody outside the class can call the constructor! Since all objects must call the constructor to be initialized, you just can't declare the object at all.

The constructor is called on the very line where you create the object:

```
ChessBoard board; // calls ChessBoard constructor
```

or when you allocate memory:

```
//calls ChessBoard constructor as part of memory allocation
ChessBoard *board = new ChessBoard;
```

If you declare multiple objects:

```
ChessBoard a;
ChessBoard b;
```

The constructors are run in the order that the objects are declared (first a then b).

Just like normal functions, a constructor can take any number of arguments, and you can have multiple constructors overloaded by argument type if the object can be initialized in different ways. For example, you could make a second constructor for ChessBoard that takes the size of the board:

```
Class ChessBoard
{
      ChessBoard ();
      ChessBoard (int board_size);
};
```

Defining the function works the same way as any other class method:

```
ChessBoard::ChessBoard (int size)
{
      // ... code
}
```

You pass the argument to the constructor like so:

```
// 8 is an argument to the constructor of ChessBoard
ChessBoard board( 8 );
```

When using new, argument passing looks as though you were directly calling the constructor:

```
ChessBoard *p_board = new ChessBoard( 8 );
```

One small note on syntax—although you use parentheses to pass arguments to a constructor, you can't use parentheses when declaring an object with a no-argument constructor.

BAD CODE
```
ChessBoard board();
```

The correct way to write the above bad code is

```
ChessBoard board;
```

It is, however, ok to use parentheses when you use new:

```
ChessBoard *board = new ChessBoard();
```

This is an unfortunate quirk of how C++ is parsed (the details are extraordinarily obscure). Avoid using parentheses when declaring an object that has a constructor that takes no parameters.

What happens if you don't create a constructor?

If you don't create a constructor, then C++, friend that it is, will create one for you. This constructor will take no arguments, but it will initialize all of the fields of the class by calling their default constructors (it won't initialize primitive types like `int` or `char` though—so watch out). I generally recommend that you create your own constructor to make sure that everything is initialized to your liking.

As soon as you declare a constructor for your class, C++ will no longer automatically generate a default constructor for you—the compiler assumes that you know what you are doing and that you want to create all the constructors for the class. In particular, if you create a constructor that takes arguments, your code will no longer have a default constructor unless you specially declare one.

This can have surprising consequences. If your code uses the auto-generated default constructor and you then add your own non-default constructor taking one or more arguments, code that depended on the auto-generated default constructor will no longer compile. You have to manually provide a default constructor since the compiler isn't creating one for you anymore.

Initializing members of the class

Each member of a class needs to be initialized in the constructor. Imagine that we have a string as a member of our `ChessBoard` class:

```
class ChessBoard
{
public:

      ChessBoard ();
```

```
        string getMove ();
        ChessPiece getPiece (int x, int y);
        void makeMove (
                int from_x,
                int from_y,
                int to_x,
                int to_y
        );

private:
        PlayerColor _board[ 8 ][ 8 ];
        string _whose_move;
};
```

You can of course simply assign to the _whose_move variable:

```
ChessBoard::ChessBoard ()
{
        _whose_move = "white";
}
```

The actual code that executes here might be a bit surprising though. First, right at the beginning of the ChessBoard constructor, the constructor for _whose_move will be called. This is good because it means that you can safely use any of your class's fields in the constructor—if the constructors of those members weren't called, they couldn't be used—the whole point of the constructor is to make the object usable!

You can pass arguments to the constructor of a class member, if you want, rather than having the default constructor run. The syntax for this is a bit unusual, but it works:

```
ChessBoard::ChessBoard ()
        // the colon is followed by the list of variables,
        // with the argument to the constructor
        : _whose_move( "white" )
{
        // at this point, _whose_move constructor has been
        // called and it contains the value "white"
}
```

The term for this is an **initialization list**. We'll see them come up a couple of times, and I'll usually use this syntax when initializing members of a class. Members of the initialization list are separated by commas. For example, if we added a new member to ChessBoard to count the number of moves that had been made, we could initialize it in the initialization list:

```
class ChessBoard
{
public:

        ChessBoard ();

        string getMove ();
        ChessPiece getPiece (int x, int y);
        void makeMove (
                    int from_x,
                    int from_y,
                    int to_x,
                    int to_y
            );

private:
        PlayerColor  _board[ 8 ][ 8 ];
        string _whose_move;
        int _move_count;
};

ChessBoard::ChessBoard ()
        // the colon is followed by the list of variables,
        // with the argument to the constructor
        : _whose_move( "white" )
        , _move_count( 0 )
{
}
```

Using the initialization list for const fields

If you declare a field of your class as const, then that field *must* be initialized in the initialization list:

```
class ConstHolder
{
public:
        ConstHolder (int val);

private:
        const int _val;
};

ConstHolder::ConstHolder ()
        : _val( val )
{}
```

You cannot initialize a const field by assigning to it because those fields are already set in stone. The initialization list is the only place where the class is not yet fully formed, and so it's safe to set immutable objects. For that same reason, if you have a field that is a reference, it too must be initialized in the initialization list.

We will come across one more use of initialization lists when we get to inheritance.

Object destruction

Just as a constructor initializes an object, sometimes you need to have code that cleans up when your object is no longer needed. For example, if your constructor allocates memory (or any other resources), then those resources eventually need to be returned to the operating system when your object is no longer in use. Dealing with this cleanup is called destroying the object, and it takes place in a special method called the **destructor**. Destructors are called when an object is no longer required—for example, when you call delete on a pointer to that object.

Let's look at an example. Suppose you have a class that represents a linked list. To implement this class, you might have a field that stores the current head of the list:

```
struct LinkedListNode
{
        int val;
        LinkedListNode *p_next;
};

class LinkedList
{
public:
        LinkedList (); // constructor
        void insert (int val); // adds a node

private:
        LinkedListNode * _p_head;
};
```

As we've seen in the past, the head node in a linked list, just like other elements, points to memory allocated using new. This means that at some point, if we're done with a `LinkedList` object, we need a way to clean it up. That's what the destructor is for. Let's see what it would look like to add a destructor to this type. Like the constructor, the destructor has a special name: it is the name of the class, with a tilde (~) in front of it, and like a constructor, the destructor does not have a return value. Unlike a constructor, the destructor never takes any arguments.

```
class LinkedList
{
public:
        LinkedList (); // constructor
        ~LinkedList (); // destructor, notice the tilde (~)

        void insert (int val); // adds a node

private:
        LinkedListNode *_p_head;
};

LinkedList::~LinkedList ()
{
        LinkedListNode *p_itr = _p_head;
        while ( p_itr != NULL )
        {
                LinkedListNode *p_tmp = p_itr->p_next;
                delete p_itr;
                p_itr = p_tmp;
        }
}
```

The code for the destructor is similar to what you've seen before for deleting every item in a linked list. The only difference is that we have a class that has a special method devoted to doing this cleanup. But wait, wouldn't it make more sense for each node to clean up its own data? Isn't that the whole point of the destructor? What if we did this?

```
class LinkedListNode
{
public:
        ~LinkedListNode ();
        int val;
        LinkedListNode *p_next;
};

LinkedListNode::~LinkedListNode ()
```

```
{
      delete p_next;
}
```

Believe it or not, this code initiates a chain of recursive function calls. What happens is that the call to `delete` invokes the destructor for the object pointed to by `p_next` (or does nothing, if `p_next` is NULL). That destructor, in turn, calls `delete` and invokes the next destructor. But what's the base case? How will this chain of destruction end? Eventually `p_next` will be NULL, and at that point, the call to `delete` will do nothing. So there is a base case—it just happens to be hidden inside the call to `delete`. Once we have this destructor for `LinkedListNode`, the destructor for the `LinkedList` itself simply needs to invoke it:

```
LinkedList::~LinkedList ()
{
      delete _p_head;
}
```

This call to delete starts the recursive chain, until the end of the list.

Now you might be thinking—that's a nice pattern, but why do we need a destructor? Couldn't we have created our own method and called it whatever we wanted? Well, sure, but the destructor has an advantage: it is called for you automatically when the object is no longer needed.

So what does it actually mean for an object to be "no longer needed"? It means one of three things:

1) When you delete a pointer to an object
2) When the object goes out of scope
3) When the object belongs to a class whose destructor is being called

Destruction on delete

Calling delete makes it quite explicit about when the destructor is called, as you've already seen:

```
LinkedList *p_list = new LinkedList;
// ~LinkedList (the destructor) is called on p_list
delete p_list;
```

Destruction when going out of scope

The second case, an object going out of scope, is an implicit operation. Any time an object is declared in a set of curly braces, it goes out of scope at the end of those curly braces:

```
if ( 1 )
{
      LinkedList list;
} // list's destructor is called here
```

A slightly more complicated example is when an object is declared inside of a function. If the function has a return statement, the destructor is called as part of exiting the function. The way that I think about it is that destructors for objects declared inside a block of code are executed "at the closing curly brace" when that block is exited. A block can be exited when the last statement in the block is done, or if a return statement or a break statement exits the block:

```
void foo ()
{
      LinkedList list;

      // some code...
      if ( /* some condition */ )
      {
            return;
      }
} // list's destructor is called here
```

In this case, even though the return is inside the if statement, I think of the destructor as running when the function "hits" the last curly brace. But what's most important for you to take away is that the destructor is run only once the object is no longer in scope—when it can no longer be referenced without a compiler error.

If you have multiple objects with destructors that need to run at the end of a block of code, the destructors are run in the opposite order that the objects were constructed. For example, in the code

```
{
      LinkedList a;
      LinkedList b;
}
```

The destructor for b is run before the destructor for a.

Destruction due to another destructor

Finally, if you have an object that is contained inside another class, the destructor for that object is called after running the destructor for the class. For example, if you have a very simple class:

```
class NameAndEmail
{
/* there would normally be some methods here */
private:
    string _name;
    string _email;
};
```

Here, the destructor for the _name and _email fields will be called once the destructor for NameAndEmail finishes running. This is very convenient—you don't need to do anything special to clean up any object in your class! You really only need to clean up pointers by calling delete (or other resources like file handles or network connections).

By the way, even if you don't add a destructor to your class, then the compiler will still make sure to run the destructor for any objects that are part of the class.

The idea of using a constructor to initialize a class and a destructor to clean up memory or other resources belonging to a class has a name: **resource allocation is initialization** or **RAII**. The basic meaning is that in C++, you should create classes to handle resources, and when you create classes, the constructor should do all the initialization and the destructor should handle all the cleanup. No special handling should be required of users of the class. Often, this results in classes like the NameAndEmail class above: the two strings clean up after themselves, so NameAndEmail doesn't need its own hand-written destructor.

Copying classes

The third stop on our tour of important class-related concepts is handling copying instances of a class. In C++, it's common to create new classes that you want to be able to copy—for example, you might write:

```
LinkedList list_one;
LinkedList list_two;
```

```
list_two = list_one;
LinkedList list_three = list_two;
```

In C++, there are two functions that you can define to make sure these kinds of copy operations work properly. One function is the assignment operator, and the other function is called the copy constructor. We'll start off by looking at the assignment operator and then talk about the copy constructor.

You might wonder—why do I need these functions, shouldn't it Just Work? The answer is that yes, sometimes it will Just Work; C++ will provide you with default versions of the copy constructor and assignment operator.

However, there are some cases where you can't rely on the default version—sometimes the compiler just isn't smart enough to know what you want. For example, the default version of the copy constructor and of the assignment operator will do what's known as a **shallow copy** of pointers. A shallow copy is when you assign a second pointer to point to the same memory as the first pointer. This is considered shallow because none of the pointed-to memory is copied, just the pointer itself. Sometimes a shallow copy may be fine, but there are situations where it is a problem.

For example, let's say we have our LinkedList class, and we write code like this:

```
LinkedList list_one;
LinkedList list_two;

list_one = list_two;
```

The trouble is that the default assignment operator generates the following code:

```
list_one._p_head = list_two._p_head;
```

You can visualize it like so:

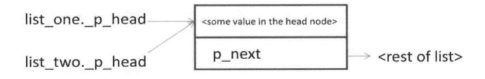

Now we have two objects with the same pointer value, and the destructor for each object will try to free the memory associated with that pointer.

When the destructor for `list_two` runs, it will delete `list_two._p_head`. (The destructor for `list_two` runs first because destructors run in the reverse order of constructors, and `list_two`'s constructor ran second.) Then the destructor for `list_one` will run, deleting `list_one._p_head`. The problem is that `list_two._p_head` was already deleted, and if you delete a pointer twice, your program is going to crash!

Clearly once one of the destructors runs, the other list is no longer good! Assignment operators are the way to handle just this kind of situation. So let's see what it should look like.

The assignment operator

The assignment operator is called when assigning an object to a pre-existing object, such as when you write:

```
list_two = list_one;
```

To implement an assignment operator requires a small amount of new syntax to be able to define an operator. Fortunately, it's not too hairy:

```
LinkedList& operator= (
        LinkedList& lhs,
        const LinkedList& rhs
);
```

This should look a lot like a normal function declaration—this function takes two arguments: a non-const reference to a `LinkedList` and a const reference to a `LinkedList`, and it returns a reference to a `LinkedList`. The only weird thing is the name of the function: `operator=`. But what this means is that rather than defining a new function, we are defining what it means for the equals sign to be used with the `LinkedList` class. The first argument is the left-hand side of the equals sign—the thing being assigned to—so it is non-const. The second argument is the right-hand side, and it is the value being assigned (and it should be const, since you don't have a reason to modify it, though making it const is not strictly required):

```
lhs = rhs;
```

The reason for returning a reference to a `LinkedList` is so that you can chain together assignments:

```
linked_list = lhs = rhs;
```

Now, most of the time, rather than declaring a stand-alone function for `operator=`, a class will typically make the `operator=` function a member function so that `operator=` can work with private fields of the class (as opposed to just declaring a free-floating function like I did above). Let's see what that looks like:

```
class LinkedList
{
public:
        LinkedList (); // constructor
        ~LinkedList (); // destructor, notice the tilde
        LinkedList& operator= (const LinkedList& other);

        void insert (int val); // adds a node

private:
        LinkedListNode * _p_head;
};
```

Notice that one argument is missing: that's because all member functions of a class implicitly take the class as an argument. In this case, the `operator=` method is used when the class is the left-hand side of an assignment. In other words, in the code:

```
lhs = rhs;
```

The `operator=` function is called on the variable `lhs`. It's as though you'd written:

```
lhs.operator=( rhs );
```

And after the function finishes, `lhs` will have the same value as `rhs`. Okay, so let's talk about how we should write the `operator=` function for our `LinkedList` class.

```
LinkedList& LinkedList::operator= (const LinkedList& other)
{
      // what goes here?
}
```

From the discussion above, we already know that just copying the pointer address isn't good enough.

What we want to do instead is to copy the whole structure. The logic will be: first free our existing list (since it's no longer needed), and then copy each list node so we can have two separate lists. Finally, since we need to return a value, we'll return a copy of the class we're working with.

That last bit requires one more piece of new syntax—we need some way to refer to the current object. To do this in C++, we can use a special variable, called the **this** pointer. The `this` pointer is a pointer that points to the instance of the class. For example, if you write `list_one.insertElement( 2 );` then inside of `insertElement`, you can use the keyword `this`, and it points to `list_one`. We'll also use the `this` pointer to add a bit of safety to the method.

```
LinkedList& LinkedList::operator= (const LinkedList& other)
{
      // make sure we aren't assigning to ourself--we can
      // just ignore that if it happens. Notice that we're
      // using 'this' here to ensure that the other value
      // isn't the same address as our object
      if ( this == & other )
      {
            // return this object to keep the chain of
            // assignments alive
            return *this;
      }
      // before copying over the new values, we need to
      // free the old memory, since it's no longer used
      delete _p_head;
      _p_head = NULL;


      LinkedListNode *p_itr = other._p_head;
      while ( p_itr != NULL )
      {
            insert( p_itr->val );
      }
      return *this;
```

```
}
```

A few notes about this function: first, notice that we are checking for self-assignment—this is the kind of thing you don't normally expect to happen, but there's no reason not to be sure it's safe. Writing code like

```
a = a;
```

should be completely safe and make no changes at all.

Next, we need to free the memory associated with the old list, since we're done with it—by deleting _p_head we can delete the whole list, just like in the destructor.

Finally, we need to repopulate the list with the right new values, which we can do by looping over the old list and inserting each element from that list into our own list. And voila, we have a class that can be copied!

Fortunately, not all classes require such sophisticated copying. If none of your class members are pointers, you probably don't need an assignment operator at all! That's right—C++, benevolent and thoughtful, will provide you with an assignment operator that by default will copy each element by running *its* assignment operator (if it's an object of a class) or by copying its bits (if it's a pointer or other value). So if you don't have a pointer in your class, you can rely on the default assignment operator in most cases. One good rule of thumb is that if you need to write your own destructor, you probably also need to write your own assignment operator. The reason for this rule is that if you have a destructor, it's probably to free some memory, and if you free the memory, you need to make sure that copies of the class get their own copies of the memory.

The copy constructor

There's one final case to think about; what if you want to construct one object to be just like another object:

```
LinkedList list_one;
LinkedList list_two( list_one );
```

This is just a special case of using a constructor—a constructor that takes an object of the same type as the object being constructed. This constructor is called a **copy constructor**. A copy constructor should make the new object a direct copy of the original. Here, list_two should be initialized so that it looks just like list_one. This is a bit like an assignment operator, except instead of having an existing class, you are starting with a completely uninitialized class. This is a good thing because it means that you don't need to waste any CPU time constructing the class, only to overwrite the values. The copy constructor is generally quite easy to implement and usually looks a lot like the assignment operator. Here's what it would look like for LinkedList:

```cpp
class LinkedList
{
public:
        LinkedList (); // constructor
        ~LinkedList (); // destructor, notice the tilde
        LinkedList& operator= (const LinkedList& other);
        LinkedList (const LinkedList& other);


        void insert (int val); // adds a node
private:
        LinkedListNode * _p_head;
};

LinkedList::LinkedList (const LinkedList& other)
        : _p_head( NULL ) // start off with NULL in case the
                          // other list is empty
{
        // notice that this code is quite similar to
        // operator= . It would make sense to create a helper
        // method that does this work in a real program
        LinkedListNode *p_itr = other._p_head;
        while ( p_itr != NULL )
        {
                insert ( p_itr->val );
        }
}
```

See, easy as pie.

The compiler will provide you a default copy constructor if you don't write your own. This copy constructor behaves like the default assignment operator: it runs the copy constructor for each object of the class, and it does a regular copy for values like integers and pointers. In most cases, if you needed to create an assignment operator, you probably also need to include a copy constructor.

There's one thing you should know about the copy constructor that sometimes surprises beginners—it sure surprised me the first time I saw it. If you write this code:

```
LinkedList list_one;
LinkedList list_two = list_one;
```

What do you think will happen—will it call the assignment operator? Nope, turns out that the compiler is smart enough to recognize that `list_two` is being initialized based on `list_one`, and it will actually call the copy constructor for you, saving some extraneous object initialization. Isn't that nice?

The full list of compiler generated methods

You've now seen every method that the compiler will automatically generate for you:

1) Default constructor
2) Default destructor
3) Assignment operator
4) Copy constructor

For every class you create, you should consider whether you can accept the compiler's default implementations for these methods or not. Many times, you can, but when you are working with pointers, you will often want to declare your own destructor, assignment operator and copy constructor. (Generally, if you need one, you need them all.)

Preventing copying entirely

Sometimes you just don't need to be able to copy objects at all. Wouldn't it be nice to say, "don't allow this object to be copied"? Doing so would let you avoid implementing the copy constructor or assignment operator *and* there'd be no risk of the compiler generating dangerous versions of these methods.

There are also situations where it is simply wrong for an object to be copyable. For example, if you have a computer game with a class representing the current user's spaceship, you don't really want to have copies of that spaceship—you want only a single spaceship that contains all the information about the current user.

You can prevent copying by *declaring* the copy constructor and assignment operator but never *implementing* them. Once you've declared the method, the compiler won't auto-generate it for you anymore. If you try to use it, you will get an error at link time because you used an undefined function. This can be a little bit confusing, because the linker won't tell you the exact line of code that has the problem. You can get much better error messages by making the methods private as well; this way, the error will occur at the compiler stage in most cases, giving easier-to-understand error messages. Let's see how to do that:

```
class Player
{
public:
      Player ();
      ~Player ();

private:
      // prohibited, by declaring but not defining these
      // methods, the compiler will not generate them for
      // us
      operator= (const Player& other);
      Player (const Player& other);

      PlayerInformation *_p_player_info;
};

// No implementation of the assignment operator or copy
// constructor
```

In summary, you should almost always choose one of the following options:

1) Use both the default copy constructor and assignment operator
2) Create both your own copy constructor and assignment operator
3) Make both the copy constructor and assignment operator private, without any implementation

If you do nothing, you will get option 1 thanks to the compiler. It's often easiest to start with option 3, and later add the assignment operator and copy constructor if you find a need for them.

Quiz yourself

1. When do you need to write a constructor for a class?

A. Always, without the constructor you can't use the class
B. Whenever you need to initialize the class with non-default values
C. Never, the compiler will provide a constructor for you all the time
D. Only if you need to have a destructor too

2. What is the relationship between the destructor and the assignment operator?
A. There isn't any
B. Your class's destructor is called before running the assignment operator
C. The assignment operator needs to specify what memory should be deleted by the destructor
D. The assignment operator must make sure that it is safe to run both the destructors of the copied class and the new class

3. When do you need to use an initialization list?
A. When you want to make your constructors as efficient as possible and avoid constructing empty objects
B. When you are initializing a constant value
C. When you want to run the non-default constructor of a field of the class
D. All of the above

4. What function is run on the second line of this code?
```
string str1;
string str2 = str1;
```
A. The constructor for str2, and the assignment operator for str1
B. The constructor for str2, assignment operator for str2
C. The copy constructor for str2
D. The assignment operator for str2

5. Which functions are called in this code, and in what order?
```
{
        string str1;
        string str2;
}
```
A. The constructor for str1, the constructor for str2
B. The destructor for str1, the constructor for str2
C. The constructor for str1, the constructor for str2, the destructor for str1, the destructor for str2
D. The constructor for str1, the constructor for str2, the destructor for str2, the destructor for str1

6. If you know a class has a non-default copy constructor, what should be true about its assignment operator?
A. It should have a default assignment operator
B. It should have a non-default assignment operator
C. It should have a declared, but not implemented, assignment operator
D. Either B or C is valid

(View solution on page 509)

Practice problems

1. Implement a vector replacement that operates only on integers, vectorOfInt (you don't need to use templates like the normal STL). Your class should have the following interface:

- A no-argument constructor that allocates a 32-element vector
- A constructor that takes an initial size as the argument
- A method get, taking an index and returning the value at that index
- A method set, that takes an index and a value, and sets the value at that index
- A method pushback that adds an element to the end of the array, resizing if necessary
- A method pushfront that adds an element to the beginning of the array
- A copy constructor and assignment operator

Your class should not leak memory; any memory it allocates must be deleted. Try to think carefully about how your class can be misused, and how you should handle those scenarios. What do you do if a user gives a negative initial size? What about accessing a negative index?

Chapter 26

Inheritance and Polymorphism

So far we've been talking about how to make a full-fledged, usable type out of your classes by providing clean public interfaces and supporting creating, copying, and cleaning up objects. Now let's take the idea of interfaces a bit further. Let's say that you have a car. Your car is a little bit old and rusted. Unfortunately, you live in a world where every car maker has a different steering mechanism—some car makers use steering wheels, some use joysticks, some use mice. Some have gas pedals, and some require you to drag a scroll bar.[69] Wouldn't that be pretty awful? Every time you wanted to use a car, you'd have to learn how to control it, all over again. Every time you wanted to rent a car, or buy a new car, you'd have to either learn how to drive it all over again.

Fortunately, cars follow certain standards. Any time you get into a car, it has the same interface—steering wheel, gas pedal. The only real distinction is that some cars have automatic transmissions, and some cars have manual transmissions. There are two interfaces that a car can have: automatic or manual.

As long as you know how to use an automatic transmission, you can drive any car that has an automatic transmission. When you are driving the car, the

---

[69] Yeah, steering with a scroll wheel would probably cause a lot of accidents.

details of the engine don't matter. All that matters is that it presents the same methods for steering, accelerating and braking as every other car.

What does this have to do with C++? In C++, it is actually possible to write code that expects a specific, well-defined interface (in the analogy above, you are the code, the car's steering mechanism is the interface). The implementation of the interface (the car itself) doesn't matter—whatever specific implementation of the interface (whichever car you choose), can be used by the code (by you, the driver) because it implements an interface that the code understands. You, as the driver, may prefer some cars to other cars, but you can drive all of them.

Now, when would you write code that has a similar property? Think about a video game—you might have a bunch of different objects that can be drawn to the screen—bullets, ships, enemies. In your main game loop, for every frame you need to redraw each of these things into its new position.

You really want to be able to write code that has this form:

```
Clear the screen
Loop through a list of drawable objects
      For each drawable object, draw it
```

The list of drawable objects would, ideally, hold every kind of object that you can display on the screen. They all need to implement some common interface that allows drawing them to the screen. But you also want your bullet, and your ship, and your enemy to each be a different class—they're going to have their own different internal data (the player's ship needs hit points, the enemy ships need AI to move them, and the bullet needs to store the amount of damage it can cause).

For the loop that draws the objects, all of that stuff is irrelevant. All that matters is that each of these different classes supports an interface that allows drawing. We want a bunch of classes with the same interface but with different implementations of that interface.

How would you do this? First, let's just define what it means to be able to be drawn:

```
class Drawable
{
```

```
public:
      void draw ();
};
```

This simple class, Drawable, defines only a single method—draw. This method draws the current object. Wouldn't it be great if we could create a vector<Drawable*> and then store anything that implements the draw method in that vector?[70] If we could do that, we could write code to draw everything onto the screen just by looping over everything in the vector, and calling the draw method.

Anyone using objects stored in that vector could only use the methods that make up the Drawable interface, but that's all we need to do here anyway!

Guess what? C++ actually supports this! Let's look at how to make that happen.

Inheritance in C++

First, let's introduce a new term: **inheritance**. Inheritance means that one class gets traits from another class. In this case, the trait that is inherited will be the interface of the Drawable class, specifically the method named draw. A class that inherits traits from another class is called a **subclass**. The class being inherited from is the **superclass**.[71] A superclass often defines an interface method (or methods) that can be implemented differently by each subclass. In our example, Drawable is a superclass. Each Drawable object in the game will be a subclass of Drawable; each class will inherit the property of *having* a draw method, allowing code that gets a Drawable to know that the draw method is available. Each class will then implement its own version of the draw method—in fact, it *must* implement its own version of the draw method, guaranteeing that all subclasses of Drawable have a valid draw method.

Okay, got the basic concept? Let's move on to the syntax:

```
class Ship : public Drawable
{
};
```

---

[70] If you're wondering why I'm putting a pointer in the vector the reason is that we need to use a pointer to get the kind of behavior we're about to see.

[71] The term **parent class** is sometimes used instead of superclass, and the term **child class** is sometimes used instead of subclass. I'll use superclass and subclass in this book.

The ": public Drawable" indicates that the class Ship inherits from the class Drawable. By writing this code, Ship inherits all public methods and public data from its superclass, Drawable. Right now, Ship has inherited the method draw. The full method, in fact. If you were to write:

```
Ship s;
s.draw();
```

The call to draw would invoke the implementation of the draw method that was written into Drawable. That's not quite what we want in this case, since the Ship class should have its own way of drawing itself, rather than using the version that comes as part of the Drawable interface.

For Ship to be able to do this, Drawable must indicate that the draw method can be overridden by subclasses. You do this by making the method **virtual**—a virtual method is a method that is part of a superclass, but that can be overridden by individual subclasses.

```
class Drawable
{
public:
      virtual void draw ();
};
```

In many cases, you don't want the superclass to provide any implementation at all, but instead you want to force the subclass to have its own implementation of the method. (There may not be a good "default" way to draw an object, for example.) You can do that by making the function **pure virtual**, which looks like this (notice the = 0):

```
class Drawable
{
public:
      virtual void draw () = 0;
};
```

The syntax looks decidedly weird when you see it for the first time! There is logic to it though— setting the method to 0 is a way to indicate that it doesn't exist. When a class has a pure virtual method, its subclasses must implement the method. To do this, the subclass needs to declare the method again, without the = 0. This indicates that the class will provide a real implementation for the method:

```
class Ship : public Drawable
{
public:
      virtual draw ();
};
```

Now the method can be defined just like any normal method:

```
Ship::draw ()
{
      /* code to do the drawing */
}
```

You might ask, why do we need a superclass like Drawable at all if all we're going to do is make a draw method that doesn't have any implementation? The point is that we need the superclass in order to define the interface that all subclasses will implement. Then we can write code that expects the Drawable interface without having to know the exact type of the class being used. Some programming languages allow you to pass any object to any function, and as long as the object implements the methods that are used by that function, everything works. C++, however, requires that a function be explicit about the interfaces of its arguments. If we didn't have a Drawable interface we couldn't even put these classes all in the same vector to begin with; there wouldn't be anything "in common" that we could use to identify what should go in the vector. Let's see the code for using our vector and drawing all the objects:

```
vector<Drawable*> drawables;

// store the Ship in the vector by creating a new Ship
// pointer
drawables.push_back( new Ship() );

for ( vector<int>::iterator itr = drawables.begin(),
        end = drawables.end();
      itr != end;
      ++itr )
{
      // remember we need to use the -> syntax for calling
      // methods when we have a pointer to an object
      (*itr)->draw(); // calls Ship::Draw
}
```

We can add different kinds of `Drawable` objects to the vector (assume we have a class, Enemy, that also inherits from `Drawable`):

```
drawables.push_back( new Ship() );
drawables.push_back( new Enemy() );
```

And everything will work—we'll call the `Ship::draw` method for the ships, and the `Enemy::draw` method for the enemies.

By the way, it's very important that we had a `vector<Drawable*>` rather than a `vector<Drawable>`. That pointer makes a big difference; without using the pointer, none of this will work.

To see why, imagine, for the moment that we wrote code that holds onto the object without using a pointer:

```
vector<Drawable> drawables;
```

In memory, we'll now have memory with different `Drawable` objects, all of the same size:

```
[Drawable 1][Drawable 2][Drawable 3]
```

The vector must store the whole object if it isn't using a pointer. But each object may not be the same size—a `Ship` and an `Enemy` might have different fields, and both might be smaller than a basic `Drawable`. This just won't work correctly.

Pointers, on the other hand, are always the same size.[72] We can say:

```
[Pointer to Drawable][Pointer to Drawable][Pointer to
Drawable]
```

---

[72] This is close enough to true for our purposes. Some machines may have different pointers for different types of data, but we won't worry about that here. If you're curious, you can read more about those situations here:
http://stackoverflow.com/questions/1241205/are-all-data-pointers-of-the-same-size-in-one-platform

And if we have a [Pointer to Ship], it is going to take up exactly the same amount of memory as a pointer to a Drawable. That's why we wrote:

```
vector<Drawable*> drawables;
```

And now we can put any kind of pointer we want into the vector, as long as the pointer is to a class that inherits from Drawable, and inside the loop, each of these objects will be drawn to the screen using the subclass's draw method. (Technically, any pointer at all would fit, but just because it fits doesn't mean we want it in our vector. The whole point of the vector is to store a list of things that can be drawn. Putting in something that can't be drawn would be terribly troublesome.)

Just remember: whenever you want to have a class inherit an interface from a superclass, you need to pass the class around using a pointer.

Now that we've gone through all the nitty-gritty details of this example, let's take a step back and look at exactly what we did:

1) First we defined an interface, Drawable, that can be inherited by subclasses.

2) Any function can take a Drawable, or any code can work with a Drawable interface. This code can call the draw method that is implemented by the particular object that is pointed to.

3) This allows existing code to use new types of objects, so long as these objects implement the Drawable interface. We can add new items to our game—icons for power-ups or extra lives, background images, whatever—and the code that processes them doesn't need to know anything about them, except that they are Drawable.

This all about reuse. The reuse comes from existing code working with newly created classes. New classes can be written to work with existing code (like the game loop that draws each element of the game) without someone having to change the existing code to be aware of the new classes. (We do have to add the objects of that new class into our vector of Drawable objects, but the loop itself doesn't change.)

The name for this behavior is called **polymorphism**. Poly means many, and morph means form—many forms. In other words, every class that implements a particular interface is one form, and since code that is written to use just the interface can handle multiple different classes, that code can support multiple forms of the interface—just like a person who can drive a car can drive a gas-powered car, a hybrid, or a pure electric car.

Other uses and misuses of inheritance

Polymorphism depends on inheritance, but inheritance can be used for more than inheriting an interface. As I alluded to earlier, it's also possible to use inheritance to pick up the implementation of a function.

For example, if the `Drawable` interface had another non-virtual method, that method would be inherited by every object that implemented `Drawable`. Sometimes people believe that inheritance is about getting reuse from inheriting methods (which avoids having to write the method for each subclass). But that is a pretty limited form of reuse. You can certainly get some savings by inheriting full method implementations, but if you do so, then you have one big challenge: how do you make sure that the implementation of that method is correct for every single subclass? This requires carefully thinking about whether something is always valid.

Let's look at why this is hard. Imagine that you have objects `Player` and `Ship`, both of which implement the `Drawable` interface, and both of these classes also have a `getName` method. You might decide to add the `getName` method to your `Drawable` class so that these two classes could share the same implementation of this method.

```
class Drawable
{
public:
     string getName ();
     virtual void draw () = 0;
};
```

Since `getName` is not virtual, all subclasses will inherit the implementation of this method. What happens when you decide to add a new class, like `Bullet`, that you wish to draw? Does every bullet really need a name? Definitely not! It might not seem like a big deal to have a useless `getName` method on the `Bullet` class, and for one class, one bad method isn't the end of the world.

The problem is that doing this again and again will build up confusing and complicated class hierarchies, where the purpose of the interface isn't really clear.

Inheritance, object construction and object destruction

When you inherit from a superclass, the subclass constructor calls the constructor of the superclass—just as it invokes the constructors of all the fields on the class.

For instance, take the following code:

```
#include <iostream>

using namespace std;
// Foo is a common placeholder name in computer programming
class Foo
{
public:
        Foo () { cout << "Foo's constructor" << endl; }
};

class Bar : public Foo
{
public:
        Bar () { cout << "Bar's constructor" << endl; }
};

int main ()
{
        // a lovely elephant ;)
        Bar bar;
}
```
Sample Code 59: constructor.cpp

When `bar` is initialized, first the `Foo` constructor runs and then the `Bar` constructor runs. The output of this code is:

```
Foo's constructor
Bar's constructor
```

Having the superclass constructor run first allows it to initialize all fields of the superclass before the subclass constructor might use those fields. Running the superclass constructor before the subclass constructor ensures that the subclass may use the fields in the superclass, knowing that they have been initialized already.

This is all done automatically for you by the compiler—you don't have to do anything for the superclass constructor to get called. Similarly, after the destructor for the subclass runs, the destructor for the superclass will again be automatically called. Here's an example of that in code:

```cpp
#include <iostream>

using namespace std;
// Foo is a common placeholder name in computer programming
class Foo
{
public:
        Foo () { cout << "Foo's constructor" << endl; }
        ~Foo () { cout << "Foo's destructor" << endl; }
};

class Bar : public Foo
{
public:
        Bar () { cout << "Bar's constructor" << endl; }
        ~Bar () { cout << "Bar's destructor" << endl; }
};

int main ()
{
        // a lovely elephant ;)
        Bar bar;
}
```
Sample Code 60: destructor.cpp

Here, the output is

```
Foo's constructor
Bar's constructor
Bar's destructor
Foo's destructor
```

Notice that the constructor and the destructor are called in opposite order; this ensures that Bar's destructor can safely use methods inherited from Foo because the data those methods operate on is still in a valid, usable state. This is very similar to the reasoning behind the superclass constructor running before the subclass constructor.

In some cases, you may wish to call a non-default constructor in the superclass. Initialization lists allow you to do this by providing the name of the superclass in the initialization list.

```
class FooSuperclass
{
public:
      FooSuperclass (const string& val);
};

class Foo : public FooSuperclass
{
public:
      Foo ()

            // sample initialization list
            : FooSuperclass( "arg" )
      {}
};
```

The call to the superclass constructor should appear before the fields of the class in the initialization list.

Polymorphism and object destruction

One tricky situation is the destruction of an object, and how it works when the object is destroyed via an interface. For example, you might have code like this:

```
class Drawable
{
public:
      virtual void draw () = 0;
};

class MyDrawable : public Drawable
{
public:
      virtual void draw ();
      MyDrawable ();
      ~MyDrawable ();

private:
      int * _my_data;
};

MyDrawable::MyDrawable ()
```

```
{
        _my_data = new int;
}

MyDrawable::~MyDrawable ()
{
        delete _my_data;
}

void MyDrawable::draw ()
{
        /* code to do the drawing */
}

void deleteDrawable (Drawable *drawable)
{
        delete drawable;
}

int main ()
{
        deleteDrawable( new MyDrawable() );
}
```

So what happens inside of deleteDrawable? Remember that the destructor is called when delete is used, so the line

```
        delete drawable;
```

is making a function call on the object. But how will the compiler know how to find the destructor for MyDrawable? It doesn't know the exact type of the drawable variable—it just knows that it is a Drawable, something with a method called draw. It only knows how to find the destructor associated with Drawable, not the destructor for MyDrawable itself. Unfortunately, since the MyDrawable class allocates memory in its constructor, it's important that the MyDrawable destructor run to free that memory.

You might think—isn't this exactly the sort of problem that a virtual function is supposed to fix? And the answer is—yes, exactly! What we need to do is declare the destructor virtual in the Drawable class, so that the compiler knows to look for an overridden destructor when delete is called on a pointer to a Drawable.

```
class Drawable
```

```
{
public:
      virtual void draw ();
      virtual ~Drawable ();
};

class MyDrawable : public Drawable
{
      public:
      virtual void draw ();
      MyDrawable ();
      virtual ~MyDrawable ();
private:
      int * _my_data;
};
```

By making the destructor in the superclass virtual, whenever a `Drawable` interface is freed using delete, the overridden destructor will be called.

As a general rule, whenever you make any method in a superclass virtual, you should make the superclass destructor virtual. Once you make a single method virtual, you are saying that someone can pass around the class to methods that take an interface. Those methods can do anything they want, including deleting the object, so make the destructor virtual in order to ensure that the object is properly cleaned up.

The slicing problem

The **slicing problem** is another issue to be aware of when working with inheritance. Object slicing happens when you have code similar to the following:

```
class Superclass
{};

class Subclass : public Superclass
{
      int val;
};

int main()
{
      Subclass sub;
      Superclass super = sub;
}
```

The field val, from Subclass, is not copied as part of the assignment to super! Unfortunately, this is generally not what you want (despite the fact that C++ allows it) because the object is only partially there. This kind of slicing can sometimes work, but it can often lead to crashes.[73]

Fortunately, there is a way to get the compiler to tell you about this kind of problem. You can declare the copy constructor for Superclass private and not implement it:

```
class Superclass
{
public:
        // note that since we are declaring the copy
        // constructor we now need to provide our own default
        // constructor
        Superclass () {}
private:
        // prohibited, we will not define this method
        Superclass (const Superclass& other);
};

class Subclass : public Superclass
{
        int val;
};

int main ()
{
        Subclass sub;
        // now this line of code causes a compilation error
        Superclass super = sub; }
```

But what if you actually want to have a copy constructor? Another way to avoid this problem is to make it so that any superclass you create has at least one pure virtual function. This ensures that if you ever even write:

```
Superclass super;
```

The code will not compile because you cannot create an object with a pure virtual function. On the other hand, you can still write:

```
Superclass *super = & sub;
```

---

[73] Especially if the class has virtual functions that expect the subclass's fields to be there.

So you get the benefits of polymorphism without the problem of slicing.

Sharing code with subclasses

So far we've talked about using both public and private protection—public methods are available to anyone outside the class, private data and methods are available only to other methods and data of the class.

But what if you want a superclass to provide methods that can be called by the subclasses, but not by external classes? First off, would you ever want to do this? You might. It's pretty common for subclasses to share some implementation code.

For example, imagine that we have a method that helps objects draw themselves by clearing a region of the screen. We'll call this method clearRegion:

```
class Drawable
{
public:
        virtual void draw ();
        virtual ~Drawable ();
        void clearRegion (int x1, int y1, int x2, int y2);
};
```

The purpose of using inheritance here is not to inherit the interface; it is to allow subclasses to access common implementation code. This is a valid use of inheritance since the subclasses all need to use this method, or at least might need to use it. Since it isn't part of the public interface of the class, it's just an implementation detail of the class hierarchy being created.

But how do we prevent this method from being part of the interface for the class? Making it public, as shown above, allows anyone to call this method—even though that's not really what you want. On the other hand, you can't make the method private, since subclasses cannot access private fields or methods, and blocking access by subclasses would defeat the whole point!

Protected data

The answer is to use the third and final access modifier—**protected**. Any methods in the protected section of the class can be accessed by subclasses, unlike private methods, but are unavailable outside the class, unlike public methods. The syntax for protected is just like public and private:

```
class Drawable
{
public:
      virtual void draw ();
      virtual ~Drawable ();
protected:
      void clearRegion (int x1, int y1, int x2, int y2);
};
```

Now only subclasses of Drawable can access clearRegion.

Protected methods are frequently useful, but I do not ever recommend using protected data. There's no need to expose full access to the data to the entire class hierarchy for the same reason that you don't want to expose data anywhere else—you want to be able to change it in the future. Instead, use protected methods to provide access to that data in subclasses.

Class-wide data

So far all you've been able to do with a class is store data in individual instances of objects. In many cases, this is enough, but there are some cases where you really want to be able to hold data that is specific not to a particular object, but instead to the class as a whole. One example is if you created a class that required each object to have a unique serial number. Each object should have its own serial number, but how do you keep track of the next serial number you want to assign? You need to have some place to store the "next serial number" at the class level, so that each time a new object is constructed, you know the value to give it. (Why might you do something like this? For one thing, using serial numbers for each object can make it easy to identify the objects in log statements. The serial number can be used to trace the object across multiple lines of the log file.)

The way you create class-wide data is by using a **static** member of the class. Unlike normal instance data, static data is not part of any individual object; it is available to all objects of the class and, if it is public, to everyone. In fact, a static variable is very similar to a global variable, except that to access a static variable from outside the class, you need to prefix the name of the class to the variable name.

Let's see what that looks like. Here's a class that declares a static variable:

```
class Node
{
public:
      static int serial_number;
};
// not inside the class declaration--so we need to use
// Node:: as a prefix
static int Node::serial_number = 0;
```

In addition to having static variables, you can also have static methods—methods that are part of a class, but that can be used without an instance of the object. Let's take a look at creating a serial number for each node by adding a private static method called _getNextSerialNumber.

```
class Node
{
public:
      Node ();

      private:
      static int _getNextSerialNumber ();

      // static, one copy for the whole class
      static int _next_serial_number;

      // non-static, available to each object, but not to
      // static methods
      int _serial_number;
};

// not inside the class declaration--so we need to use
// Node:: as a prefix
static int Node::serial_number = 0;

Node::Node ()
      : _serial_number( _getNextSerialNumber() )
{ }

int Node::_getNextSerialNumber ()
{
      // use the postfix version of ++ to return the value
      // that was previously in the variable
      return _next_serial_number++;
}
```

Just remember, when you use a static method, that method is part of the class, but it has no access to object-specific fields. It only has access to static data. The static method does not have a `this` pointer passed into it.

How is polymorphism implemented?

Note: how the compiler implements polymorphism is an advanced topic, and it will take you deep into the implementation of this area of C++. I've included this section because it is a neat implementation technique, and I couldn't bear not to share it with you. It isn't critical that you learn this stuff the first (or second) time you're introduced to polymorphism. If you're curious how the magic of polymorphism is implemented, read on; if you get a headache, don't sweat it. You can always come back to this section later when you need to understand more of the details.

The key idea of polymorphism is that when the compiler encounters a function operating on an interface, rather than a concrete subclass, it does not know exactly what machine code will be run for that call. For example, in the code:

```
vector<Drawable*> drawables;

void drawEverything ()
{
        for ( int i = 0; i < drawables.size(); i++ )
        {
              drawables[ i ]->draw();
        }
}
```

The call to `drawables[ i ]->draw()` can't be compiled into a specific function call because the `draw` method is virtual. Depending on which object inherited from `Drawable`, it could call any number of different methods: drawing a bullet, the user's spaceship, an enemy spaceship, or a power-up.

Moreover, `drawEverything` is calling code that it knows nothing about. The code that calls the `draw` method needs to see only the `Drawable` interface. It doesn't have to know about anyone who actually implements `Drawable`. But how can this be if it is going to call a method on a subclass of `Drawable`?

The object carries around a list of virtual methods as a hidden field in the object—in this case, there would be one entry, with the address of the `draw` method. Each method on a particular interface is assigned a number (draw would be method 0); when calling a virtual method, the number associated with that method is used as an index into the list of virtual methods for the object. A call to a virtual method compiles into a lookup of a method in the list of virtual methods followed by a call to the looked-up method. In the code above, the call to `draw` becomes a lookup of method 0 in the table of methods, followed by a call to that address. This list of virtual methods is called a **vtable** (short for **virtual table**).

Here is what this looks like visually:

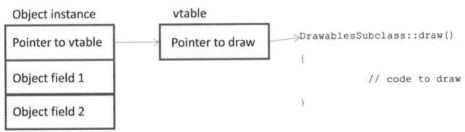

Because the object carries around its own table of methods to use, the compiler can change the addresses in the table when compiling different classes in order to provide a specific implementation of a virtual method. Of course you don't do this yourself—the compiler does it for you. The code that uses the table just has to know exactly the right index to use for each virtual method to find it in the table.

A virtual table will only contain methods declared to be virtual—non-virtual methods do not need this mechanism, so they do not have virtual table entries. If you write a class with no virtual methods at all, then your class will not have a virtual table.

When a virtual method is called, this amounts to the code accessing the vtable and finding the method by index. Writing

```
drawables[ i ]->draw();
```

is treated by the compiler as saying:

1. Get the pointer stored in `drawables[ i ]`

2. From that pointer, find the address of the virtual table for the group of methods associated with the interface of type `Drawable` (in this case, there is just one method).

3. Find the function with the given name (in this case, `draw`) in that table of functions. This table is literally a set of addresses that stores the memory location of each function.

4. Call that function, with the associated arguments.

Usually step 2 is accomplished not by using the actual name of the function, but instead by the compiler turning each function name into an index into the table. This ensures that at run time making a virtual function call is incredibly fast— there is very little performance difference between making a virtual function call and making a normal function call.

You can think of the code the compiler generates as looking like this (I made up the `call` syntax of course...)

```
call drawables[ i ]->vtable[ 0 ];
```

On the other hand, there is one real drawback to using virtual functions. Your object needs to carry about one vtable per inherited interface. This means that each virtual interface expands the size of the object by a couple of bytes. In practice, this is a serious concern only for code that creates a very large number of objects that have few member variables.

Quiz yourself
1. When does the destructor for a superclass get run?
A. Only if the object is destroyed via a call to delete on a pointer to the superclass
B. Prior to the destructor of the subclass being called
C. After the destructor of the subclass is called
D. While the destructor of the subclass is called

2. Given the following class hierarchy, what would you need to do in the constructor for `Cat`?
```
class Mammal {
public:
        Mammal (const string& species_name);
```

```
};

class Cat : public Mammal
{
public:
        Cat ();
};
```
A. Nothing special
B. Use the initializer list to call `Mammal`'s constructor with an argument of "cat"
C. Call `Mammal`'s constructor from within the `Cat` constructor with an argument of "cat"
D. You should remove the `Cat` constructor and use the default constructor, which will solve this problem for you

3. What is wrong with the following class definition?
```
class Nameable
{
        virtual string getName ();
};
```
A. It doesn't make the `getName` method public
B. It doesn't have a virtual destructor
C. It doesn't have an implementation `getName`, but it doesn't declare `getName` to be pure virtual
D. All of the above

4. When you declare a virtual method in an interface class, what does a function need to do to be able to use the interface method to call a method on a subclass?
A. Take the interface as a pointer (or a reference)
B. Nothing, it can just copy the object
C. It needs to know the name of the subclass to call the method on
D. I'm lost! What's a virtual method?

5.How does inheritance improve reuse?
A. By allowing code to inherit methods from its superclasses
B. By allowing a superclass to implement virtual methods for a subclass
C. By allowing code to be written expecting an interface, rather than a concrete class, allowing new classes to implement the interface and use that old code
D. By allowing new classes to inherit the traits of a concrete class that can be used with virtual methods

6. Which of the following is a correct statement about class access levels?
A. A subclass can access only public methods and data of its parent class
B. A subclass can access private methods and data of its parent class
C. A subclass can access only protected methods and data of its parent class
D. A subclass can access protected or public methods and data of its parent class

(View solution on page 511)

Practice problems

1. Implement a `sort` function that takes a vector of pointers to an interface class, `Comparable`, that defines a method, `compare(Comparable& other)`, and returns 0 if the objects are the same, 1 if the object is greater than `other`, and -1 if the object is less than `other`. Create a class that implements this interface, create several instances, and sort them. If you're looking for some inspiration for what to create—try a `HighScoreElement` class that has a name and a score, and sorts so that the top scores are first, but if two scores are the same, they are sorted next by name.

2. Provide another implementation of your sort function, this time taking an interface called `Comparator`, which has a method `compare(const string& lhs, const string& rhs)` that follows similar rules to the previous compare method: return 0 if the two values are the same, 1 if `lhs > rhs` or -1 if `lhs < rhs`. Write two different classes to do comparison: one that does a case-insensitive comparison and one that sorts in reverse alphabetical order.

3. Implement a logging method that takes an interface class, `StringConvertable`, as an argument. `StringConvertable` has a method `toString` that converts the resulting object into a string representation of itself. The logging method should print out the date and time as well as the object itself. (You can find information on getting the date at the following URL: http://www.cplusplus.com/reference/clibrary/ctime/). Again notice how we are able to reuse our logging method simply by implementing an interface.

Chapter 27
Namespaces

As you start to create more and more classes, you might start wondering, "Hasn't someone else written code that does this? And can I use it?" At times, the answer is going to be, "yes". Many core algorithms and data structures, like linked lists or binary trees, have already been implemented in rock solid, reusable ways, and you'll want to use that code. But if you are using code that someone else created, you have to be careful to avoid name conflicts.

For example, you might want to write a class called `LinkedList`, to store your implementation of a linked list. But it's possible that some of the code you are using has a class with the same name but a different implementation. Something has to give—you can't have two classes with the same name.

Using namespaces

To avoid this conflict, you can extend the basic name of the type by creating a **namespace**. For example, I might put my linked list class into the namespace called `com::cprogramming`, so that the fully qualified name of the type is `com::cprogramming::LinkedList`. Using a namespace drastically reduces the chance of a naming conflict. The `::` operator used here is the same as the one used for accessing static members of a class or declaring a method, but instead of being used to access elements of a class, it is being used to access elements of a namespace.

Now you might be wondering, if namespaces are so great, why doesn't the standard library code use them? Isn't this just a lot of typing for nothing?

It turns out that you have seen namespaces already. At the top of every program, we've put

```
using namespace std;
```

This is so that we can avoid having to use fully qualified names when referring to objects like `cin` and `cout`. If we didn't write this statement, we'd have to write `std::cin` or `std::cout` every time we wanted to use those objects! This technique works as long as you don't actually need to use the namespaces to avoid a naming conflict in that particular file, providing a convenient shortcut when you know that there are no collisions. When there are collisions, all you need to do is omit the using declaration for the namespace and fully qualify each type in the file.

Let's see how that would work with the earlier example. If I have two different classes called `LinkedList`, most of my files would have `using namespace com::cprogramming` at the top. If I had a file that had conflicts between the names, I'd change that file so that it referred to my `LinkedList` class as `com::cprogramming::LinkedList`. Instead of having to change all of my code everywhere, I only need to change the files where I need to use both kinds of `LinkedList`. In those files, I'd use the fully qualified name, removing the `using namespace com::cprogramming` statement.

Here's an example of how you would declare some code to be part of a namespace—in this case, a single variable:

```
namespace cprogramming
{
      int x;
} // <-- notice that no semicolon is needed
```

Now I must refer to x as `cprogramming::x` or say:

```
using namespace cprogramming;
```

And then I can just write `x` in the file that contains the line `using namespace cprogramming`.

It is possible to nest namespaces, one inside the other. You might want this if you were working at a large company with many different units, each of which needed to do some individual development. In a case like that, you might use the name of your company for the outer namespace and use an inner namespace for each individual group inside the company. Here's a simple example of declaring a nested namespace for com::cprogramming.

```
namespace com {
namespace cprogramming
{
     int x;
} }
```

Now the full name for x is com::cprogramming::x. (In this example, I don't indent for every namespace—if you use multiple namespaces and you indented for each one, the tabs would really get out of hand!)

You can write

```
using namespace com::cprogramming;
```

To access the elements of that namespace.

Namespaces are "open," meaning that you can put code into a namespace in multiple files. For example, if you create a header file to contain a class, and you put that class into a namespace:

```
namespace com {
namespace cprogramming
{
class MyClass
{
public:
     MyClass ();
};
} }
```

In the corresponding source file, you can write:

```
#include "MyClass.h"

namespace com {
namespace cprogramming
{
```

```
        MyClass::MyClass ()
        {}
} }
```

Both files are able to add code within the namespace. Just like you'd want.

When to write "using namespace"

In general, you should only put using declarations inside of cpp files and not into header files. The problem is that every file that uses that header will be subject to naming collisions—each individual cpp file should control the namespaces that it is using. In general, I recommend using fully qualified names in header files and including using declarations only within your cpp files.

There are some well-known exceptions to this rule. The standard library itself actually violates it—although for a good reason.

If you write:

```
#include <iostream.h>
```

instead of

```
#include <iostream>
```

Then you no longer need to include a using declaration for std. It turns out the content of `iostream.h` is basically:

```
#include <iostream>
using namespace std;
```

This is done for backward compatibility with programs that were created before namespaces were added to the language, so that if you had a program like this:

```
#include <iostream.h>

int main ()
{
        cout << "Hello world";
}
```
Sample Code 61: iostream_h.cpp

It would still compile when namespaces were added to the standard library.

For new code, I recommend using the newer header file (without the .h) so that you don't have this namespace pollution. It doesn't cost you much to put using `namespace std;` into each file, and it keeps you using the "most current" C++.

When should you create a namespace?

In general, if you're working on a program that is only a couple of files, creating your own namespaces is probably unnecessary. Namespaces are really intended for when you start to create programs with dozens or hundreds of files in multiple directories, where you might really start seeing naming conflicts. Quick one-off programs or multi-file programs don't really need to have their own namespace. I'd suggest you start putting code into a namespace when you think you'll reuse it later or when your program is growing so large that you need to break it into multiple directories. Any time your code reaches that level of complexity, you should be using all the tools you have available to keep it organized.

Although namespaces are hardly the most earth-shattering feature of C++ you'll learn about, they do come in handy when you are working on larger codebases. Understanding what namespaces are for—and why you'll see other people use them—will help you integrate other people's code into your own code.

Quiz yourself

1. When should you use a using namespace directive?
A. In all header files, right after the include
B. Never, they are a dangerous crutch
C. At the top of any cpp file where there's no namespace conflict
D. Right before you use a variable from that namespace

2. Why do we need namespaces?
A. To provide compiler writers some interesting work
B. To provide more encapsulation of code
C. To prevent name conflicts in large codebases
D. To help clarify what a class is for

3. When should you put code in a namespace?
A. Always

B. When you're developing a program that's large enough that it's more than a few dozen files

C. When you're developing a library to be shared with other people

D. B and C

4. Why shouldn't you put a using namespace declaration into a header file?

A. It isn't legal

B. There's no reason not to; the using declaration is only valid within the header file itself

C. It forces the using declaration onto anyone who includes the header file, even if it would cause conflicts

D. It can cause conflicts if multiple header files include using declarations

(View solution on page 513)

Practice problems

1. Take your implementation of a vector from the practice problem at the end of chapter 25 and add it to a namespace.

Chapter 28
File I/O

Files are the lifeblood of the computer—without files, everything a computer does would ultimately be impermanent, lasting only until the user reboots—or the application terminates. C++, naturally, has the ability to read and write into files. Working with files is known as **file I/O** (I/O stands for input and output).

File I/O basics

Reading and writing to files looks an awful lot like using `cout` and `cin`. Unlike `cin` and `cout`, which are global variables, you have to declare your own objects to read and write from files.[74] This means you need to know the actual types.

The two data types are the **ifstream** and the **ofstream**. The names stand for **i**nput **f**ile **stream** and **o**utput **f**ile **stream**. A **stream** is just a bunch of data that you can read from or write to. What these types do is take a file and turn it into a long stream of data that you can access, as though you were interacting with the user. Both of these types require the `fstream` header file (`fstream` stands for **f**ile **stream**).

Reading from files

Let's talk about reading from files first. To read from a file, we'll use the `ifstream` type. We can initialize an `ifstream` instance with the name of a file that we want to read from:

---

[74] For convenience, I have sometimes called them functions but they are really just objects on which methods are called.

```
#include <fstream>

using namespace std;
int main ()
{
      ifstream file_reader( "myfile.txt" );
}
```
Sample Code 62: ifstream.cpp

This small program will attempt to open the file `myfile.txt`; to find `myfile.txt` it will look in the directory where the program is executed (this is called the **working directory** of the program). You can also give a full path, if you prefer, such as `c:\myfile.txt`.

Notice that I said this program attempts to open the file. The file might not exist. You can check the result of creating an `ifstream` to see if it did, in fact, open the file by calling the method `is_open`, which indicates if the `ifstream` object has successfully opened a file:[75]

```
#include <fstream>
#include <iostream>


using namespace std;
int main ()
{
      ifstream file_reader( "myfile.txt" );
      if ( ! file_reader.is_open() )
      {
            cout << "Could not open file!" << '\n';
      }
}
```
Sample Code 63: ifstream_error_checking.cpp

When you work with files, you have no choice but to write code that handles possible failures. Files may not exist, or they may be corrupted, or they may be in use by another process on the system. In all of these cases, certain file operations may fail. Whenever you work with files, you need to be prepared for failures—disk failures, corrupted files, power loss, bad hard drive sectors—all of these things can make a file operation fail.

---

[75] You can find out about these standard functions by using web sites like http://en.cppreference.com/w/cpp or http://cplusplus.com/reference/

Once the file is open, you can use an `ifstream` just like you would use `cin`. This code reads a number from a text file:

```cpp
#include <fstream>
#include <iostream>


using namespace std;
int main ()
{
      ifstream file_reader ( "myfile.txt" );
      if ( ! file_reader.is_open() )
      {
            cout << "Could not open file!" << '\n';
      }
      int number;
      file_reader >> number;
}
```
Sample Code 64: read_file.cpp

Just as if it were reading input typed by a user, this line will read digits from the file until it finds a space or other separator. For example, if the file had the text

```
12 a b c
```

Then `number` would store 12 after the program ran.

Since we are working with files, we need to know if an error occurred. In C++, the way to check that you have successfully read in a value is to check the result of the function that performs the read operation. We can do this like so:

```cpp
#include <fstream>
#include <iostream>

using namespace std;
int main ()
{
      ifstream file_reader ( "myfile.txt" );
      if ( ! file_reader.is_open() )
      {
            cout << "Could not open file!" << '\n';
      }
      int number;
      // here, we're checking if reading in an integer
      // succeeded or not
```

```
        if ( file_reader >> number )
        {
                cout << "The value is: " << number;
        }
}
```
Sample Code 65: read_error_checking.cpp

By checking the result of the call to `file_reader >> number` we'll find out about problems reading from the disk media as well as problems with the format of the data being read. Remember way back in the beginning of the book we talked about the possibility of a user typing a letter when we want a number? This is how you guard against that kind of problem. You check the return value of the input routine; if it's true, then everything is ok and you can trust the data; if it's false, then something went wrong and you need to treat it as an error.

File formats

When you ask for input from a user, you can tell the user what you want, and if the user gives bad input, you can provide guidance on how to correct it. When you read from a file, you don't have that luxury. The file has already been written, possibly even before your program was created. To read the data back in, you need to know the **file format**. A file format is the layout of the file, although it does not need to be complex. For example, let's say that you had a high score list that you wanted to save between runs of a program. A simple file format might consist of ten lines, each with a single number.

A sample high score list might look like this

```
1000
987
864
766
744
500
453
321
201
98
5
```
Sample file 1: highscores.txt

You could write a program to read in this high score list:

```
#include <fstream>
#include <iostream>
#include <vector>

using namespace std;
int main ()
{
        ifstream file_reader( "highscores.txt" );
        if ( ! file_reader.is_open() )
        {
                cout << "Could not open file!" << '\n';
        }
        vector<int> scores;
        for ( int i = 0; i < 10; i++ )
        {
                int score;
                file_reader >> score;
                scores.push_back( score );
        }
}
```

Sample Code 66: highscore.cpp

This code is quite simple—it just opens the file and reads in one score at a time—in fact, it doesn't even really rely on the scores being separated by newline characters—it would work with spaces. But this is an accident of the implementation, not a feature of the file format. Other programs that work with the file format might not be as forgiving in what they expect to read in. A good principle when working with file formats, called Postel's Law, is: "Be liberal in what you accept, and conservative in what you send." In other words, code that produces a file should be very careful to follow the specification, but code that reads the file format should be robust to small errors made by less well-written programs. In the example program above, we are being liberal in accepting space separators in addition to newline separators.

End of file

This code is written to conform to a very specific file format, and you'll notice that it doesn't try to handle errors at all. For example, if there are fewer than ten entries, this code won't stop reading from the file, even once it reaches the end of the file. We might have fewer than ten entries if there aren't ten scores yet—for example, if the game has only been played twice. The expression EOF is often used to refer to the state of being at the end of the file.

We can make our code robust (liberal in what we accept), by handling cases where the file has fewer than ten items. We can handle this case by once again checking the result of the method used to read input.

```cpp
#include <fstream>
#include <iostream>
#include <vector>

using namespace std;

int main ()
{
        ifstream file_reader( "myfile.txt" );
        if ( ! file_reader.is_open() )
        {
                cout << "Could not open file!" << '\n';
        }
        vector<int> scores;
        for ( int i = 0; i < 10; i++ )
        {

                int score;
                if ( ! ( file_reader >> score ) )
                {
                        break;
                }

                scores.push_back( score );
        }
}
```
Sample Code 67: highscore_eof.cpp

When the code runs on a file with fewer than ten entries, it will stop reading as soon as it reaches the end of the file. By using a vector, rather than a fixed sized array, we can easily handle short files. The vector will hold exactly the input that was read in, and nothing else. If we had done the same thing with an array, we'd need to keep track of how many entries were actually stored in the array—we couldn't assume the whole array was filled.

Sometimes when you are working with a file, you'll want to read in all the data from a file until you hit the end of the file. In cases like this, you need to be able to distinguish between a read failure because you're at the end of the file, and a read failure due to an error in the file. The method `eof` will indicate if you're at the end of the file. You can write a loop that reads as much data as it can, checking the read result each time, until a failure occurs. Then you can check whether eof returns true; if so, you're at the end of the file; if not, there was an error. You can check for other failures by calling the fail method, which returns true if bad input was given or if there was a problem reading from the device. Once you've hit the end of file, you must call the clear method in order to do further file operations. We'll soon see an example using all of these methods, in the section below that writes a new score to the high score list.

There is another important difference between reading from files and interacting with the user. What would happen if we changed our high score list to include the name of the player in addition to the score? We'd need to read in the name of the player as well as the score—and we'd have to change our code to handle it. Older versions of our program will be unable to read the new file format. This can be a major headache if you have a lot of users and you want to update your file format! There are techniques you can use to **future proof** your file format by adding optional fields, or giving older programs the ability to ignore new elements of the format. These techniques, however, are outside the scope of this book. For now, just know that defining a file format is (in some ways) a bigger commitment than defining a basic interface.

Writing files

The type we need to use for writing files is called the ofstream, which stands for output file stream. This type is almost exactly like an ifstream, except that instead of using it like you use cin, you use it like cout.

Let's look at a simple program that writes out the values 0 through 9 into a file called highscores.txt (we'll soon make this code produce something a bit more like a high score list).

```
#include <fstream>
#include <iostream>
#include <cstdlib>

using namespace std;

int main ()
{
    ofstream file_writer( "highscores.txt" );
    if ( ! file_writer.is_open() )
    {
        cout << "Could not open file!" << '\n';
        return 0;
    }
```

```
    // since we don't have any real scores, we'll output
    // the numbers 10 to 1
    for ( int i = 0; i < 10; i++ )
    {
            file_writer << 10 - i << '\n';
    }
}
```

Sample Code 68: ofstream.cpp

We don't need to worry about reaching the end of file in this code. When you write to the file and you are at the end of the file, the ofstream will extend the file for you. This is called **appending** to the file.

Creating new files

When you use an ofstream to write to a file, by default, it will create the file if the file does not already exist, or overwrite it if it does. If you're saving a high score list, you probably don't mind overwriting your file each time since you're just going to write back all the data. But if you are keeping a running log—for example, if you keep track of the date and time each time someone launches your program—you definitely don't want to overwrite your log each time.

The ofstream constructor takes a second argument that specifies how the file should be handled:

ios::app	Append to the file, setting the position to the end after each write
ios::ate	Set the current position to the end
ios::trunc	Delete everything in the file (**trunc**ate it)
ios::out	Allow output to the file
ios::binary	Allow binary operations on the stream (also available when reading from a file)

If you want to select multiple options, for example opening a file for appending and using binary I/O (which we'll cover soon), you can combine the options with the pipe (|):[76]

```
ofstream a_file( "test.txt", ios::app | ios::binary );
```

This code opens the file without destroying the current contents, allowing binary data to be written at the end of the file.

File position

When a program reads to a file (or writes into a file), the file I/O code needs to know where the read or write will take place. Think of it like the cursor on your screen, telling you where the next character you type will show up.

For basic operations, you don't need to worry about the position—you can just have your code read whatever is next in the file, or write wherever will next be written to. But you can also change your position in the file without doing a read. This is often necessary when working with files that store complicated data, such as ZIP files or PDF files, or if you have a large file for which reading in every byte would be slow or impossible (such as if you were implementing a database).

There are actually two different positions in the file—one for where the program will next read and one for where the program will next write. You can get your current position using the tellg and tellp methods. These give you the current position for reading (g stands for get) and writing (p stands for put).

You can also set your position in the file, moving from your current position, by using seekp and seekg. As you probably guessed from the names, moving around in a file is called **seeking**. When you seek in a file, you move the read position or the write position to a new location. These two methods take two parameters, a distance to seek, and a source for the seek operation. The distance to seek is measured in bytes, and the source is either your current position, the start of the file or the end of the file. After seeking, you will be able

---

[76] The pipe character is a bitwise operator, bitwise-or. Each of the ios:: options sets a single bit to true, and you can combine options using the bitwise-or. For more information on bitwise operators, take a look at
 http://www.cprogramming.com/tutorial/bitwise_operators.html

to read (or write) starting at the new position in the file. Changing one position by a seek has no impact on the other position.

The three flags for the position in the file are:

ios_base::beg	Seek from the beginning of the file
ios_base::cur	Seek from the current position
ios_base::end	Seek from the end of the file

For example, to move to the start of the file before writing it, you could say:

```
file_writer.seekp( 0, ios_base::beg );
```

The value returned from `tellp` and `tellg` is a special variable type called `streampos`, defined by the standard library. It allows conversion to and from integers, but by using `streampos`, we are able to be more explicit about the type. An integer can be used anywhere, but a `streampos` is meant for a specific purpose. A `streampos` can be used to store positions in files and seek to those positions. Using the right variable type in our code makes it clear what the variable is for.

```
streampos pos = file_reader.tellg();
```

In some cases, you will not need to seek in a file—reading or writing the file from beginning to end will be enough. However, many file formats are optimized for adding new data to the file. When you add new data into a file, it is much faster to add to the end of the file than insert into the middle of the file. The problem with inserting into the middle is that you have to move everything in the file that comes after the place you're inserting into—just like inserting an element into the middle of an array.[77]

Let's modify our high scores program from earlier to add a new high score to the file. To make things interesting, we'll insert the value into the correct position in the file.

---

[77] There is one special case: if you are just overwriting existing data with new data of the exact same length, you don't need to move anything and it is just as fast as writing to the end of the file.

To do this, we need to be able to both read and write the file, so we'll use the fstream class, which allows both reading and writing to the file. Think of it as ofstream and ifstream smushed together. First we'll read in a new high score from the user; then we'll read in each line of the file, until we find a score that's less than the score that was entered. This is where we'll insert the new score. We'll save this position, read in every remaining line in the file into a vector, and then return to this position. We'll write out the new score, and then write the rest of the scores back out, replacing the lines that were already there.

Since we're using an fstream, we'll get all the benefits of being able to both read and write, but we now need to explicitly tell the constructor to open the file for both reading and writing. We'll use the flags ios::in | ios::out to make that clear. You'll need to create it a high score file before running the program; it doesn't create an empty file for you.

```cpp
#include <fstream>
#include <iostream>
#include <vector>

using namespace std;

int main ()
{
        fstream file (
                "highscores.txt",
                ios::in | ios::out
        );
        if ( ! file.is_open() )
        {
                cout << "Could not open file!" << '\n';
                return 0;
        }
        int new_high_score;
        cout << "Enter a new high score: ";
        cin >> new_high_score;

        // the while loop below searches the file until it
        // finds a value less than the current high score; at
        // this point, we know we want to insert our high
        // score right before that value. To make sure that
        // we know the right position, we keep track of the
        // position prior to the current score; the
        // pre_score_pos
        streampos pre_score_pos = file.tellg();
        int cur_score;
```

```cpp
while ( file >> cur_score )
{
    if ( cur_score < new_high_score )
    {
        break;
    }
    pre_score_pos = file.tellg();
}

// if fail is true, and we aren't at eof, there was
// some bad input
if ( file.fail() && ! file.eof() )
{
    cout << "Bad score/read--exiting";
    return 0;
}
// without calling clear, we won't be able to write
// to the file if we hit eof
file.clear();

// return to the point right before the last score we
// read, for reading so that we can read in all the
// scores that are less than our high score, and move
// them one position later in the file
file.seekg( pre_score_pos );

// now we will read in all the scores, starting with
// the one we previously read in
vector<int> scores;
while ( file >> cur_score )
{
    scores.push_back( cur_score );
}
// we expect to reach the end of file via this read
// loop because we want to read in all scores in the
// file
if ( ! file.eof() )
{
    cout << "Bad score/read--exiting";
    return 0;
}
// since we hit eof, we need to clear the file again
// so that we can write to it
file.clear();

// seek back to the position we want to do our insert
file.seekp( pre_score_pos );
// if we are not writing to the beginning of the
// file, we need to include a newline. The reason is
```

```
        // that when a number is read in it stops at the
        // first whitepsace, so the position we are at prior
        // to writing is at the end of the number rather than
        // at the start of the next line
        if ( pre_score_pos != std::streampos(0) )
        {
                file << endl;
        }
        // write out our new high score
        file << new_high_score << endl;
        // loop through the rest of the scores, outputting
        // all of them

        for ( vector<int>::iterator itr = scores.begin();
              itr != scores.end();
              ++itr )
        {
                file << *itr << endl;
        }
}
```
Sample Code 69: file_position.cpp

Accepting command line arguments

When writing programs that interact with files, you often want to let users provide the file name as an argument on the command line. This is often easier to use, and it makes it easier to write scripts that call your program. Let's take a brief pause from looking at reading from and writing to files so that we can spiff up our programs with this feature.

Command-line arguments are given after the name of a program and are passed in to the program from the operating system:

```
C:\my_program\my_program.exe arg1 arg2
```

Command line arguments are passed directly into your main function—to use command line arguments, you must provide the full declaration of the main function (previously all the main functions we've seen have had an empty argument list). In fact, main takes two parameters: one parameter is the number of command line arguments, and the other parameter is a full list of all of the command line arguments.

The full declaration of main looks like this:

```
int main (int argc, char *argv[])
```

The integer, argc, is the **arg**ument **c**ount. It is the number of arguments passed into the program from the command line, including the name of the program. You might wonder why you have not needed to include these arguments in every program; the answer is simply that if you don't put them in, the compiler ignores the fact that they are passed in to the function.

The array of character pointers is the listing of all the arguments. argv[0] is the name of the program, or an empty string if the name is not available. After that, every element number less than argc is a command line argument. You can use each argv element just like a string. argv[argc] is a NULL pointer.

Let's look at an example program that takes a command line argument—in this case, a program that takes the name of a file and outputs the entire text of it onto the screen.

```
#include <fstream>
#include <iostream>

using namespace std;

int main (int argc, char *argv[])
{
        // argc should be 2 for correct execution, the
        // program name and the filename

        if ( argc != 2 )
        {
                // when printing out usage instructions, you
                // can use argv[ 0 ] as the file name
                cout << "usage: " << argv[ 0 ] << " <filename>"
                        << endl;
        }
        else
        {
                // We assume argv[ 1 ] is a filename to open
                ifstream the_file( argv[ 1 ] );
                // Always check to see if file opening
                // succeeded
                if ( ! the_file.is_open() )
                {
                        cout << "Could not open file "
                                << argv[ 1 ] << endl;
```

```
                      return 1;
            }

            char x;
            // the_file.get( x ) reads the next character
            // from the file into x, and returns false if
            // the end of the file is hit or if an error
            // occurs
            while ( the_file.get( x ) )
            {
                      cout << x;
            }
      } // the_file is closed implicitly here by its
        // destructor
}
```
Sample Code 70: cat.cpp

This program uses the full function declaration of main to access the command line parameters. First it checks to ensure the user provided a file name. The program then checks to see if the file is valid by trying to open it. If the file is valid, it is opened—if not, the program reports an error to the user. If the file is opened successfully, then it prints out each character of the file onto the screen.

Dealing with numeric command line arguments

If you wish to take a command line parameter and use it as a number, you can do so by reading it as a string and calling the atoi function (atoi stands for ASCII **to** integer). The atoi function takes a char * and returns the integer represented by the string, and you must include the cstdlib header to use it. For example, this program reads a command line argument, converts it to a number, and prints the square of that number:

```
#include <cstdlib>
#include <iostream>

using namespace std;
int main (int argc, char *argv[])
{
      if ( argc != 2 )
      {
            // when printing out usage instructions, you
            // can use argv[ 0 ] as the file name
            cout << "usage: " << argv[ 0 ] << " <number>"
                  << endl;
      }
      else
      {
```

```
        int val = atoi( argv[ 1 ] );
        cout << val * val;
    }
    return 0;
}
```
Sample Code 71: atoi.cpp

Binary file I/O

So far we've seen how to work with files that contain textual data; now let's turn our attention to working with **binary files**, which are often used for maximal efficiency. Binary files require different programming techniques than text files. Now, don't be confused—every single file on your system is stored in binary. But in many cases, the file is written in a way that the user can read. For example, C++ source files are filled entirely with characters that a basic text editor can read. This kind of file, where every byte of the file is part of a character that can be read, is called a **text file**.

However, not all files contain just text. Some files are made up of bytes that are not printable characters. Instead, these files are just raw binary data from one or more data structures that have been written directly to disk.

For example, let's say that you have a structure that represents a player:

```
struct player
{
    int age;
    int high_score;
    string name;
};
```

If you were to write this structure into a file, you'd have two options for how to do it. First, we could record `age` and `high_score` as text fields, along with `name`, so that our file could be opened in notepad. It might look like this:

```
19
120000
Tom
```

This representation takes six characters to represent the high score. As we have learned, a character takes one byte to store, which means storing the high score will take six bytes. But the high score is an integer, and an integer usually is only four bytes (on a 32-bit system), so shouldn't we only need four bytes to store it?

The answer is yes! But if we were to write the number out using only four bytes, we can no longer open up the file in a text editor and see the actual number. Why? Because when we write 120000 into the file as a string of characters, it is encoded so that each character uses a byte to store the actual digit as a character. When you put the number into the file directly, the bytes are not encoded into characters at all. So you now have the four bytes that make up an integer written into the file. If a text editor reads the file, it will treat the four bytes as four characters, but the characters it prints will have no relation to the number we are showing! The result will be meaningless because we were encoding the file differently.

Binary file formats use less space. In the example above, we saw that storing the number 120000 in characters takes 50% more space than using the binary representation. You can imagine that this could have a big impact if you're sending data over a network, or if your hard drive isn't very fast or big. On the other hand, binary files are more difficult to look at and understand—you can't just open up a binary file in a text editor to see what data is inside it. File format designers face a tradeoff between creating efficient formats and creating formats that any human can understand and modify. Text-based markup languages like XML are often used to create file formats that take up more space, but that are very easy for a human to understand.

When space is an issue, processors are fast enough that it is possible to use compression technologies like ZIP to reduce the space required while maintaining an otherwise text-based file after it has been unzipped. Since it is very easy to unzip a file, these files are still easy for humans to work with, while being much smaller than the uncompressed text file would be.

Binary files are still common, however—many existing file formats are binary, and many file formats really must be binary—anything that stores images, video or audio doesn't have a meaningful, full fidelity textual representation. And when maximal performance or space saving is necessary, binary files still win out—for example, in Office 2007 Microsoft introduced new file formats that were based on XML inside of a ZIP file. But they also added one binary format for Excel (.xlsb) for users who need maximal performance. In other words, binary files are here to stay, and any time you need to design a file format, you must evaluate the trade-offs between easier implementation and representation (text-based formats) versus performance and size (binary formats).

So, you might ask, how do you actually work with a binary file?

Working with binary files

Step one is to open a file in binary mode:

```
ofstream a_file( "test.bin", ios::binary );
```

Once the file is open, you can't use the input and output functions we've used before—we'll need to use functions that are specific to working with binary data. We need to write bytes directly into the file from a block of memory. The method that we will use is called `write`, and it takes a pointer to a block of memory and the size of memory to write into the file. The pointer type is a `char*`, but your data doesn't have to be characters. So why are we using a char? In C++, the way to work with individual bytes is to use a single byte variable, the `char`, or a pointer to a series of bytes, the `char*`. When you want write a literal series of bytes to a file, you need to provide a `char*` in order to put individual bytes into the file. In order to write an integer to the file, we want to treat it as a series of bytes, `char*`, and pass that pointer to a method that will write the bytes from memory directly into the file. To do that, the write method will write out each character, each byte, one by one, in order. For example, suppose you have the number 255. In memory, this is represented by the byte 0xFF (255 in hex). If you have an integer that stores the byte 0xFF, it will look like this in memory:

```
0x000000FF
```

Or, byte for byte,

```
00 00 00 FF
```

To write an integer into a file, we need a way of referring directly to this set of bytes. That's why we use a char*: it isn't for its ability to represent ASCII characters; it's for its ability to work with bytes.

We will also need a way to tell the compiler that it should treat our data as though it were an array of characters.

Converting to char*

So how do we tell the compiler to treat a variable as a pointer to a char, rather than a pointer to its true type? Asking the compiler to treat a variable as a different type is called **typecasting**. A typecast tells the compiler—"no, really, I know what I'm doing; I really want this variable to be used this way". We want to treat a variable as a series of individual bytes, so we need to use a cast in order to force the compiler to give you access to each individual byte.

The two most basic typecasts are `static_cast` and `reinterpret_cast`. A `static_cast` is used when you want to cast between related types—for example, telling the compiler to treat a `double` as an `integer` so that you can truncate it—e.g. `static_cast<int>( 3.4 )`. The type being cast to is provided in brackets after the name of the cast.

In this case, though, we want to completely ignore the type system and have the compiler reinterpret a series of bytes as belonging to a totally different type. To achieve this feat, we need `reinterpret_cast`. For example, to treat an array of integers as an array of characters, we can write

```
int x[ 10 ];
reinterpret_cast<char*>( x );
```

By the way, working with binary data is one of the few places where a `reinterpret_cast` is a good idea. Whenever you see a `reinterpret_cast`, be suspicious! It is a powerful way of making the compiler to do things that it normally wouldn't do, and, as a result, the compiler will not check the code that uses the cast as carefully as it checks other code. In this particular case, we really are trying to get memory that is just a sequence of bytes, so it's what we need; but if that's not your intent, it's not a good idea to use `reinterpret_cast`.

An example of binary I/O

Finally, we can demonstrate binary input and output! This sample code fills an array and then writes it into the file. It uses the `write` method we saw earlier, taking a `char*` for the source data, and the size of the data to write from that source. In this case, the source is our array, and the size of the array is the length of the array in bytes.

```
int nums[ 10 ];
```

```
for ( int i = 0; i < 10; i++ )
{
    nums[ i ] = i;
}
a_file.write(
    reinterpret_cast<char*>( nums ),
    sizeof( nums )
);
```

We start with an array of integers, but by casting it to a char*, it will be treated as simply an array of bytes, which will be written directly to disk. When we later read in those bytes again, it will put back into memory exactly the same set of bytes, and we can then cast that memory back to an integer to get the exact same value.

Notice that the size to write is provided by the sizeof operator. The sizeof command is very useful for getting the size of a particular variable. In this case, it returns the total number of bytes that make up the array nums.

Be careful when using sizeof on a pointer, though. When you give it a pointer, it gives you the size of the pointer, not the size of the memory pointed to. The code above works because nums is declared as an array rather than a pointer, and sizeof knows the total size of the array. If you have a pointer variable, int *p_num, the size of that variable is (usually) four bytes because that's all it needs to hold an address. If you want the size of the pointed-to thing, you can write sizeof(*p_num). Here, the result will be the same as sizeof(int). If the pointer points to an array (if you had written int *p_num = new int[length]), you can get the total size like so: sizeof(* p_num) * length.

You can also use the write method to write a structure directly into your file. For example, let's say that you have a structure

```
struct PlayerRecord
{
    int age;
    int score;
};
```

You can simply create an instance of PlayerRecord and write it into the file:

```
PlayerRecord rec;
```

```
rec.age = 10;
rec.score = 890;

a_file.write(
      reinterpret_cast<char*>( & rec ),
      sizeof( rec )
);
```

Notice that we take the address of rec in this case, to pass in a pointer to the structure.

Storing classes in a file

What if we decided to add a non-basic data type to our structure? For example, what if we put a string into the structure?

```
struct PlayerRecord
{
      int age;
      int score;
      string name;
};
```

In this case, we've simply added the name of the player as a string to the structure. But now if we were to write it into the file, what would happen when we got to the string? It would write the information that is stored inside the string—but it probably wouldn't write the content of the string itself.

The string type is implemented as a pointer to a string (possibly along with some other data, such as the length of the string). When we write out the struct as binary data, it will write out what is stored directly in the string—the pointer and the length. But this pointer is only meaningful while your program is running! The actual pointer value—the memory address—isn't useful once your program quits because there's no longer anything at that address. The next time someone reads in the structure, it will get a pointer that points to memory that hasn't been properly allocated, or that points to data that has nothing to do with the string.

We need to come up with a fixed, well-defined format to represent our binary data on disk, rather than blindly writing out the structure itself directly to disk. Our format will be that we write the characters of the string and the size of the string (the size is needed for reasons that will become clear very soon). Let's see what that would look like.

```
PlayerRecord rec;
rec.age = 11;
rec.score = 200;
rec.name = "John";

fstream a_file(
     "records.bin",
     ios::trunc | ios::binary | ios::in | ios::out
);


a_file.write(
     reinterpret_cast<char*>( & rec.age ),
     sizeof( rec.age )
);
a_file.write(
     reinterpret_cast<char*>( & rec.score ),
     sizeof( rec.score )
);
int len = rec.name.length();
a_file.write(
     reinterpret_cast<char*>( & len ),
     sizeof( len )
);
a_file.write( rec.name.c_str(), len + 1 );
// + 1 for the null terminator
```

First, notice the use of the c_str method to get a pointer to the string of characters in memory, as opposed to using the string object itself, which has no guaranteed layout in memory. If your string reads "abc", then calling c_str will give you the address of a sequence of characters with the letters "abc". This string will end with a character having the value 0; this 0 byte is called the null terminator, and it indicates the end of the string.[78] A string in this format is called a C string because in C, the C string was the only string format universally available.

It's ok that we are writing character data into the binary file; even though we're writing characters into the file, this is still writing binary data—it just happens to be binary data that is also human-readable.

---

[78] Sometimes you will see the null terminator written as '\0'. This is perfectly legitimate way of writing it. The difference between 0 and '\0' is that if you write '\0' then the native variable type is a char, otherwise it is an integer that is converted into a char. For our purposes, either one is fine.

It's also perfectly fine that we aren't writing out the exact structure we started with—what matters is that we can convert the format of the file on disk into an object in memory, not that we directly write the bytes from memory onto the disk. A file format is a representation of data; a structure is another representation of data. The two are storing the same data, but the format of the structure in memory doesn't need to be the same as the format of the data in the file.

Reading from a file

To read back from a binary file, we will use the aptly named `read` method. The read method's arguments are nearly equivalent to the arguments to `write`: a place to put the data and the amount of data to read.[79] To read back an integer from a file, we would write this code:

```
int x = 3;
a_file.read( reinterpret_cast<char*>( & x ), sizeof( x ) );
```

When you work with files, you will need ways to both write and read each kind of data structure you want to store in the file. Let's look at how to read back a `PlayerRecord`. First, we'll do the easy part, resetting our file position and then reading in the fields `age` and `score` that were written directly to disk without changing their format.

```
a_file.seekg( 0, ios::beg );

PlayerRecord in_rec;

if ( ! a_file.read(
        reinterpret_cast<char*>( & in_rec.age ),
        sizeof( in_rec.age )
) )
{
        // handle error
}
if ( ! a_file.read(
        reinterpret_cast<char*>( & in_rec.score ),
        sizeof( in_rec.score )
```

---

[79] One notable difference is that the pointer passed to `write` may be const, meaning you can pass a pointer to a const object to be written. In this case, by the way, if you're passing in a const object, you need to use `reinterpret_cast<const char*>` (notice `const` in the cast).

```
) )
{
      // handle error
}
```

Now what about reading in the string? We can't just read in the char* from the file in on top of our string. The format in memory is different from the format on disk. We have to read in the char* and then create a new string.

Now you can see why we needed to store the length of the string: we need to know how much space to allocate to hold the char*. We will read in the length of the string; then we will allocate memory for it, and finally we will read the string into that memory.

```
int str_len;

if ( ! a_file.read(
      reinterpret_cast<char*>( & str_len ),
      sizeof( str_len )
) )
{
      // handle error
}
// perform a sanity check to ensure we don't try to
// allocate too much memory!
else if ( str_len > 0 && str_len < 10000 )
{
      char *p_str_buf = new char[ str_len ];
      // + 1 for null terminator
      if ( ! a_file.read( p_str_buf, str_len + 1 ) )
      {
            // handle error
      }
      // validate that the string is null-terminated
      if ( p_str_buf[ str_len ] == 0 )
      {
            in_rec.name = string( p_str_buf );
      }
      delete[] p_str_buf;
}

cout << in_rec.age << " " <<in_rec.score << " " <<
in_rec.name << endl;
```

Here's a full working program for you to experiment with.

```cpp
#include <fstream>
#include <string>
#include <iostream>

using namespace std;

struct PlayerRecord
{
      int age;
      int score;
      string name;
};

int main ()
{
      PlayerRecord rec;
      rec.age = 11;
      rec.score = 200;
      rec.name = "John";

      fstream a_file(
            "records.bin",
            ios::trunc | ios::binary | ios::in | ios::out
      );

      a_file.write(
            reinterpret_cast<char*>( & rec.age ),
            sizeof( rec.age )
      );
      a_file.write(
            reinterpret_cast<char*>(  & rec.score ),
            sizeof( rec.score )
      );

      int len = rec.name.length();
      a_file.write(
            reinterpret_cast<char*>( & len ),
            sizeof( len )
      );

      a_file.write(
            rec.name.c_str(),
            rec.name.length() + 1
      );

      PlayerRecord in_rec;

      a_file.seekg( 0, ios::beg );
      if ( ! a_file.read(
```

```
                    reinterpret_cast<char*>( & in_rec.age ),
                    sizeof( in_rec.age )
        ) )
        {
                cout << "Error reading from file" << endl;
                return 1;
        }
        if ( ! a_file.read(
                    reinterpret_cast<char*>(& in_rec.score ),
                    sizeof( in_rec.score )
        ) )
        {
                cout << "Error reading from file" << endl;
                return 1;
        }

        int str_len;

        if ( ! a_file.read(
                    reinterpret_cast<char*>( & str_len ),
                    sizeof( str_len )
        ) )
        {
                cout << "Error reading from file" << endl;
                return 1;
        }
        // perform a sanity check to ensure we don't try to
        // allocate too much memory!
        if ( str_len > 0 && str_len < 10000 )
        {
                char *p_str_buf = new char[ str_len + 1];
                if ( ! a_file.read( p_str_buf, str_len + 1 ) )
                // + 1 for null terminator
                {
                        delete[] p_str_buf;
                        cout << "Error reading from file"
                             << endl;
                        return 1;
                }
                // validate that the string is null-terminated
                if ( p_str_buf[ str_len ] == 0 )
                {
                        in_rec.name = string( p_str_buf );
                }
                delete[] p_str_buf;
        }
        cout << in_rec.age << " " <<in_rec.score << " "
             << in_rec.name << endl;
```

}
Sample Code 72: binary.cpp

After you run this program, try opening the file in Notepad or another text editor. You'll be able to read the name John, because it is stored as characters of a string, but nothing else will make sense.

Quiz yourself

1. Which type can you use to read from a file?

A. `ifstream`

B. `ofstream`

C. `fstream`

D. A and C

2. Which of the following statements is true?

A. Text files use less space than binary files

B. Binary files are easier to debug

C. Binary files are more space efficient than text files

D. Text files are too slow to use in real programs

3. When writing to a binary file, why can't you pass a pointer to a `string` object?

A. You must always pass a `char*` in to the write method

B. The string object may not be held in memory

C. We don't know the layout of a string object, it may contain pointers that would be written to the file

D. Strings are too large and must be written piece by piece

4. Which of the following statements is true of a file format?

A. File formats are as easy to change as any other input

B. Changing a file format requires thinking about what happens when an old version of a program reads a new version of a file

C. Designing a file format requires thinking about what happens if a new version of a program opens an old version of a file

D. B and C

(View solution on page 514)

Practice problems

1. Reimplement the text file version of the high-score program that inserts into the correct file position, but do it using a binary file format instead of a text file format. How can you tell if your program is working? Create a program that displays the file as a text file.

2. Modify the HTML parser you implemented in Chapter 19   More about Strings so that it can read data from a file on disk.

3. Create a simple XML parser. XML is a basic formatting language, similar to HTML. The document is a tree structure of nodes, of the form <node>[data]</node>, where [data] is either some text or another nested node. XML nodes may have attributes, of the form <node attribute="value"></node>. (The true XML specification includes many more details, but that would be a lot more work to implement.) Your parser should accept an interface class with several methods that it calls when something interesting happens:

   1) Whenever a node is read, it calls a method nodeStart, with the name of the node.

   2) Whenever an attribute is read, it calls a method, attributeRead; this method should always be called immediately after the nodeStart method for the node with which the attribute is associated.

   3) Whenever a node has body text, call nodeTextRead, with the content of the text as a string. If you have a situation like this <node>text<sub-node>text</sub-node>more text</node>, there should be separate calls to nodeTextRead for the text before the sub- node and the text after the sub-node.

   4) Whenever an end-node is read, call nodeEnd, with the name of the node.

   5) You may treat any < or > character as part of a node tag. If an XML author wants < or > to appear in the text, it should be written as < or > (for less-than and greater-than). Since ampersands must also be escaped, they must appear as &. You do not need to perform translation of < and > or & in your code, however.

Here are a few example XML documents for you to use as test input data:
```
<address-book>
<entry>
<name>Alex Allain</name>
      <email>webmaster@cprogramming.com</email>
</entry>
<entry>
      <name>Joe Doe</name>
      <email>john@doe.com</email>
</entry>
</address-book>
```

And

```
<html>
      <head>
            <title>Doc title</title>
      </head>
      <body>This is a nice <a
href="http://www.cprogramming.com">link</a> to a
website.</body>
</html>
```

To test that your parser is working correctly, you can write a piece of code that displays each element of the file as it is parsed, and validate that it gets the elements that you expect. Or you can implement the next exercise, which will show an example of your parser in use.

4. Rewrite your HTML parser so that it uses your XML parser instead of the hand-coded parsing you had before. Add support for displaying lists. You should be able to read the <ul> tag or the <nl> tag for unordered and numbered lists. Each list item should be between <li> and </li> tags. The display for
```
<ul>
<li>first item</li>
<li>second item</li>
</ul>
```

Should be
```
* first item
* second item
```

And for
```
<nl>
<li>first item</li>
```

```
<li>second item</li>
</nl>
```

Should be
```
1. first item
2. second item
```

Make sure that you restart your numbering if a second numbered list appears!

Chapter 29
Templates in C++

So far you've had to specify the types for everything you've done in C++. Declare a variable? You need a type. Declare a function—you need the types for all the parameters, the return value, and all its local variables.

Sometimes, though, you want to write code that is generic—it doesn't matter what type you are using because the logic is the same for all types. You've already seen some examples of this type of code written by someone else—the STL (see page 317). The STL is a collection of data structures (and also algorithms) that operate in a generic fashion—they can hold any type that you, the programmer, ask for. When you store items in an STL vector, you tell the vector the type of data it will store; you don't have to work with just pre-defined possibilities. The authors of the STL wrote one vector implementation capable of storing all types of data.

How did they achieve this wonderful property? They used a feature of C++ called **templates**. Templates allow you to write a "template" of a function or class, without writing in all of the types; then when support for a particular type is needed, the compiler can create, or **instantiate**, a version of the template with all the types filled in. That's what happens when you write `vector<int> vec`; the compiler fills in the `vector` template with the `int` type, creating a usable class.

Using templates, as you've already seen, is pretty straightforward. This chapter is all about *creating* your own template functions and template classes. We'll start by looking at template functions.

Template functions

Templates are perfect for making more generic functions. For example, you might consider writing a small helper function to compute the area of a triangle:

```
int triangleArea (int base, int height)
{
     return base * height * .5;
}
```

What if you wanted to find the area of a triangle with a height of .5 and a base of .5? The values will be truncated to zero since both arguments are integers, so the function will return 0, even though the area isn't zero.

The other alternative is to write another method:

```
double triangleAreaDouble (double base, double height)
{
     return base * height * .5;
}
```

This code looks exactly like the code from the first function...except for the line where we declared all of the types to be doubles instead of integers. If we want to do the same thing with another type—maybe a custom number class—we're going to have to write a third implementation of this function.

C++ templates are perfect for this kind of thing. The template allows you to "factor out" the types. In exchange for the caller of the function listing the types to be used, the compiler will generate a function for each of the requested types.

Template declaration syntax looks a little bit intimidating, but I'll break it down so that it makes sense. Here's how you would write this function using template syntax:

```
template <typename T>
T triangleArea (T base, T height)
{
```

```
        return base * height * .5;
}
```

First, we declare that the function is a template using the **template** keyword. Following this, we list the **template parameters**, in angle brackets—these parameters are the values that the template user will specify (e.g. int in the expression vector<int>). The template parameter is supposed to be a type rather than a value, so we use the **typename** keyword. Right after typename we put the name of the parameter, T—the whole thing is quite similar to declaring an argument to a function. When the caller of the function provides the type as a template parameter, the template will treat any reference to the parameter, T, as if it were that type. Again, it's just like using a function argument to get the value passed into the function.

For example, if the caller writes

```
triangleArea<double>( .5, .5 );
```

Then everywhere that T appears in the code, it will be replaced with double. It will be as though we'd written the triangleAreaDouble function. The code we wrote was literally a template that the compiler used to create the specific specialized function that handled the double type.

Put another way, you can think of the whole line

```
template <typename T>
```

as reading: "the function (or class) that follows is a template; inside it, I will use the letter T as a type—such as int, double, char—or the name of a specific class. When someone needs to use the template, a specific type must be provided for T. This is done by putting the type inside the angle brackets(<>) before the name of the function (or class)."

Type inference
In some cases, the caller of a template function doesn't even need to explicitly provide the template parameter—the compiler is often able to infer the values for the template parameters based on the arguments to the function. For example, if you wrote

```
triangleArea( .5, .5);
```

The compiler would be able to figure out that T was supposed to be a double. That's because the template parameter, T, is used to declare the arguments to the function. Because the compiler knows the types of the arguments, it can infer what T is supposed to be.

Type inference works any time a template parameter is used as the type for one of the function arguments.

Duck typing

There's a saying that if it, "looks like a duck, walks like a duck, and talks like a duck, it is a duck". Amazingly, this saying is often used in relation to C++ templates. Here's why:

When you pass in a template parameter, the compiler needs to decide whether that template parameter is valid for the template. For example, in our triangleArea template, the kinds of values passed to the function must support the arithmetic operator for multiplication:

```
return base * height * .5;
```

But some types can't be multiplied. Integers and doubles, as different kinds of numbers, can be multiplied. But what about vector<int>? The idea of multiplying a vector is absurd—it doesn't mean anything and the vector class doesn't support it.

If you tried to pass in three vectors to triangleArea, the function call would not compile:

BAD CODE
```
int main ()
{
        vector<int> a, b, c;
        triangleArea ( a, b, c );
}
```

In fact, the compiler is very precise, and will tell you which operations vector<int> does not support:

```
template_compile.cc: In function 'T compute_equation(T, T,
T) [with T = std::vector<int, std::allocator<int> >]':
```

```
template_compile.cc:13:   instantiated from here
template_compile.cc:5: error: no match for 'operator*' in
'base * height'
```

This error message is long, but we can break it down. The first line tells you which template function has a problem (`triangleArea`); the second line tells you the line on which you tried to use that template function. That's usually the line you want to actually look at in your code. (By the way, the phrase "instantiated from here" just means "where you tried to use a template." **Instantiate** is programmer-ese for create—in this case, you tried to create an implementation of `compute_equation` with the template parameter `vector<int>`.)

The next lines tell you exactly why the compile failed. In this case, it says, "no match for 'operator*' in 'base * height'". What this means is that it couldn't figure out how to multiply `base` and `height` (there is no * operator defined for vectors). Because both variables are vectors, you can guess that this means vectors don't support multiplication.[80]

The vector, in other words, does not act like a number—it doesn't "look like a number, walk like a number, or talk like a number". Whenever a template function is used, the compiler determines whether the type that is given can actually work inside the template. It doesn't care about anything except whether the type supports the specific methods and operations that are called on it. It just needs to "look like" a type that works.

Duck typing is very different from the way that polymorphic functions work; a polymorphic function takes a pointer to an interface class and can only call methods defined on that interface class. With templates, there is no pre-defined interface that any particular template parameter must conform to. As long as the template parameter can be used the way the function is written, the function will compile. In other words, if the template type "looks like a duck, walks like a duck, and talks like a duck" our template would treat it like a duck. Normally, templates expect less aquatic qualities from the template parameters, but I hope you now see why we say templates use **duck typing**—all

---

[80] You might wonder why the compiler does not complain about adding vectors. It would have, if it had gotten that far. But the compiler saw the problem with multiplication and gave up before reaching the addition.

that matters is that the type supports the methods that are needed to make the template work.

Template classes

Template classes are often the purview of library writers who want to create classes like `vector` and `map`. But everyday programming can benefit from the ability to make code more generic. Don't use templates just because you can, but look for opportunities to remove classes that differ only by the types involved. You'll probably find yourself writing template methods more often than you write template classes, but it's handy to know how to use them—for example if you want to implement your own custom data structure.

Declaring a template class is very much like declaring a template function.

For example, we could build a small class to wrap an array:[81]

```
template <typename T> class ArrayWrapper
{
private:
      T * _p_mem;
};
```

Just like with a template function, we start off by declaring that we are going to introduce a template, using the `template` keyword, and then add the list of template parameters. In this case, we have only a single template parameter: T.

We can use the type T wherever we want to use the type that the user would specify—just like working with a template function.

When you define a function for a template class, you must also use the template syntax. Let's say that we add a constructor for the `ArrayWrapper` template:

```
template <typename T> class ArrayWrapper
{
```

---

[81] In programming, the term **wrapping** is used when one function calls another function to implement most of the functionality, but the outer function also does some small amount of additional work such as logging or error checking. In this case, the main method is the one that is used to implement the outer method, and the outer method is said to wrap the main method.

```
public:
      ArrayWrapper (int size);

private:
      T *_p_mem;
};

// now, to define the constructor outside of the class, we
// need to start off by marking the function as being a
// template
template <typename T>
ArrayWrapper<T>::ArrayWrapper (int size)
      : _p_mem( new T[ size ] )
{ }
```

We begin with same basic template prelude, redeclaring the template parameter. The only difference from before is that the class name includes the template (`ArrayWrapper<T>`), making it clear that this is part of a template class, and not a template function on a non-template class called `ArrayWrapper`.

In this method implementation, we can use the template parameter as a stand-in for the type provided, just as with template functions. Unlike with a template function, the caller of the function does not ever need to provide the template parameter—the parameter is taken from the initial declaration of the template type. For example, when you get the size of a vector of integers, you don't write `vec.size<int>()` or `vec<int>.size()`; you just write `vec.size()`.

Tips for working with templates

It is often easier to write a class for a specific type first and then rewrite the code using templates. For example, you might declare a class using integers, and then from that declaration, come up with a generic template. This approach is not required, and you don't need to do it if you are comfortable with templates—but when you're writing your first templates, it can help you separate issues with the syntax for templates from issues with the algorithm.

For example, let's look at a simple calculator class that works only on integers—at first.

```
class Calc
{
public:
      Calc ();
```

```
        int multiply (int x, int y);
        int add (int x, int y);
};

Calc::Calc ()
{}

int Calc::multiply (int x, int y)
{
        return x * y;
}

int Calc::add (int x, int y)
{
        return x + y;
}
```

This little class works very well for integers. Now we can turn it into a template so that we can make calculators for non-integer types:

```
template <typename Type>
class Calc
{
public:
        Calc ();
        Type multiply (Type x, Type y);
        Type add (Type x, Type y);
};

template <typename Type> Calc<Type>::Calc ()
{}

template <typename Type> Type Calc<Type>::multiply (
            Type x,
            Type y
        )
{
        return x * y;
}

template <typename Type> Type Calc<Type>::add (
            Type x,
            Type y
        )
{
        return x + y;
```

```
}

int main ()
{
    // demonstrate a declaration
    Calc<int> c;
}
```
Sample Code 73: calc.cpp

Several modifications were required for this transformation: we had to declare that there was a template type called `Type`:

```
template <typename Type>
```

Then we had to add this template declaration before the class and before each function definition:

```
template <typename Type> class Calc
```

```
template <typename Type> int Calc::multiply (int x, int y)
```

We also had to modify each function definition to indicate that it was part of a template class:

```
template <typename Type> int Calc<Type>::multiply (
        int x,
        int y
)
```

Finally, we had to replace `int` everywhere with `Type`:

```
template <typename Type> Type Calc<Type>::multiply (
        Type x,
        Type y
    )
```

Once you are used to templates, turning a class defined for a specific type into a template class that works for many types is a mechanical transformation.[82] Over time, you will become comfortable enough with the template syntax to write template classes from scratch without any intermediate code.

---

[82] Be careful that you don't over-generalize. For example, if you had a loop counter that was also an integer, you wouldn't want to change its type.

Templates and header files

So far we've looked at templates that were written directly into `.cpp` files. What would happen if we want to put the template declaration into a header file? The problem is that the code that uses a template function (or template class) must have access to the entire template definition for each function call to a template function (and for each member function called on a template class). This is very different from how normal functions work, which require only that the caller know the function declaration. For example, if you were to put the `Calc` class into its own header file, you would have to also put the full definition of the constructor and the `add` method into the header file, rather than placing them into a `.cpp` file as you normally would. Otherwise, any attempt to use `Calc` would fail.

This unfortunate property of templates has to do with the way that templates are compiled; the compiler mostly ignores templates when it first parses them. It is only when you use the template with a specific concrete type (when you say `Calc<int>`) that the compiler will generate the code for the template for that specific type (`int`, in this case). In order to do that code generation, most compilers need to have the template available to generate the code. As a result, you must include all of the template code in every file that uses the template. Moreover, when you compile a file that contains a template, you might not learn about syntax errors in the template until someone tries to use the template for the first time.

When you create a template class, generally the easiest approach is simply to put all of the template definitions in the header file. It can be helpful to use a different extension than `.h` to make it clear that your file is a template—for example, `.hxx`.

Summarizing templates

Templates allow you to create generic code—code that will work for any type, rather than being restricted to just, say, an integer. Templates are used frequently to implement C++ libraries (such as the standard template library). You will probably find that you do not often need to write template code, but be on the lookout for code that has the exact same structure but with different types. For example, you might find that you are writing code to loop over multiple different kinds of vectors, and that the operation you perform is the same for each. In fact, many of the times where you need a template will come from working with another type that is already templated, such as the STL containers.

For example, you might write a function to add the values in a vector and another function to append all of the strings in a vector. Both of these functions have the same basic structure of looping over a vector and using the + operator, but they do the work on different types. If you see code like this, follow the principle, "don't repeat yourself." If you write code doing the same thing for two different types, use a template instead of writing two separate implementations.

Diagnosing template error messages

The downside of templates is that most compilers give hard-to-understand error messages when you misuse a template—even if you didn't write the template (this might happen, for example, when you use the STL). You may get flooded with a page of error messages for a single mistake. Template error messages are difficult to read because they expand out template parameters to their full types—even template parameters that you don't normally use (because they are provided as default parameters).

For example, take this innocent looking declaration of a vector:

```
vector<int, int> vec;
```

There's one tiny problem with this declaration—it should have only one template parameter. But when you compile it, you get a crazy number of errors:

```
/usr/lib/gcc/x86_64-redhat-
linux/4.1.2/../../../../include/c++/4.1.2/bits/stl_vector.h
: In instantiation of 'std::_Vector_base<int, int>':
/usr/lib/gcc/x86_64-redhat-
linux/4.1.2/../../../../include/c++/4.1.2/bits/stl_vector.h
:159:   instantiated from 'std::vector<int, int>'
template_err.cc:6:   instantiated from here
/usr/lib/gcc/x86_64-redhat-
linux/4.1.2/../../../../include/c++/4.1.2/bits/stl_vector.h
:78: error: 'int' is not a class, struct, or union type
/usr/lib/gcc/x86_64-redhat-
linux/4.1.2/../../../../include/c++/4.1.2/bits/stl_vector.h
:95: error: 'int' is not a class, struct, or union type
/usr/lib/gcc/x86_64-redhat-
linux/4.1.2/../../../../include/c++/4.1.2/bits/stl_vector.h
:99: error: 'int' is not a class, struct, or union type
```

```
/usr/lib/gcc/x86_64-redhat-
linux/4.1.2/../../../../include/c++/4.1.2/bits/stl_vector.h
: In instantiation of 'std::_Vector_base<int,
int>::_Vector_impl':
/usr/lib/gcc/x86_64-redhat-
linux/4.1.2/../../../../include/c++/4.1.2/bits/stl_vector.h
:123:   instantiated from 'std::_Vector_base<int, int>'
/usr/lib/gcc/x86_64-redhat-
linux/4.1.2/../../../../include/c++/4.1.2/bits/stl_vector.h
:159:   instantiated from 'std::vector<int, int>'
template_err.cc:6:   instantiated from here
/usr/lib/gcc/x86_64-redhat-
linux/4.1.2/../../../../include/c++/4.1.2/bits/stl_vector.h
:82: error: 'int' is not a class, struct, or union type
/usr/lib/gcc/x86_64-redhat-
linux/4.1.2/../../../../include/c++/4.1.2/bits/stl_vector.h
:86: error: 'int' is not a class, struct, or union type
/usr/lib/gcc/x86_64-redhat-
linux/4.1.2/../../../../include/c++/4.1.2/bits/stl_vector.h
: In instantiation of 'std::vector<int, int>':
template_err.cc:6:   instantiated from here
/usr/lib/gcc/x86_64-redhat-
linux/4.1.2/../../../../include/c++/4.1.2/bits/stl_vector.h
:161: error: 'int' is not a class, struct, or union type
/usr/lib/gcc/x86_64-redhat-
linux/4.1.2/../../../../include/c++/4.1.2/bits/stl_vector.h
:193: error: no members matching 'std::_Vector_base<int,
int>::_M_get_Tp_allocator' in 'struct
std::_Vector_base<int, int>'
/usr/lib/gcc/x86_64-redhat-
linux/4.1.2/../../../../include/c++/4.1.2/bits/stl_vector.h
: In destructor 'std::vector<_Tp, _Alloc>::~vector() [with
_Tp = int, _Alloc = int]':
template_err.cc:6:   instantiated from here
/usr/lib/gcc/x86_64-redhat-
linux/4.1.2/../../../../include/c++/4.1.2/bits/stl_vector.h
:272: error: '_M_get_Tp_allocator' was not declared in this
scope
/usr/lib/gcc/x86_64-redhat-
linux/4.1.2/../../../../include/c++/4.1.2/bits/stl_vector.h
: In constructor 'std::_Vector_base<_Tp,
_Alloc>::_Vector_base(const _Alloc&) [with _Tp = int,
_Alloc = int]':
/usr/lib/gcc/x86_64-redhat-
linux/4.1.2/../../../../include/c++/4.1.2/bits/stl_vector.h
:203:   instantiated from 'std::vector<_Tp,
_Alloc>::vector(const _Alloc&) [with _Tp = int, _Alloc =
int]'
template_err.cc:6:   instantiated from here
```

```
/usr/lib/gcc/x86_64-redhat-
linux/4.1.2/../../../../include/c++/4.1.2/bits/stl_vector.h
:107: error: no matching function for call to
'std::_Vector_base<int,
int>::_Vector_impl::_Vector_impl(const int&)'
/usr/lib/gcc/x86_64-redhat-
linux/4.1.2/../../../../include/c++/4.1.2/bits/stl_vector.h
:82: note: candidates are: std::_Vector_base<int,
int>::_Vector_impl::_Vector_impl(const
std::_Vector_base<int, int>::_Vector_impl&)
/usr/lib/gcc/x86_64-redhat-
linux/4.1.2/../../../../include/c++/4.1.2/bits/stl_vector.h
: In member function 'void std::_Vector_base<_Tp,
_Alloc>::_M_deallocate(_Tp*, size_t) [with _Tp = int,
_Alloc = int]':
/usr/lib/gcc/x86_64-redhat-
linux/4.1.2/../../../../include/c++/4.1.2/bits/stl_vector.h
:119:    instantiated from 'std::_Vector_base<_Tp,
_Alloc>::~_Vector_base() [with _Tp = int, _Alloc = int]'
/usr/lib/gcc/x86_64-redhat-
linux/4.1.2/../../../../include/c++/4.1.2/bits/stl_vector.h
:203:    instantiated from 'std::vector<_Tp,
_Alloc>::vector(const _Alloc&) [with _Tp = int, _Alloc =
int]'
template_err.cc:6:    instantiated from here
/usr/lib/gcc/x86_64-redhat-
linux/4.1.2/../../../../include/c++/4.1.2/bits/stl_vector.h
:133: error: 'struct std::_Vector_base<int,
int>::_Vector_impl' has no member named 'deallocate'
```

What on earth is going on? Who is the devil who designed this error message? The problem is this: vector has a second parameter that is a default template parameter—normally the compiler auto-supplies it. But when you fill in the second `int`, it tries to use `int` as the second template parameter, but this parameter cannot be an `int`. The compiler does actually tell you this near the start of the error message list:

```
error: 'int' is not a class, struct, or union type
```

The template code is trying to use the template parameter in a way that an integer cannot be used. For example, if you have code like this:

```
template <typename T>
class Foo
{
      Foo ()
```

```
        {
                T x;
                x.val = 1;
        }
};
```

Then `T` can't be an integer because `x` (which is of type `T`) must have a field called `val` and integers do not have fields at all, and they definitely don't have a field called `val`.

If we write

```
Foo<int> a;
```

The code would fail to compile.

It's duck typing again (see Duck typing on page 444)—the template doesn't care about the exact type it is given, but it does care that the type "fit" into the code. In this case, an integer doesn't support the "`x.val`" syntax, so the compiler rejects it.

The `vector` template has a similar constraint on its second parameter—it needs to be a type that supports more functionality than a basic integer provides. All of the errors are complaining about the many different ways that `int` would be an invalid type for that template parameter!

When confronted by this massive wall of text, it is best, as always, to start at the top of the error message and try to fix a single error at a time. I'm going to pull out only the text up to the point where I see the word "error".

```
/usr/lib/gcc/x86_64-redhat-
linux/4.1.2/../../../../include/c++/4.1.2/bits/stl_vector.h
: In instantiation of 'std::_Vector_base<int, int>':
/usr/lib/gcc/x86_64-redhat-
linux/4.1.2/../../../../include/c++/4.1.2/bits/stl_vector.h
:159:   instantiated from 'std::vector<int, int>'
template_err.cc:6:   instantiated from here
/usr/lib/gcc/x86_64-redhat-
linux/4.1.2/../../../../include/c++/4.1.2/bits/stl_vector.h
:78: error: 'int' is not a class, struct, or union type
```

Okay, that's much better, right? It's only a few lines—almost like what we saw in the earlier section on duck typing (see Duck typing on page 444). We can handle this!

Let's go through this simpler error message. Notice the first line says "In instantiation of `std::_Vector_base<int, int>`." A template instantiation just means, "When trying to compile a template with this set of template parameters. " This error indicates that there is a problem creating a template with those parameters (`_Vector_base` is a helper class used to implement vector). The next line indicates that the `Vector_base` template failed to compile because of an attempt to create the template `vector<int,int>`, and it tells you that it comes from the file `template_err.cc` on line 6; `template_err.cc` is our code, so now we know the line of code that caused the problem.

Finding the line of code containing the problem is always the first step to figuring out what went wrong. You can often tell what is wrong just by looking at your own code. If it isn't obvious at first glance, we can keep going through the list of instantiations, until we get to the actual error message: `error: 'int' is not a class, struct, or union type`. This tells you that the compiler was expecting an `int` to be a class or structure, rather than a built-in type like `int`. Vectors should be able to hold any type, so this suggests that there is a problem with a template parameter given to the vector. At this point, you should double-check how to declare a vector and you would see that you need only a single template parameter.

Now that we have a diagnosis for the first problem, it's time to fix it and recompile. Normally you'd be able to figure out at least a couple of compiler errors at once, but, with templates, the first error often causes all of the other errors. It's better to fix one issue at a time and avoid lots of head-scratching over errors that are already fixed.

In this example, with over a page of error messages, every single error in the program was due the addition of the second `int` template parameter.

Quiz yourself
1. When should you use templates?
A. When you want to save time
B. When you want your code to go faster

C. When you need to write the same code multiple times with different types
D. When you need to make sure you can reuse your code later

2. When do you need to provide the type for a template parameter?
A. Always
B. Only when declaring an instance of a template class
C. Only if the type cannot be inferred
D. For template functions, only if the type cannot be inferred; for template classes, always

3. How does the compiler tell if a template parameter can be used with a given template?
A. It implements a specific C++ interface
B. You must specify the constraints when declaring the template
C. It tries to use the template parameter; if the type supports all required operations, it accepts it
D. You must list all valid template types when declaring the template

4. How is putting a template class in a header different from putting a regular class in a header file?
A. There is no difference
B. The regular class cannot have any of its methods defined in the header file
C. The template class must have all of its methods defined in the header file
D. The template class does not need a corresponding .cpp file, but the class does

5. When should you make a function a template function?
A. From the beginning—you never know when you'll need to use the same logic for a different type, so you should always make template methods
B. Only if you cannot cast to the types that the function currently requires
C. Whenever you just wrote nearly the same logic but for a different type with similar properties to the type used by the first function
D. Whenever two functions do "about" the same thing, and you can tweak the logic with a few extra Boolean parameters

6. When will you learn about most errors in your template code?
A. As soon as you compile the template
B. During the linking phase
C. When you run your program

D. When you first compile code that instantiates the template

(View solution on page 515)

Practice problems

1. Write a function that takes a vector and sums all the values in the vector, no matter what type of numerical data the vector holds.

2. Modify the vector replacement class implemented as a practice problem in chapter 25, but make it a template so that it is can store any type.

3. Write a search method that takes a vector, of any type, and a value, of any type, and returns true if the value is in the vector, or false if it is not.

4. Implement a sort function that takes a vector of any type and sorts the values by their natural sort order (the order you get from using < or >).

Part 4: Miscellaneous Topics

You've already learned the tools you need to write fun, large programs. A few topics, while useful, do not fit into the narrative of the book; these topics include getting arguments from the command line and performing nice formatting of input and output. These topics are related more to the user interface of your program than to algorithmic logic, but they are just as important. Without communicating with the user, your program is not going to be very interesting!

You could approach the topics in this section in any order, depending on what you want to accomplish—you might even find that you want to read some of these sections before you finish the rest of the book, especially if you are covering some of these topics as part of a class that are you are taking.

Chapter 30

Formatting Output Using Iomanip

Creating cleanly formatted output is a common request from your pesky end users (next thing you know, they'll want your program to work!) In C++, you can create nicely formatted output with `cout` by using functions in the `iomanip` header file.

Dealing with spacing issues

The most common formatting issue is poor spacing. Nicely formatted output uses spacing that looks just right. There aren't columns of text that are too long or too short, and everything is appropriately aligned. So let's learn how to do it!

Setting the field width with setw

The `setw` function allows you to set the minimum width of the next output via the insertion operator. If the next output is less than the minimum width, then the output is padded with spaces. If the output is longer than the minimum width, nothing is done—importantly, the output is not truncated.

The actual usage of `setw` is a bit odd—you call the function and pass the value into `cout`:

```
#include <iostream>
#include <iomanip>

using namespace std;
```

```
int main()
{
        cout << setw( 10 ) << "ten" << "four" << "four";
}
```
Sample Code 74: setw.cpp

The output from the above program looks like this:

```
        tenfourfour
```

If you call setw without passing it to cout, it has no effect whatsoever. As you can see from the sample program, a call to setw affects only the very next output.

You'll notice that by default, the string is aligned to the right (the padding is placed to the left of the string)—in other words, the string is prefixed with the padding character. You can set the alignment of your output by passing in the alignment direction, either left or right, into cout. This sample program will align the text to the left rather than the right, making the output a bit more readable.

```
#include <iostream>
#include <iomanip>

using namespace std;

int main()
{
        cout << setw( 10 ) << left << "ten" << "four" <<
"four";
}
```
Sample Code 75: setw_left.cpp

The output from the above would look like this:

```
ten       fourfour
```

The result has been aligned to the left this time.

setw allows you to decide the width of a column of output at runtime. For example, to display several columns of data, you can figure out the widest string in each column, and pad every entry of that column so that each one is slightly wider than the longest element of the column.

Changing the padding character

There are times where you may not want to use spaces for your padding. You can call setfill to change the padding character. setfill works like setw, in that you pass it directly into cout.

If we take the original example of padding, but add a setfill of dash:

```
cout << setfill( '-' ) << setw( 10 ) << "ten" << "four"
    << "four";
```

It would look like this:

```
-------tenfourfour
```

Permanently changing settings

You can also globally change the padding character using the fill member function on cout. For example, this code:

```
cout.fill( '-' );

cout << setw( 10 ) << "A" << setw( 10 ) << "B"
    << setw( 10 ) << "C" << endl;
```

Will print out as:

```
---------A---------B---------C
```

The fill method returns the previous fill character, so that you can restore it later. This return value is useful if all you're doing is avoiding multiple setfill calls. For example:

```
const char last_fill = cout.fill( '-' );

cout << setw( 10 ) << "A" << setw( 10 ) << "B"
    << setw( 10 ) << "C" << endl;

cout.fill( last_fill );

cout << setw( 10 ) << "D" << endl;
```

The last line will now print out as:

```
         D
```

You can permanently set the alignment of padded text by calling the `setf` member function of `cout`. You can pass in flags to the `setf` function for left or right with the flags `ios_base::left` or `ios_base::right`.[83]

```
cout.setf( ios_base::left );
```

As with `fill`, this call returns the previous value so that you can later restore it if you want to.

Try adding the above call to `setf` to the previous example to see the difference in formatting.

Putting your knowledge of iomanip together

Let's put together some of the previous methods and write code that prints first and last names into two columns, making sure that the two columns are nicely aligned, like this:

```
Joe     Smith
Tonya   Malligans
Jerome  Noboggins
Mary    Suzie-Purple
```

We need to set the width of the columns correctly, just a bit larger than the largest element in each column. We can loop through the code and find the maximum length and then use `setw` with the maximum length (optionally adding some padding) to display the names. Let's see the code that does it:

```cpp
#include <iostream>
#include <vector>
#include <iomanip>
#include <string>

using namespace std;

struct Person
{
    Person (
            const string& firstname,
            const string& lastname
    )
```

---

[83] `setf` stands for **set** **flag**.

```cpp
        : _firstname( firstname )
        , _lastname( lastname )
        {}

        string _firstname;
        string _lastname;
};

int main ()
{
        vector<Person> people;

        people.push_back( Person( "Joe", "Smith" ) );
        people.push_back( Person( "Tonya", "Malligans" ) );
        people.push_back( Person( "Jerome", "Noboggins" ) );
        people.push_back( Person( "Mary", "Suzie-Purple" ) );


        int firstname_max_width = 0;
        int lastname_max_width = 0;

        // get the max widths

        for ( vector<Person>::iterator iter = people.begin();
              iter != people.end();
              ++iter )
        {
              if ( iter->_firstname.length()
                      >
                   firstname_max_width )
              {
                    firstname_max_width =
                          iter->_firstname.length();

              }
              if ( iter->_lastname.length()
                      >
                   lastname_max_width )
              {
                    lastname_max_width =
                          iter->_lastname.length();

              }
        }

        // print the elements of the vector
        for ( vector<Person>::iterator iter = people.begin();
              iter != people.end();
              ++iter )
        {
              cout << setw( firstname_max_width ) << left
```

```
                        << iter->_firstname;
            cout << " ";
            cout << setw( lastname_max_width ) << left
                        << iter->_lastname;
            cout << endl;
        }
}
```
Sample Code 76: column_alignment.cpp

Printing numbers

Creating nice output sometimes requires correctly formatting numbers; when printing out a hexadecimal value, it's nice to prefix it with "0x" to show the base. It's also much prettier if you set the number of trailing zeros after a decimal place to something appropriate for your application (2, if you're working with money).

Setting the precision of numerical output with setprecision

The setprecision function sets the maximum number of digits displayed when printing a number. Like setw, the return value of setprecision should be inserted into the stream. In fact, its usage is very similar to setw in all respects. To print the number 2.71828 with three total digits:

```
std::cout << setprecision( 3 ) << 2.71828;
```

Calling setprecision will properly round the output—so the output here is 2.72, rather than the truncated 2.71. On the other hand, if you'd printed 2.713, it would come out as 2.71.

Unlike most of the other commands that are inserted into streams, setprecision will change the precision until the next time it is passed into a given stream. So changing the above example like so,

```
cout << setprecision( 3 ) << 2.71828 << endl;
cout << 1.412 << endl;
```

will print out

```
2.72
1.41
```

You might wonder what happens if you print a number with more digits before the decimal point than the precision provided to setprecision. The answer depends on whether you are printing a floating-point number or an integer. An integer is printed in full, and a floating-point number is printed in scientific notation with the requested number of digits:

```
cout << setprecision( 2 ) << 1234.0 << endl;
```

Results in the text

```
1.2e3
```

That e3, by the way, is the same thing as writing $* 10^3$.

While

```
cout << setprecision( 2 ) << 1234 << endl;
```

Results in the text

```
1234
```

What do you do about money?

You might have noticed that so far, there really hasn't been a good way of printing numbers that represent money, where you typically want to always have two decimal places, but you never want to have any rounding.

The short answer is that you probably shouldn't store money in a `double` anyway! The reason is that `double` values are not perfectly precise, so small rounding errors can get introduced, shaving off parts of a cent here or there. For most applications, a better way to store money is to store the total number of cents in an integer. When you want to display the value, for perfect precision, you can then divide by 100 to get the number of dollars, and use modulus to get the number of cents, and display each value separately.

```
int cents = 1001; // $10.01
cout << cents / 100 << "." << setw(2) << setfill('0')
     << cents % 100;
```

It would, of course, make sense to create a standard helper function that does this calculation for you and a class that stores money, hiding the precise details of what numerical format is used.

Output in different bases

When programming, you frequently want to display numbers in octal or hexadecimal. You can use the `setbase` function to do so. When inserted into a stream, `setbase` sets the base to 8, 10, or 16. For instance,

```
cout << "0x" << setbase( 16 ) << 32 << endl;
```

will print out

```
0x20
```

Which is 32 written in hexadecimal. Note that you can use `dec`, `oct`, and `hex` as shorthand for `setbase( 10 )`, `setbase( 8 )`, and `setbase( 16 )` respectively when inserting into a stream.

While the code above explicitly prints the `0x`, you can use `setiosflags` to indicate that `cout` should display the base automatically. If you pass the result of `setiosflags( ios_base::showbase )` into `cout`, then decimal numbers will be displayed normally, hex numbers will be prefixed with `0x`, and octal numbers will be prefixed with `0`.

```
cout << setiosflags( ios_base::showbase ) << setbase( 16 )
    << 32 << endl;
```

will print out

```
0x20
```

Like `setprecision`, the changes made by `setiosflags` are permanent. You can disable the prefix using `noshowbase` as an argument.

With these tools in hand, you should have the ability to create much more pleasing output!

Chapter 31
Exceptions and Error Reporting

As you build larger programs, you will need a clean way to handle error reporting from your functions. There are two classic ways of reporting errors: using error codes and using exceptions. Using error codes doesn't require any new language features, but it means that each function (that can fail) returns an error code (or a success code) that indicates the result of the function. This technique has the advantage of being relatively simple to understand:

```
int failableFunction ();

const int result = failableFunction();

if ( result != 0 )
{
      cout << "Function call failed: " << result;
}
```

On the other hand, this error code handling technique has the disadvantage of requiring each function to return an error code, even if you want to get another value from the function. In order to have a function return a computed value, you need to use a reference or pointer parameter:

```
int failableFunction (int& out_val);

int res_val;
```

```
const int result = failableFunction( res_val );

if ( result != 0 )
{
     cout << "Function call failed: " << result;
}
else
{
     // use the res_val to do something
}
```

Although this approach works, the code no longer shows the natural flow you'd expect.

Exceptions, on the other hand, are an entirely new language feature. The way exceptions work is that when a function wants to report an error, it immediately stops executing and throws an **exception**. When an exception is thrown, the program searches for an exception handler, which will handle the exception.

One way to think about what an exception means is to imagine that the function immediately returns, without returning a value. Moreover, instead of returning to the caller of the function, execution returns to the place that can actually handle the exception. If there is nowhere to return to, then the program will crash due to an unhandled exception. Otherwise, it will return to the point that handles the exception, and the program will continue from there. This allows you to write code that has a single place to which any failure will "return", handling them all at once.

In order to specify where a failed function should return to, you use a try/catch block:

```
try
{
     // code that can fail by throwing an exception
}
catch ( ... )
{
     // place where the exception is handled (i.e. where
     // the function returns to)
}
```

Any function in the try block can throw an exception that will be handled in the catch block. There may be multiple kinds of exceptions, each a different class, which allows you to write multiple catch blocks, each of which handles a different kind of failure. If you catch ..., as in the above code, then any exception not caught by another, more specific, catch block will be handled by that catch block. You can think of ... as a catch-all. The first catch block that can handle an exception will handle that exception, so if you want to have a catch-all, you should put it last, after all other catch blocks:

```
try
{
    // code that can fail by throwing an exception
}
catch ( const FileNotFoundException& e )
{
    // Handle failures due to not being able to find a
    // file
}
catch ( const HardDriveFullException& e )
{
    // Handle failures due to running out of space on the
    // hard drive
}
catch ( ... )
{
    // place where other exceptions are handled (i.e.
    // where the function returns to)
}
```

Releasing resources during exceptions

If you call a function that throws an exception, you do not necessarily need to catch the exception—the exception will propagate out from your function, and it may find a catch block in a higher-level function. This is perfectly valid, as long as you don't need to do anything in response to the exception. As a matter of fact, you often *don't* need to do anything because the destructors of all local objects are called when a function is exited due to an exception. For example:

```
int callFailableFunction ()
{
    const string val( "abc" );
    // call code that throws an exception
    failableFunction();
}

int main ()
{
    try
```

```
    {
          callFailableFunction();
    }
    catch ( ... )
    {
          // handle failure
    }
}
```

Here, if `failableFunction` throws an exception, then the string `val`, constructed in `callFailableFunction`, will be destroyed when the exception is thrown, cleaning up any resources that were allocated to store the string. This feature is called **stack unwinding**—each stack frame that doesn't catch the exception is cleaned up, or unwound, by calling the destructors for each object in that frame. Remember, even if you didn't explicitly write a destructor, the object has the default destructor that will do some cleanup.

Manual cleanup of resources in a catch block
Sometimes you actually need to clean up some resource manually when an exception is thrown. In most cases, you should try to write a guard object that cleans up that resource, but if you don't have this option, you can always catch the exception, do the cleanup, and then rethrow the exception. For example:

```
int callFailableFunction ()
{
      const int* val = new int;
      // call code that throws an exception
      try
      {
            failableFunction();
      }
      catch ( ... )
      {
            delete val;
            // Notice the use of throw; to rethrow the
            // exception
            throw;
      }
      // notice that we have to put delete  here, too. The
      // catch block does not execute if there is no
      // exception. The only way to ensure that code is
      // always run is to put it in the destructor of
      // a local object.

      delete val;
}
```

```
int main ()
{
      try
      {
            callFailableFunction ();
      }
      catch ( ... )
      {
            // handle failure
      }
}
```

Throwing exceptions

So far, you've seen lots about how to catch and handle an exception—but how do you create an exception and throw it? Creating an exception class is nothing special—it is just a normal class. You put into that exception any fields that you think are important, and provide accessor methods for reading information about the exception. A typical exception will have an interface like this:

```
class Exception
{
public:
      virtual ~Exception () = 0;
      virtual int getErrorCode () = 0;
      virtual string getErrorReport () = 0;
};
```

Then each specific kind of error would inherit from Exception and implement these virtual methods:

```
class FileNotFoundException : public Exception
{
public:

      FileNotFoundException (
            int err_code,
            const string& details
      )
            : _err_code ( err_code )
            , _details ( details )
      {}

      virtual ~FileNotFoundException ()
      {}
```

```
        virtual int getErrorCode ()
        {
                return _err_code;
        }

        virtual string getErrorReport ()
        {
                return _details;
        }

private:

        int _err_code;
        string _details;
};
```

You can then throw the exception as though you were constructing an instance of that class:

```
throw FileNotFoundException( 1, "File not found" );
```

One advantage of inheriting all exceptions from a common base class is that exceptions can be caught by the superclass. For example, you can write:

```
catch ( const Exception& e )
{
}
```

And it will catch any exception that inherits from the Exception class. Using a carefully defined exception hierarchy allows you to write code that can handle a variety of errors in a single catch block. For example, all input and output errors might inherit from a class called IOException, thereby allowing all I/O exceptions to be handled as a single unit—while in specific cases where different subclasses need different handling, the code can still catch specific subclasses of IOException.

The standard superclass exception for native C++ constructs in the standard library is std::exception. You do not have to define your own exception hierarchy with this as the parent class, but if you are using the standard library it would make sense to use std::exception as a common base class so that you can use it to catch all exceptions thrown in your program—both by the standard library and by your own code.

Throw specifications

Okay, so you can throw an exception when you reach an error, and you can catch an exception if you know that a function will fail. But how do you know whether a function will throw an exception, anyway? In C++, you can specify the exceptions that you expect your function might throw by using a **throw spec**. A throw spec is a list of exceptions, possibly empty, that appears at the end of your function declaration and your function definition.

In the header:

```
void canFail () throw (FileNotFoundException);
void cannotFail () throw ();
```

In the cpp file:

```
void canFail () throw (FileNotFoundException)
{
      throw FileNotFoundException();
}

void cannotFail () throw ()
{
}
```

The problem with exception specifications is that **they are not checked at compile time**; they are only checked at run time. Even worse, if a function throws an exception that is not expected, your program may simply terminate immediately. This means that you can't truly rely on the exception specification being accurate, but you can definitely expect them to cause your program to crash. Some tools, such as PC-Lint (http://www.gimpel.com/html/pcl.htm), provide compile time checking of exceptions and mitigate many of the issues that people have with exception specifications. In the new C++ standard, C++11, full exception specs have been deprecated, which means they are unlikely to continue as part of the language in the future.[84]

The net result of this is that you have to rely on the author of a function properly documenting the exceptions that the function can throw, and if you write a function that throws an exception, you need to document that your function throws an exception.

---

[84] The specification maintains the ability to say that a function definitely does not throw an exception, which can sometimes improve performance.

Benefits of exceptions

The two primary benefits of exceptions are to simplify the error handling logic, by putting it all into a single catch block rather than having to have many checks for a return code, and to improve error reporting by giving more information than just an error code.

The first benefit, allowing errors to be handled in a single catch block, can turn code like this:

```
if ( funCall1 ()  == ERROR )
{
       // handle error
}
if ( funCall2 ()  == ERROR )
{
       // handle error
}
if ( funCall3 ()  == ERROR )
{
       // handle error
}
```

Into

```
try
{
       funCall1 ();
       funCall2 ();
       funCall3 ();
}
catch ( const Exception& e )
{
       // handle error
}
```

All of the error handling code is in one place, and the mainline use case is very simple to follow.

The second benefit, of allowing the error to report additional information, is also very useful. With an error code, you only get back, well, the error code. With an exception, each error can provide additional information about the error. A `FileNotFoundException` can contain the name of the file, for example.

Misuse of exceptions

While exceptions are a fantastic tool for reporting errors, they can also be abused because of their power to immediately return from a function to an earlier caller on the stack. In general, you should not use exceptions to handle expected, non-error situations. For example, you could in theory use an exception to report the result of a function, rather than returning a value. But this would be both much slower than returning (there is some runtime cost to handle a thrown exception) and it would be confusing. As you saw before, using exceptions to report errors simplifies the mainline logic of a function. If you start to use exceptions as part of your mainline logic, then you lose that simplicity.

Let's look at how you could take code that uses exceptions for mainline use cases and rewrite it without exceptions, using an example of a snippet of parser code. A parser is a piece of code that reads in a well-defined language—such as HTML—and interprets its structure. Often a parser will have functions to parse individual elements of the program structure. For example, in HTML there might be functions to parse links and tables.

One way to write a parser would be to have `parseLink` and `parseTable` report whether they were able to parse the next piece of text, and use an exception if not:

```
try
{
     parseLink();
     return;
}
catch ( const ParseException& e )
{
     // not a link, try the next type
}
try
{
     parseTable();
     return;
}
catch ( const ParseException& e )
{
     // not a table, try the next type
}
```

The problem here is that if the next piece of text is not a link or a table, that's not an error; it's normal. It would be better to write the parser like this:

```
if ( expectLink() )
{
      parseLink();
}
else if ( expectTable() )
{
      parseTable();
}
```

Since HTML usually indicates within a few characters what the next element on the page is, you can easily write methods that check if the next part of the document is a link or a table, and now you have simple if statements rather than complex exceptions.

Exceptions in summary

Exceptions are a clean way of reporting errors without having to litter your code with specific error handling logic. Thanks to stack unwinding and destructors that clean up your objects, exceptions allow most of your code to be about the mainline logic of the algorithm rather than checking error codes.

Throwing an exception does have some performance implications, so you should use exceptions when an error occurs, not as part of an algorithm's control flow. For example, your parser might throw exceptions if it reads in characters that are known to be always invalid; it shouldn't throw exceptions for situations that can be part of the normal format for a file. This makes it clear which situations are truly errors. It also ensures the best performance for your code, by running exception handling only in the rare case that there is a true problem. These cases almost always result in termination of the algorithm, so it's ok if they are slower than usual.

In many real world programs, error handling plays a major role in the time it takes to develop products, so you will start to see and hear more about exceptions as you advance past the basics that we've covered in this book.

Chapter 32
Final Thoughts

You've now learned a great deal about C++, but your journey is not at an end. In truth, you are really at the beginning of a lifetime of learning about programming. You now have the tools to write many interesting, sophisticated programs. The next step is to start doing it: build complex systems and practice implementing algorithms and data structures. There is more to programming than the language you are using—there are questions about how to design programs, how to design algorithms, how to design the user interface, what libraries you should use, how to organize a team of programmers, and even how to figure out what to build in the first place. In other words, there is a lot of **software engineering** to be done. This book has of course touched on some of these areas, but they are entire topics in their own right, not to be taken lightly.

Like learning to speak any human language, there is much more to learn than the basic grammar and syntax of the language. You won't go straight from speaking English to writing a great novel. Similarly, you won't go from writing C++ to creating an operating system. But what is important is that you now have the foundation to learn the concepts and ideas that are necessary to take the next step. Here are a few suggestions for what you should do next:[85]

1) Start to read books about software engineering and algorithm design. Books like *Programming Pearls* by Jon Bentley will give you an

---

[85] Several of my suggestions were inspired by the outstanding essay "Teach Yourself Programming in Ten Years", by Peter Norvig: http://norvig.com/21-days.html

entertaining introduction to some of the non-language aspects of programming, including basic algorithm analysis, design and estimation.

2) Write programs. Start by imitating other existing software—write clones of existing tools, learning the libraries that you need to do it. Then get involved—find an internship or work on an open source project. The more code you write, the more bad code you will write, but it is only by writing bad code that you will eventually learn to write good code.

3) Read about other disciplines—not just programming. Learn about software testing; learn about project management; learn about product management; learn about marketing. In the end, the more you understand about the entire software development process, the closer you will come to being a well-rounded developer, architect or executive.

4) Find other programmers—work with them, learn from them. This is one of the benefits of taking a course at a university or an internship.

5) Find a mentor who has walked your path. Words on a page can't answer the questions an author didn't think of; having someone like you can help you leap over many roadblocks. Be respectful, but don't be afraid to ask questions and show that you don't know something. A state of confusion is a great learning opportunity!

6) Enjoy programming. If you aren't having fun, then you probably don't want to do it full time as a career. Keep it fun. Don't do boring things that make you not want to program.

You've now reached the end of this book, but the beginning of your career. Good luck!

Quiz Solutions

Chapter 2 quiz solution

1. What is the correct value to return to the operating system upon the successful completion of a program?
A. -1
B. 1
C. 0
D. Programs do not return a value.

2. What is the only function all C++ programs must contain?
A. `start()`
B. `system()`
C. `main()`
D. `program()`

3. What punctuation is used to signal the beginning and end of code blocks?
A. { }
B. -> and <-
C. `BEGIN` and `END`
D. (and)

4. What punctuation ends most lines of C++ code?
A. .
B. ;
C. :
D. '

5. Which of the following is a correct comment?
A. `*/ Comments */`

B. ** Comment **
C. /* Comment */
D. { Comment }

6. What header file do you need to use to get access to cout?
A. stream
B. nothing, it is available by default
C. iostream
D. using namespace std;

Chapter 3 quiz solution

1. What variable type should you use if you want to store a number like 3.1415?

A. `int`

B. `char`

C. `double`

D. `string`

2. Which of the following is the correct operator to compare two variables?

A. `:=`

B. `=`

C. `equal`

D. `==`

3. How do you get access to the string data type?

A. It is built into the language, so you don't need to do anything

B. Since strings are used for I/O, you include the `iostream` header file

C. You include the `string` **header file**

D. C++ doesn't support strings

4. Which of the following is not a correct variable type?

A. `double`

B. `real`

C. `int`

D. `char`

5. How can you read in an entire line from the user?

A. use `cin>>`

B. Use `readline`

C. use `getline`

D. You cannot do this easily

6. What would be displayed on the screen for this expression in C++: `cout  <<  1234/2000?`

A. 0

B. .617

C. Roughly .617, but the result cannot be precisely stored in a floating-point number

D. It depends on the types of the two sides of the equation

7. Why does C++ need a char type if there are already integers?

A. Because characters and integers are completely different kinds of data, one is a number, one is a letter

B. For backward compatibility with C

C. To make it easy to read in, and print out, actual characters rather than numbers, even though chars are stored as numbers

D. For internationalization support, to handle languages like Chinese and Japanese, that have many characters

Chapter 4 quiz solution

1. Which of the following is true?

A. 1

B. 66

C. .1

D. -1

E. All of the above

2. Which of the following is the Boolean operator for Boolean and?

A. &

B. `&&`

C. |

D. | &

3. What does the expression `!( true && ! ( false || true ) )` evaluate to?

A. `true`

B. `false`

4. Which of the following shows the correct syntax for an if statement?

A. `if expression`

B. `if { expression`

C. `if ( expression )`

D. `expression if`

Chapter 5 quiz solution

1. What is the final value of x when the code int x; for(x=0; x<10; x++) {} is run?

A. 10

B. 9

C. 0

D. 1

(If this confuses you, consider what happens if you add a cout statement after the end of the for loop.)

2. When does the code block following while(x<100) execute?

A. When x is less than one hundred

B. When x is greater than one hundred

C. When x is equal to one hundred

D. While it wishes

3. Which is not a loop structure?

A. for

B. do-while

C. while

D. repeat until

4. How many times is a do-while loop guaranteed to loop?

A. 0

B. Infinitely

C. 1

D. Variable

Chapter 6 quiz solution

1. Which is not a proper prototype?

A. `int funct(char x, char y);`

B. `double funct(char x)`

C. `void funct();`

D. `char x();`

(Note the missing semicolon.)

2. What is the return type of the function with prototype: `int func(char x, double v, float t);`

A. `char`

B. `int`

C. `float`

D. `double`

3. Which of the following is a valid function call (assuming the function exists)?

A. `funct;`

B. `funct x, y;`

C. `funct();`

D. `int funct();`

4. Which of the following is a complete function?

A. `int funct();`

B. `int funct(int x) {return x=x+1;}`

C. `void funct(int) {cout<<"Hello"}`

D. `void funct(x) {cout<<"Hello";}`

Chapter 7 quiz solution

1. Which follows the case statement?

A. :

B. ;

C. –

D. A newline

2. What is required to avoid falling through from one case to the next?

A. `end;`

B. `break;`

C. `Stop;`

D. You need a semicolon

3. What keyword covers unhandled possibilities?

A. `all`

B. `contingency`

C. `default`

D. `other`

4. What is the result of the following code?

```
int x = 0;
switch( x )
{
        case 1: cout << "One";
        case 0: cout << "Zero";
        case 2: cout << "Hello World";
}
```

A. One

B. Zero

C. Hello World

D. ZeroHello World

Chapter 8 quiz solution

1. What will happen if you don't call `srand` before calling `rand`?
A. `rand` will fail
B. `rand` will always return 0
C. `rand` will return the same sequence of numbers every time your program runs
D. Nothing

2. Why would you seed `srand` with the current time?
A. To ensure your program always runs the same way
B. To generate new random numbers each time your program is run
C. To make sure that the computer generates real random numbers
D. This is done for you, you only need to call `srand` if you want to set the seed to the same thing each time

3. What range of values does `rand` return?
A. The range you want
B. 0 to 1000
C. 0 to RAND_MAX
D. 1 to RAND_MAX

4. What does the expression 11 % 3 return?
A. 33
B. 3
C. 8
D. 2

5. When should you use `srand`?
A. Every time you need a random number
B. Never, it's just window dressing
C. Once, at the start of your program
D. Occasionally, after you've used `rand` for a while, to add more randomness

Chapter 10 quiz solution

1. Which of the following correctly declares an array?
A. `int anarray[ 10 ];`
B. `int anarray;`
C. `anarray{ 10 };`
D. `array anarray[ 10 ];`

2. What is the index number of the last element of an array with 29 elements?
A. 29
B. 28
C. 0
D. Programmer-defined

3. Which of the following is a two-dimensional array?
A. `array anarray[ 20 ][ 20 ];`
B. `int anarray[ 20 ][ 20 ];`
C. `int array[ 20, 20 ];`
D. `char array[ 20 ];`

4. Which of the following correctly accesses the seventh element stored in foo, an array with 100 elements?
A. `foo[ 6 ];`
B. `foo[ 7 ];`
C. `foo( 7 );`
D. `foo;`

5. Which of the following properly declares a function that takes a two-dimensional array?
A. `int func ( int x[][] );`
B. `int func ( int x[ 10 ][] );`
C. `int func ( int x[] );`
D. `int func ( int x[][ 10 ] );`

Chapter 11 quiz solution

1. Which of the following accesses a variable in structure b?

A. b->var;

B. b.var;

C. b-var;

D. b>var;

2. Which of the following is a properly defined structure?

A. struct {int a;}

B. struct a_struct {int a};

C. struct a_struct int a;

D. struct a_struct {int a;};

3. Which properly declares a structure variable of type foo with the name my_foo?

A. my_foo as struct foo;

B. foo my_foo;

C. my_foo;

D. int my_foo;

4. What is the final value output by this code?

```cpp
#include <iostream>

using namespace std;

struct MyStruct
{
      int x;
};

void updateStruct (MyStruct my_struct)
{
      my_struct.x = 10;
}

int main ()
{
      MyStruct my_struct;
      my_struct.x = 5;
      updateStruct ( my_struct );
      cout << my_struct.x << '\n';
}
```

A. 5
B. 10
C. This code will not compile

Chapter 12 quiz solution

1. Which of these is NOT a good reason to use a pointer?
A. You want to allow a function to modify an argument passed to it
B. You want to save space and avoid copying a large variable
C. You want to be able to get more memory from the operating system
D. You want to be able to access variables more quickly

2. What does a pointer store?
A. The name of another variable
B. An integer value
C. The address of another variable in memory
D. A memory address, but not necessarily another variable

3. Where can you get more memory from during your program's execution?
A. You can't get any more memory
B. The stack
C. The free store
D. By declaring another variable

4. What can go wrong when using pointers?
A. You could access memory that you cannot use, causing a crash
B. You could access the wrong memory address, corrupting data
C. You could forget to return memory to the OS, causing the program to run out of memory
D. All of the above

5. Where does memory for a normal variable declared in a function come from?
A. The free store
B. The stack
C. Normal variables do not use memory
D. The program's binary itself (that's why EXEs are so large!)

6. Once you allocate memory, what do you need to do with it?
A. Nothing, it is yours forever
B. Return it to the operating system when you're done using it
C. Set the value pointed to to 0
D. Store the value 0 in the pointer

Chapter 13 quiz solution

1. Which of the following is the proper declaration of a pointer?

A. `int x;`

B. `int &x;`

C. `ptr x;`

D. `int *x;`

2. Which of the following gives the memory address of integer variable `a`?

A. `*a;`

B. `a;`

C. `&a;`

D. `address ( a );`

3. Which of the following gives the memory address of a variable pointed to by pointer `p_a`?

A. `p_a;`

B. `*p_a;`

C. `&p_a;`

D. `address ( p_a );`

4. Which of the following gives the value stored at the address pointed to by the pointer `p_a`?

A. `p_a;`

B. `val ( p_a );`

C. `*p_a;`

D. `&p_a;`

5. Which of the following properly declares a reference?

A. `int *p_int;`

B. `int &my_ref;`

C. `int &my_ref = & my_orig_val;`

D. `int &my_ref = my_orig_val;`

6. Which of the following is not a good time to use a reference?

A. To store an address that was dynamically allocated from the free store

B. To avoid copying a large value when passing it into a function

C. To force that a parameter to a function is never NULL

D. To allow a function to access the original variable passed to it, without using pointers

Chapter 14 quiz solution

1. Which of the following is the proper keyword to allocate memory in C++?
A. new
B. malloc
C. create
D. value

2. Which of the following is the proper keyword to deallocate memory in C++?[86]
A. free
B. delete
C. clear
D. remove

3. Which of the following statements is true?
A. Arrays and pointers are the same
B. Arrays cannot be assigned to pointers
C. Pointers can be treated like an array, but pointers are not arrays
D. You can use pointers like arrays, but you cannot allocate pointers like arrays

4. What are the final values in x, p_int, and p_p_int in the following code (note that because integers and pointers are different types, compilers will not accept this code directly, but the exercise is useful for working through on paper what is going on with multiple pointers):

```
int x = 0;
int *p_int = & x;
int **p_p_int = & p_int;
*p_int = 12;
**p_p_int = 25;
p_int = 12;
*p_p_int = 3;
p_p_int = 27;
```

A. x = 0, p_p_int = 27, p_int = 12
B. x = 25, p_p_int = 27, p_int = 12
C. x = 25, p_p_int = 27, p_int = 3
D. x = 3, p_p_int = 27, p_int = 12

---

[86] Okay, if you answered malloc and free to these last two questions, you're also right as these are the functions from C—but you might not have read the chapter!

5. How can you indicate that a pointer has no valid value that it points to?
A. Set it to a negative number
B. Set it to NULL
C. Free the memory associated with that pointer
D. Set the pointer to `false`

Chapter 15 quiz solution

What is an advantage of a linked list over an array?
A. Linked lists take up less space per element
B. Linked lists can grow dynamically to hold individual new elements without copying existing elements
C. Linked lists are faster at finding a particular element than an array
D. Linked lists can hold structures as elements

2. Which of the following statements is true?
A. There is no reason to ever use an array
B. Linked lists and arrays have the same performance characteristics
C. Linked lists and arrays both allow constant time access to elements by index
D. It is faster to add an element into the middle of a linked list than to the middle of an array

3. When would you normally use a linked list?
A. When you only need to store one item
B. When the number of items you need to store is known at compile time
C. When you need to dynamically add and remove items
D. When you need instant access to any item in a sorted list without having to do any iteration to access it

4. Why is it ok to declare a linked list with a reference to the type of the list item? (`struct Node { Node* p_next; };`)
A. This isn't allowed
B. Because the compiler is able to figure out that you don't actually need the memory for self-referencing items
C. Because the type is a pointer, you only need enough space to hold a single pointer; the memory for the actual next node is allocated later
D. This is allowed so long as you do not actually assign `p_next` to point to another structure

5. Why is it important to have a NULL at the end of the linked list?
A. It indicates where the list ends and prevents the code from accessing uninitialized memory
B. It prevents the list from becoming a series of circular references
C. It is a debugging aid—if you try to go too far down the list, the program will crash

D. If we don't store a NULL, then the list will need infinite memory because of the self-reference

6. How are arrays and linked lists similar?
A. Both allow you to quickly add new elements in the middle of your current list
B. Both allow you to store data sequentially and sequentially access that data
C. Both arrays and linked lists can easily grow larger by incrementally adding elements
D. Both provide fast access to every element in the list

Chapter 16 quiz solution
1. What is tail recursion?
A. When you call your dog
B. When a function calls itself
C. When a recursive function calls itself as the last thing it does before returning
D. When you can write a recursive algorithm as a loop

2. When would you use recursion?
A. When you can't write the algorithm as a loop
B. When it is more natural to express an algorithm in terms of a sub-problem than in terms of a loop
C. Never, really, it's too hard ☹
D. When working with arrays and linked lists

3. What are the required elements for a recursive algorithm?
A. A base case and a recursive call
B. A base case and a way of breaking down the problem into a smaller version of itself
C. A way recombining the smaller versions of a problem
D. All of the above

4. What can happen if your base case is incomplete?
A. The algorithm might finish early
B. The compiler will detect it and complain
C. This isn't a problem
D. You may have a stack overflow

Chapter 17 quiz solution

1. What is the primary virtue of a binary tree?
A. It uses pointers
B. It can store arbitrary amounts of data
C. It allows fast lookups of data
D. It is easy to remove from the binary tree

2. When would you consider using a linked list instead of a binary tree?
A. When you need to maintain data in a way that allows fast lookups
B. When you want to be able to access the elements in sorted order
C. When you need to be able to quickly add to the front or end, but never access items in the middle
D. When you don't need to free the memory you are using

3. Which of the following is a true statement?
A. The order in which you add items to a binary tree can change the tree structure
B. A binary tree should have items inserted in sorted order to provide the best structure
C. A linked list will be faster than a binary tree for finding elements if the elements are inserted in random order to the binary tree
D. A binary tree can never be reduced to having the same structure as a linked list

4. Which of the following describes why binary trees are fast at finding nodes?
A. They aren't—having two pointers means you have to do more work to traverse the tree
B. Each level you go down the tree, you cut the number of remaining nodes you have to search through approximately in half
C. They aren't really any better than linked lists
D. Recursive calls on binary trees are faster than looping over a linked list

Chapter 18 quiz solution

1. When is using a vector appropriate?
A. You need to store an association between key and value
B. You need to be able to maximize performance when changing the collection of items
C. You don't want to worry about the details of updating your data structure
D. Like a suit at a job interview, a vector is always appropriate

2. How do you remove all items at once from a map?
A. Set the item to an empty string
B. Call `erase`
C. Call `empty`
D. Call `clear`

3. When should you implement your own data structures?
A. When you need something really fast
B. When you need something more robust
C. When you need to take advantage of the raw structure of the data, such as building an expression tree
D. You really won't implement your own data structures, unless you like it

4. Which of the following properly declares an iterator you can use with `vector<int>`?
A. `iterator<int> itr;`
B. `vector::iterator itr;`
C. `vector<int>::iterator itr;`
D. `vector<int>::iterator<int> itr;`

5. Which of the following accesses the key of the element an iterator over a map is currently on?
A. `itr.first`
B. `itr->first`
C. `itr->key`
D. `itr.key`

6. How do you tell if an iterator can be used?
A. Compare it with `NULL`

B. Compare it to the result of calling end() **on the container you are iterating over**

C. Check it against 0

D. Compare it with result of calling begin() on the container you are iterating over

Chapter 19 quiz solution

1. Which of the following is valid code?
A. `const int& x;`
B. `const int x = 3; int *p_int = & x;`
C. `const int x = 12; const int *p_int = & x;`
D. `int x = 3; const int y = x; int& z = y;`

2. Which of these function signatures allows the following code to compile:
`const int x = 3; fun( x );`
A. `void fun (int x);`
B. `void fun (int& x);`
C. `void fun (const int& x);`
D. `A and C`

3. What's the best way to tell if a string search failed?
A. Compare the result position to 0
B. Compare the result position to -1
C. Compare the result position to `string::npos`
D. Check if the result position is greater than the length of the string

4. How do you create an iterator for a const STL container?
A. Declare the iterator `const`
B. Use indices to loop over it rather than using an iterator
C. Use a `const_iterator`
D. Declare the template types to be `const`

Chapter 21 quiz solution

1. Which of the following is not a part of the C++ build process?

A. Linking

B. Compiling

C. Preprocessing

D. Postprocessing

2. When would you get an error related to an undefined function?

A. During the link phase

B. During the compilation phase

C. At program startup

D. When you call the function

3. What can happen if you include a header file multiple times?

A. Errors about multiple declarations

B. Nothing, header files are always loaded only once

C. It depends on how the header file is implemented

D. Header files can only be included by one source file at a time, so this isn't a problem

4. What advantage is there to having separate compile and link steps?

A. None, it's confusing and it probably makes things slower since you have multiple programs running

B. It makes it easier to diagnose errors because you know whether the problem is from the linker or compiler

C. It allows only changed files to be recompiled, saving compilation and linking time

D. It allows only changed files to be recompiled, saving compilation time

Chapter 22 quiz solution

1. What is the advantage of using a function instead of directly accessing data?
A. The function can be optimized by the compiler to provide faster access
B. The function can hide the implementation of the function from callers, making it easier to change the caller of the function
C. Using functions is the only way to share the same data structure across multiple source code files
D. There is no advantage

2. When should you put code into a common function?
A. Whenever you need to call it
B. When you have started calling the same code from more than a couple of places
C. When the compiler starts to complain about the functions being too big to compile
D. B and C

3. Why would you want to hide the representation of a data structure?
A. To make the data structure easier to replace
B. To make the code that uses the data structure easier to understand
C. To make it easier to use the data structure in new parts of the code
D. All of the above

Chapter 23 quiz solution

1. Why would you want to use a method rather use the field of a structure directly?

A. Because the method is easier to read

B. Because the method is faster

C. You wouldn't, you should use the field directly

D. So that you can change the representation of the data

2. Which of the following defines the method associated with the structure
`struct MyStruct { int func(); };`

A. `int func() { return 1; }`

B. `MyStruct::int func() { return 1; }`

C. `int MyStruct::func() { return 1; }`

D. `int MyStruct func () { return 1;  }`

3. Why would you want to include a method definition inline with the class?

A. So that users of the class can see how it works

B. Because it always makes the code faster

C. You don't! It leaks details about the implementation

D. You don't, it makes the program run more slowly

Chapter 24 quiz solution

1. Why would you use private data?
A. To make data safe from hackers
B. To prevent other programmers from ever touching that data
C. To make it clear what data is supposed to be used only for the implementation of a class
D. You shouldn't, it makes it harder to program

2. How is a class different from a structure?
A. Not at all
B. A class defaults to everything being public
C. A class defaults to everything being private
D. A class lets you say whether fields are public or private, a structure doesn't

3. What should you do with data fields of your class?
A. Make them public by default
B. Make them private by default, but move to public if needed
C. Never make them public
D. Classes don't usually have data, but if they do, rock on Wayne

4. How do you decide if a method should be public?
A. Never make methods public
B. Always make methods public
C. Make methods public if they are needed to use the main features of a class, otherwise make it private
D. Make methods public if there's any chance that someone might want to use that method

Chapter 25 quiz solution

1. When do you need to write a constructor for a class?
A. Always, without the constructor you can't use the class
B. Whenever you need to initialize the class with non-default values
C. Never, the compiler will provide a constructor for you all the time
D. Only if you need to have a destructor too

2. What is the relationship between the destructor and the assignment operator?
A. There isn't any
B. Your class's destructor is called before running the assignment operator
C. The assignment operator needs to specify what memory should be deleted by the destructor
D. The assignment operator must make sure that it is safe to run both the destructors of the copied class and the new class

3. When do you need to use an initialization list?
A. When you want to make your constructors as efficient as possible and avoid constructing empty objects
B. When you are initializing a constant value
C. When you want to run the non-default constructor of a field of the class
D. All of the above

4. What function is run on the second line of this code?
```
string str1;
string str2 = str1;
```
A. The constructor for `str2`, and the assignment operator for `str1`
B. The constructor for `str2`, assignment operator for `str2`
C. The copy constructor for `str2`
D. The assignment operator for `str2`

(Because `str2` isn't initialized yet, the copy constructor is run instead of the assignment operator.)

5. Which functions are called in this code, and in what order?
```
{
        string str1;
        string str2;
}
```
A. The constructor for `str1`, the constructor for `str2`

B. The destructor for `str1`, the constructor for `str2`

C. The constructor for `str1`, the constructor for `str2`, the destructor for `str1`, the destructor for `str2`

D. The constructor for `str1`, the constructor for `str2`, the destructor for `str2`, the destructor for `str1`

6. If you know a class has a non-default copy constructor, what should be true about its assignment operator?

A. It should have a default assignment operator

B. It should have a non-default assignment operator

C. It should have a declared, but not implemented, assignment operator

D. Either B or C is valid

(And it should be private so that the compiler catches the problem early.)

Chapter 26 quiz solution

1. When does the destructor for a superclass get run?

A. Only if the object is destroyed via a call to delete on a pointer to the superclass

B. Prior to the destructor of the subclass being called

C. After the destructor of the subclass is called

D. While the destructor of the subclass is called

2. Given the following class hierarchy, what would you need to do in the constructor for `Cat`?

```
class Mammal {
public:
        Mammal (const string& species_name);
};

class Cat : public Mammal
{
public:
        Cat ();
};
```

A. Nothing special

B. Use the initializer list to call `Mammal`'s constructor with an argument of "cat"

C. Call `Mammal`'s constructor from within the `Cat` constructor with an argument of "cat"

D. You should remove the `Cat` constructor and use the default constructor, which will solve this problem for you

3. What is wrong with the following class definition?

```
class Nameable
{
        virtual string getName();
};
```

A. It doesn't make the `getName` method public

B. It doesn't have a virtual destructor

C. It doesn't have an implementation `getName`, but it doesn't declare `getName` to be pure virtual

D. All of the above

4. When you declare a virtual method in an interface class, what does a function need to do to be able to use the interface method to call a method on a subclass?

A. Take the interface as a pointer (or a reference)
B. Nothing, it can just copy the object
C. It needs to know the name of the subclass to call the method on
D. I'm lost! What's a virtual method?

5.How does inheritance improve reuse?
A. By allowing code to inherit methods from its superclasses
B. By allowing a superclass to implement virtual methods for a subclass
C. By allowing code to be written expecting an interface, rather than a concrete class, allowing new classes to implement the interface and use that old code
D. By allowing new classes to inherit the traits of a concrete class that can be used with virtual methods

6. Which of the following is a correct statement about class access levels?
A. A subclass can access only public methods and data of its parent class
B. A subclass can access private methods and data of its parent class
C. A subclass can access only protected methods and data of its parent class
D. A subclass can access protected or public methods and data of its parent class

Chapter 27 quiz solution
1. When should you use a using namespace directive?
A. In all header files, right after the include
B. Never, they are a dangerous crutch
C. At the top of any cpp file where there's no namespace conflict
D. Right before you use a variable from that namespace

2. Why do we need namespaces?
A. To provide compiler writers some interesting work
B. To provide more encapsulation of code
C. To prevent name conflicts in large codebases
D. To help clarify what a class is for

3. When should you put code in a namespace?
A. Always
B. When you're developing a program that's large enough that it's more than a few dozen files
C. When you're developing a library to be shared with other people
D. B and C

4. Why shouldn't you put a using namespace declaration into a header file?
A. It isn't legal
B. There's no reason not to; the using declaration is only valid within the header file itself
C. It forces the using declaration onto anyone who includes the header file, even if it would cause conflicts
D. It can cause conflicts if multiple header files include using declarations

Chapter 28 quiz solution

1. Which type can you use to read from a file?
A. `ifstream`
B. `ofstream`
C. `fstream`
D. A and C

2. Which of the following statements is true?
A. Text files use less space than binary files
B. Binary files are easier to debug
C. Binary files are more space efficient than text files
D. Text files are too slow to use in real programs

3. When writing to a binary file, why can't you pass a pointer to a `string` object?
A. You must always pass a `char*` in to the write method
B. The string object may not be held in memory
C. We don't know the layout of a string object, it may contain pointers that would be written to the file
D. Strings are too large and must be written piece by piece

4. Which of the following statements is true of a file format?
A. File formats are as easy to change as any other input
B. Changing a file format requires thinking about what happens when an old version of a program reads a file
C. Designing a file format requires thinking about what happens if a new version of a program opens an old version of a file
D. B and C

Chapter 29 quiz solution

1. When should you use templates?
A. When you want to save time
B. When you want your code to go faster
C. When you need to write the same code multiple times with different types
D. When you need to make sure you can reuse your code later

2. When do you need to provide the type for a template parameter?
A. Always
B. Only when declaring an instance of a template class
C. Only if the type cannot be inferred
D. For template functions, only if the type cannot be inferred; for template classes, always

3. How does the compiler tell if a template parameter can be used with a given template?
A. It implements a specific C++ interface
B. You must specify the constraints when declaring the template
C. It tries to use the template parameter; if the type supports all required operations, it accepts it
D. You must list all valid template types when declaring the template

4. How is putting a template class in a header different from putting a regular class in a header file?
A. There is no difference
B. The regular class cannot have any of its methods defined in the header file
C. The template class must have all of its methods defined in the header file
D. The template class does not need a corresponding .cpp file, but the class does

5. When should you make a function a template function?
A. From the beginning—you never know when you'll need to use the same logic for a different type, so you should always make template methods
B. Only if you cannot cast to the types that the function currently requires
C. Whenever you just wrote nearly the same logic but for a different type with similar properties to the type used by the first function
D. Whenever two functions do "about" the same thing, and you can tweak the logic with a few extra Boolean parameters

6. When will you learn about most errors in your template code?
A. As soon as you compile the template
B. During the linking phase
C. When you run your program
D. When you first compile code that instantiates the template